Computer Systems Engineering Series

DOUGLAS LEWIN, *Editor*

Real-Time Computer Systems

A.L. Freedman

R.A. Lees

Crane Russak • *New York*

Edward Arnold • *London*

Real-Time Computer Systems

Published in the United States by
Crane, Russak & Company, Inc.
347 Madison Avenue
New York, N.Y. 10017

First published in Great Britain in 1977 by
Edward Arnold (Publishers) Ltd.
25 Hill Street
London, WIX 8LL

Crane, Russak ISBN 0-8448-1003-7
Edward Arnold ISBN 0-7131-2634-5
LC 76-022844

Printed in the United States of America

Contents

Editor's Foreword

The continuing expansion of knowledge in the computer sciences means that it is now more important than ever for the professional computer engineer to keep abreast of the latest developments in his field. Moreover, due to the rapid assimilation of computer techniques into all areas of science and engineering, non-specialists are also finding it essential to acquire expertise in these disciplines. Thus, there exists a need for readable, up-to-date texts on relevant specialist topics of computer engineering which can form authoritative source books for both the practicing engineer and the academic.

This series is an attempt to fulfill such a requirement and is directed primarily at the professional engineer and graduate student in computer technology; in many cases the books will also meet the needs of specialist options offered in undergraduate courses.

The texts will embrace all aspects of computer systems design with an overall emphasis on the engineering of integrated hardware–software systems. In general the series will present established theory and techniques which have found direct application in systems design. However, promising new theoretical methods will also be covered.

All the books will follow a similar basic pattern of a review of the fundamental aspects of the subject, followed by a survey of the current state of the art, and, where applicable, design examples. An important feature will be the associated bibliography and references, which will select the more important and fundamental publications. The objective is to bring the reader up to a level in the subject where he can read current technical papers and apply the results to his own research and design activities. In the main, authors will be chosen from specialists in their field, drawn from both industrial and academic environments, and experienced in communicating technical ideas.

New books will be regularly added to the series to provide an up-to-date source of specialist texts in Computer Systems Engineering.

DOUGLAS LEWIN
Brunel University

Preface

This book has been written because we feel that the failure rate of real-time computer systems is needlessly high, whether for reasons of cost, timescale, technical limitations, or lack of usefulness. We have made an attempt to give a methodology for getting all these aspects right, including the assessment of the purpose, consideration of the technical aspects in hardware and software, and the implementation and use of the systems. Examples are drawn from many applications and practical suggestions are made which apply to most real-time computer systems. It is hoped the book will be useful not only to those designing future systems, but also to those intending users who are concerned with gaining maximum benefit from them.

The authors would like to thank the Plessey Co. Ltd. and Scientific Control Systems Ltd. (SCICON) for assistance in the preparation of this book and for opportunities to gain much of the experience on which the main theses of the book are based.

A.L.F.
R.A.L.

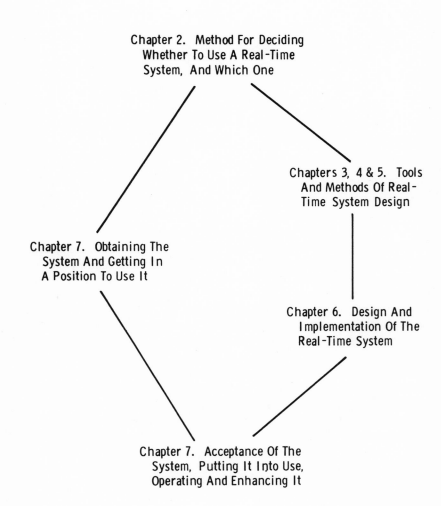

Fig. 1.1. Plan of the book.

Introduction to Real-Time Systems

1.1. Scope and Purpose of the Book

This book is about dedicated real-time systems. It sets out to clarify basic principles underlying both the design and the use of such systems. Design and use are wholly dependent on each other, since systems can only be used to the extent that they are so designed as to make them useful, and not many will be designed unless the benefits of using them exceed the cost of designing and making them. In long-established fields of technology established practices have evolved as experience accumulated. In a technology as new as real-time systems, it is essential to go back to the basic principles. There is no difficulty in grasping these principles—they appear obvious once they have been pointed out; furthermore, most of them are by no means unique to real-time systems and many of them also apply to the design and use of human systems. It is therefore hoped that the book will be meaningful to both users and designers, and will promote a closer understanding between them.

The plan of the book is indicated in Fig. 1.1. Based on the inter-dependence of use and design, Chapter 2 sets out a procedure for determining the best real-time system for a given purpose. This procedure yields both a specification of the most cost-effective system for a given use and the data for deciding whether the use of such a system would be justified. Chapters 3, 4, and 5 give background information on the technology of real-time systems. Chapter 3 surveys the equipment for the capture of data, for processing it, and for the delivery of outputs, the ways of combining such equipment to get the work done, and the methods for enabling operation to continue even in the case of a failure. Chapter 4 deals with programs and how they are written so as to make the system carry out the required processing, while Chapter 5 explains the programs which

1

control the operation of the system so as to ensure that the work needed to produce the specified outputs is done in time to achieve the required response times. Chapters 6 and 7 pick up where Chapter 2 leaves off. Given the specification of what the system is required to do and of the constraints it has to meet, Chapter 6 sets out a methodology for designing a system to meet these requirements and the way to implement it and to test it. Chapter 7 returns to the user aspects of the system; it considers the procurement of the system, the preparations for its use, acceptance testing, optimizing the use of the system, and enhancing it.

1.2. Definition of Real-Time Systems

The world's advanced economies now depend on the use of *real-time* computer systems, but there is still no generally accepted definition of these systems. In order to see what the distinctive features of real-time computer operation really are, let us consider two examples. In pre-computer days one could walk into one's bank, consult one's balance sheet, find out how much money was left, and also why it was so disappointingly little. When computers were first introduced into banks, all that one would obtain was a hand-written slip of paper stating the balance at the close of the last day's business. As this did not say which transactions had been cleared by then, the single number on the slip of paper was probably quite useless. This probably useless single number had been copied by a clerk from a list of balances of all customers of that branch which had been printed out, together with similar lists for all other branches, by a central computer sometime during the night. Since such lists of all balances for all branches represented a lot of printing, the amount of information provided for each customer had to be kept to the barest minimum. Only a very few customers inquired about their balances on any particular day, but, as nobody knew who these would be, all balances had to be printed out. Thus the bank's customers could not obtain the information they really needed because the computer was busy producing a lot of unwanted information. Then the banks changed their way of using computers: instead of printing out all the balances every evening the computer waits until a particular customer calls in at his branch with a request for his balance. The customer's name and account number are then keyed in on a terminal and transmitted to the central computer; the computer then transmits back the balance to the terminal together with, if so requested, the last, say, 10 entries in the account.

A similar contrast between two modes of computer usage can be illustrated in the case of one of the earliest computer applications, namely the preparation of the payroll. With the traditional mode of performing this task a punched card is prepared for each employee, giving details of the work done by him during the week. A stack of these cards is placed in the feeder magazine of a card reader attached to the computer. The latter will read in the first card and compute the pay and tax of that particular employee from the data on the card and from base data kept in the computer store. Having completed the computation for one employee and printed it out, the computer will then read in the next card and repeat the process. The feeding of the cards from the hopper to the reading mechanism, and thus the intake of the input data, is controlled by the computer. In the real-time mode of operation the computer is connected to the time clocks. As an employee clocks in the computer records Joe Bloggs reporting for work at such and such a time. The computer thus automatically captures all the data on the time worked by all employees during the week. When called upon to do so the computer is now in a position to provide information on the payments to be made to one or all of these employees.

There are thus two distinctly contrasting modes of using digital computers. In one case the work is organized around the computer. Before the computer can be started off on the job, all the data which it will require is separately collected and translated into a form suitable for the machine. It is then placed under the control of the computer so that it can take in the data as and when required. Similarly, the computer is instructed in advance which outputs to provide, irrespective of when these may be required, if at all. This is known as *batch processing*. In the real-time mode of operation, on the other hand, the computer is extended into a system which automatically captures its input data, as and when this data is available for capture, and delivers the processed information as and when required.

Having obtained a definition of real-time systems one may well wonder about the origin of the name. Is there such a thing as non-real time anyway? It turns out that there is, or was. Early computers had rather limited capabilities and this put a high premium on the efficiency of programs for them. To provide a measure of efficiency of these programs which would be independent of the speed of the hardware, the time taken by the program was quoted as the number of machine cycles required to do it. Thus there was a measure of time which was not the real time of the outside world. When they came to design computer systems which had to interact with the outside world the designers had to refer to the real time of the outside world. This explains the origin of the name.

A real-time system responds to external events. The real-time payroll system, for instance, responds to the insertion of an employee's clock card by capturing the time and identity of the employee. For this reason such systems are sometimes called *event driven*. Also, this implies that real-time systems have to be in continuous operation. The equipment by which the system interacts with the outside world is said to be *on line* to the computer.

These responses to the outside world have to be accomplished within a certain time. As employees queue for the clock during the rush to clock in or out, the computer has only a few seconds in which to capture this data. If the data is not captured by the time the next card is inserted into the clock, it will be irretrievably lost. Similarly, any output that may be demanded has to be furnished within a set time. In fact, the complete chain of data capture, processing, and output of the processed information may have to be completed within a specified time. Consider, for instance, a real-time system controlling a chemical plant or the jet engine of an aircraft: a change in, say, temperature has to be captured as input data, and this has to be processed to see whether an adjustment of control-valve settings is needed in consequence. If so, the new settings have to be computed and delivered to the valve actuators. All this must be accomplished within, possibly, a fraction of a second to achieve the close control which is the reason for the system being there in the first place. These various times within which data has to be captured, or processed information delivered, are known as the *response times* of the system. Depending on the job which the system has to do, they mostly range from microseconds to seconds. Achieving the required response times is what the design of real-time systems is about, for unless they are achieved the system is useless.

It follows immediately that a real-time system has to be designed for its peak load. For instance, the capacity to capture clocking-in and clocking-out data of a real-time payroll system must suffice for the morning and evening in and out rushes, just as a commuter transit system has to provide the rush-hour capacity. In consequence, a real-time system, again like a commuter transit system, may well be grossly underutilized most of the time. Some implications of this will be discussed in the next chapter.

Another major problem inherent in real-time operation is this: as the input data is captured by the system itself it is only available within the system and can only be accessed through it. This means that, in the case of a failure, not only are the functions performed by the system lost, but it is also impossible for somebody else or for something else to take over these functions unless they can acquire the data accumulated by the system. The repercussions of this will be discussed in Chapter 3.

1.3. The Development of Real-Time Systems

1.3.1. The Two Lines of Development

The few electronic computers which existed in the world in 1950 had memories of some 1000 to 2000 words, into which had to be squeezed both the numbers to be operated on and the instructions specifying the individual arithmetic operations, a number or instruction usually occupying one word. Speed of operation was mostly some 1000 instructions per second. For input they had paper-tape readers, and for output paper-tape punches and teleprinters producing 10 characters per second. Thousands of vacuum tubes consuming tens of kilowatts were used to achieve this performance. An error-free run of a few hours was considered good going. Still, they enabled scientists to do things which would have been quite impossible without them.

Engineers also became interested in automatic digital computers as they realized that, with their automatic computation capability, they could take over control functions in communications, manufacturing processes, and military applications. These engineers did not have to learn new concepts to make use of digital computers in what is now called real-time operation, because in many cases they were already operating in this manner with analog computers. They were therefore ready to start exploiting digital computers for real-time operation as soon as they became available.

Other people were assessing the potential of computers for commercial data processing. These people were not in the least interested in real time. Their problem was that early computers were particularly ill suited to commercial data processing. Here speed of computation was of secondary importance. What was needed was the ability to acquire large amounts of data, store it, process it, and then speedily print out the answers. However, this was precisely what the early computers could not do. Not surprisingly, many people concluded that electronic computers would not be useful for commercial data processing. Others thought differently, and set out to provide the missing capabilities. In 1951 the U.S. Bureau of Census put into operation a machine which could read 12,800 characters per second from magnetic tape and deliver its output at the same rate (1). The output could later be printed from the tape at 600 lines per minute. Thus began the development of *peripherals* — electromechanical and electro-optical devices for the extension of the input, storage, and output capabilities of electronic computers. As computers for commercial data processing were developed and people learned how to use them, the stage was reached where they also wanted to use them in the real-time mode. They then set out, together with the suppliers of these computers, to develop real-time systems, but did so quite separately from the developments in the technical fields. These two separate lines of development are briefly outlined in the next two subsections.

1.3.2. The Technical Line

While there were engineers ready to use computers, the computers were not ready for the engineers. They were neither fast enough nor reliable enough, and were most certainly not cheap enough. Some communications engineers by-passed this problem by designing special-purpose computers for specific applications. An example of a system based on this approach was the Magnetronic Reservisor aircraft seat-reservation system for airlines. The first of these systems was put into service by American Airlines in 1952 (2). It was located at the airline's New York Office at La Guardia Airport, and at first served sales offices in metropolitan New York. The store was a drum of 15,000 words. Operators communicated with the machine by means of specially designed key sets. A special metal plate inserted into the key set identified a selection of eight flights to the system. Lamps on the key set then displayed information on the availability of seats and the status of these flights. Transactions, such as the reservation or the return of seats, were communicated to the sytem by means of the keyboard. There were 120 key sets on the system, and by 1955 the rate of operation was 7.5 million transactions per year. By 1957 the system was replaced by a new model which maintained in the drum memory an inventory of the flights for next ten days together with information on the day's arrivals and departures. (3).

By 1961 there were 12 systems of this type in operation, including one which was handling reservations at Sheraton Hotels. Key sets of these systems spread to more than 100 cities in the USA and Canada. They communicated with their systems over telegraph circuits. A method of saving on communications lines known as *multi-drop* was used on these systems. With the multi-drop method a communications line from the system to a terminal then continues to a further terminal or terminals so that a number of terminals are connected to the system by the same line. Some method of allocating the use of the common line is then needed. Mostly this is done by the control computer addressing the terminals on the common line in turn.

An aircraft seat-reservation system provides a clear example of the problem, discussed in the previous section, of access to the *data base*, that is the data accumulated in the system, in the case of a system failure. If access to the inventory of unsold seats as maintained on the drum were lost, it would have taken a long time to reconstruct it. To reduce the possibility of system failures, the Reservisor had duplicated computers and drums operating in parallel. Some of the electrical signals within the two machines were continuously compared as a check of correct operation. When a discrepancy was discovered test routines were carried out on the computers, and the one discovered to be faulty was taken out of operation. The systems were scheduled to run 7 days a week, 22 hours a day, and did in fact achieve 99.8% of the scheduled run time.

Systems like the Magnetronic Reservisor, with their control circuits designed to perform special functions, are described as having *hard-wired control*. They lack the flexibility of a system controlled by a computer whose functions can be modified by changing the program in the store, have to be specially designed for the specific application, and, if any changes are required in their operation, the maker of the system has to be called in to design and carry out the necessary modifications to the system. Systems controlled by general-purpose computers are said to be *stored program controlled*. The first such systems were developed for military applications.

The most pressing military data-processing need was for air defense. To counter the threat posed by ever faster aircraft and missiles, capable of carrying nuclear warheads, powerful and sophisticated radars of various types were developed. All these radars generated large amounts of data at very high rates. Yet more input data came from the ground observer corps, weather people, air-traffic-control authorities, and the various weapons bases. All this data had to be captured, processed, evaluated, and made to control the various defense weapons, such as interceptor aircraft, anti-aircraft missiles, and anti-aircraft guns. In early 1950 the military authorities concluded that the problems could only be solved by automatic data processing. A contract was placed jointly by the three armed services with the Massachusetts Institute of Technology for the Lincoln Laboratory there to develop a real-time control system for air defense. The system was called SAGE, for Semi-Automatic Ground Environment (4).

The "semi-automatic" in the name of the system acknowledged that the decision-making processes were the province of the human controllers. That meant that the system had to capture all relevant data, process it, present it to the controllers for their decisions, accept their decisions, re-process the data to reflect them, and then to produce the consequent outputs required to implement these decisions. Thus SAGE is probably the first example of a so-called Management Information System, in this case the management of air-defense activities.

The area covered by SAGE was divided into 30 sectors, each under the control of a direction center. At each center over 100 air-force personnel divided between them the air-defense tasks such as surveillance, identification, weapon control, or sector command. The computer maintained at all times a complete picture of the air situation within the sector and data on the weapons bases such as the operational status of the various weapons. From this data base the computer supplied each operator with data needed for the performance of his task at the latter's request. The computer could also force high-priority data for the attention of the operator. Data was presented on a 19-inch air-situation display. This was a map-type display of data ranging from geographical features to predicted interception points. In addition, information such as weather conditions at an airfield or the reason for the rejection of an operator's request could be presented on 5-inch alphanumeric displays. Operators and controllers could also be alerted by audible alarms. Messages could be input to the computer by keyboards and switches. Special devices known as light guns (see Chapter 3) were provided to enable operators to identify to the computer a particular item on a display.

The operation of the system is outlined in Fig. 1.2. Radar data, aircraft flight plans, weather data, weapons-status data from weapons bases, and messages from adjacent centers and from command headquarters arrived in digital form and were automatically processed. Other, infrequent input data came over the telephone. If necessary, it was entered

into the computer by means of keyboards or punched cards. Digitally en-
coded outputs were automatically transmitted to interceptors over ground-
to-air data links, and to weapons bases, adjacent centers, command headquarters, and other users. The SAGE computers, designated AN/FSQ-7,
used what was then a new type of store — small magnetic rings, called
cores, which remembered zeros and ones by the direction in which they
were magnetized. A word could be read out or written into this store in
6 μs — the so-called *cycle time*. More importantly, with the new core
store there was no need to wait until the rotation of the drum brought
the required word under the read or write head. With this new type of
store the computers could carry out some 20,000 instructions per second.
Each computer had 8k words of core, the words being 32 bits long. (As
store mostly comes in multiples of 1024 words, the suffix k, when referring
to store, usually denotes 1024 rather than 1000.) The core memory was
backed by 12 magnetic drums, each with 12k words. The data base
required over 10^6-bits of store. In addition some 75,000 instructions of
program had to be stored. The central computer had some 60,000 vacuum
tubes and occupied 70 cabinets.

With the design of SAGE, most of the basic problems of real-time
system design were solved. One of these was solved by suitable design
of the computer itself. As concluded in the preceding section, the definitive feature of a real-time system is its ability of automatic capture and
delivery of data. Computers for real-time systems therefore have to be
designed so as to make this possible. Logically, the input-output method

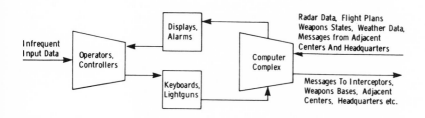

Fig. 1.2.   Summary of SAGE system.

which imposes the least load on the computer is one which deposits or, conversely, extracts information from the store without the need for any action on the part of the central processor. It is in fact perfectly feasible to provide a computer with this capability with very little increase in hardware. The only load on the central processor then is to the extent to which it is held up should it need access to the memory. This feature is known as *direct memory access*. It was provided in the SAGE computers, but its name then was *in-out break feature*.

The man-machine interface on present real-time systems is not very different from that of the SAGE system, and where today's real-time systems incorporate data-transmission facilities, they are in principle much the same as those on SAGE. To obtain continuous operation each center had two complete computer configurations. One, known as the active computer, would be doing the job with the other one on stand-by. When a fault was detected all input-output equipment would be switched automatically to the stand-by machine within a few seconds and the programs started off on that machine. This, however, still left the problem, stated in the preceding section, of the data base accumulated in the active computer. To overcome this, the active computer transmitted all changes in the data base to the stand-by machine several times a minute. The standby machine thus took over with an up-to-date data base. In current terminology this arrangement is known as a *hot start*.

By 1957 SAGE was in production following a period of trial operation of a prototype. Its design may have solved the basic problems of real-time system design, but not everybody could afford a SAGE. The situation, however, changed greatly with the development of transistors. Transistor computers were so much better than their vacuum-tube predecessors that they were termed *second-generation* computers. Size and power requirements were reduced by several orders of magnitude. As the production techniques of transistors improved, the cost of computers came down, their reliability improved, and less maintenance was needed. The electronic telephone exchange, message-switching, and air-traffic-control systems described in section 5.6 provide examples of the many application areas of real-time systems based on second-generation computers.

With the second-generation computers came suppliers of computers specially designed for real-time systems. To keep cost down these machines had short words of 12-18 bits. This was sufficient for real-time applications since 1 bit in 12 corresponds to an accuracy of 1 part in 4,000. Their stores mostly did not exceed 4000 words. Only inexpensive peripherals were available with these machines. Little was offered in the way of support software, i.e. programs to assist users in the task of writing their own programs, but this did not present much of a problem since few applications needed more than a few thousand words of program. Not having to spend their effort any more on developing computers, the designers of real-time systems could now concentrate on system design, while the cost of developing the computer did not have to be recovered in the price of the system. With the availability of these low-cost machines the business of supplying real-time systems to commerce and industry became financially viable. In the mid-sixties the new industry received a major boost through the emergence of a *third generation* of computers. The bulk of the transistors in a computer are used in functional groupings of rather limited variety. Typically such a grouping stores a single bit or adds two bits together. An extension of the transistors manufacturing process made it possible to produce not just a single transistor on a slice of silicon (or *chip* in the jargon), but a complete functional grouping. These became known as *integrated circuits*. Where a computer designer still had to generate some function using individual transistors he would say that he was using *discrete components*.

It was the combination of integrated circuits with greatly improved core stores, much cheaper ones with cycle times down to about a microsecond or less, which resulted in this new generation. Compared with the second-generation computers these machines were still smaller and still more reliable, largely because they had fewer joints and fewer connectors (these having by then become the major source of malfunctions). Their speeds were in the range of hundreds of thousands of instructions per second, while the price of minimal configurations might have been as low as $10,000. To put this development into perspective observe that many of these machines out-performed the SAGE computers which only 10 years earlier needed tens of thousands of valves to achieve their performance. With the reduction in the cost of computers, the designers of real-time systems could now afford larger stores. This allowed them to tackle more ambitious projects. It also meant that they could afford to be somewhat less efficient in their use of the store. This enabled them to produce general service programs which performed the common tasks required in a given type of system. The cost of developing this part of the software could thus be spread over a large number of systems. These common service programs are known as *control* or *executive programs* and are described in Chapter 5. The designers could also now afford to include software which made it possible for operators to communicate with the system without having to know how to program the computer.

With the availability of these third-generation computers, real-time systems spread into a wide variety of applications. Control of production and distribution, from utilities to chemical processing, was one of the major areas of expansion (5,6). An example of a so-called *process control* system is one at a chemical plant with a continuous process which nevertheless had to be shut down and re-started frequently, with the start and shut-downs executed in a precisely prescribed and controlled manner (7). This system was also required to detect malfunctions and to display continuously information on the status of the plant. It had 80 analog inputs from a variety of sensors monitoring the process, and a further 160 digital inputs providing information on the condition of the plant and the status of control elements such as valves. To optimize the process, 40 control loops had to be computed continuously. Ninety digital outputs controlled valves, pumps, motors, etc. The system was based on a third-generation computer with a word length of 12 bits and 24k of core store. The computer configuration included an alphanumeric cathode-ray-tube display, printers, and paper-tape-handling equipment. The system operated under the control of an executive program for process-control systems. The display of information on the status of the plant and process could be controlled by operators without a knowledge of programming. They did this by typing on the keyboard one or more commands from a predetermined list. A special program within the system recognized these messages and translated them into the computer instructions needed to execute them. Similarly, a list of over 50 commands for changes in the plant, e.g. "close valve so and so", was available to enable operators to specify the sequence of actions for, say, a shut-down of the plant without a knowledge of programming. The software for recognizing and translating these messages did not have to be included in the operational system software since it was only used when the operational programs were prepared or modified. Such a facility, specific to a given type of application, is sometimes referred to as a *problem-oriented language*.

To provide for failure of the control system the operators' control panel was extended to provide the operators with visual indications of the state of the process and with manual control of the system outputs. With process-control systems the possibility of providing these visual indications eliminates the problem of providing access to the data base in the case of system failure. This makes it possible to fall back on manual control or stand-by analog controls. With well-designed systems based on third-generation computers system failures may be expected not to exceed three a year. In many cases continuity of operation may be important, particularly if, as has been claimed in one case, the system pays for itself in less than 40 hours. In such cases the computers and common equipment are duplicated (7,8). Process-control systems range from simple systems with minimal computer configurations whose task is merely to log operating data on the process to hierarchical systems controlling chemical plant occupying hundreds of acres (9,10).

The introduction of the second-generation computers started off a snowball effect (or positive feedback in engineering jargon) between the advances in computer technology, computer design, and the design and spread of real-time systems. As the suppliers of computers took advantage of the advances in computer technology and components to reduce the cost of computers, the designers of real-time systems took advantage of these machines to increase the cost effectiveness of their systems, thus increasing sales and calling for a greater volume of production. This greater volume enabled the manufacturers of computer components to improve their manufacturing processes, increasing the levels of circuit integration. They could then produce circuits performing ever more complex functions on a single chip (hence the series of abbreviations *SSI*, *MSI*, and *LSI*, which stand for *small-*, *medium-*, and *large-scale integration* respectively). These more advanced components enabled the computer manufacturer to make still cheaper computers which again resulted in more cost-effective real-time systems and so on.

At the time of writing, the snowball effect has reached the stage where integrated circuits performing all the basic functions of a central processor are manufactured on a single chip, so that only a few additional chips are required to turn them into a complete central processor. These circuits are known as microprocessor chips. The most powerful of these can perform some 200,000 instructions per second on 16-bit numbers. Other, slower, microprocessor chips, mostly with 8-bit length words, are becoming so cheap that designers expect to be able soon to produce complete control systems in large quantities for under $100. This opens up a whole new range of application for computer-based systems. Among them are control of ignition and braking in automobiles, control of home appliances, and game playing add-on modules for TV sets (11,12).

1.3.3. The Commercial Line

Commercial data processing on electronic computers was made possible by the development of a wide range of peripherals for input, output, storage, and transmission of data. To assist their customers in the use of their new tools the suppliers offered them ready-made programs for the most common commercial processing tasks such as payroll or stock control. These *packages*, as they came to be known, had to suit most customers and hence were not particularly efficient for anyone. To help the customer write his own programs the suppliers provided him with *high-level languages*. These were to be used in much the same way as the problem-oriented languages mentioned in the preceding section, but were much more powerful and sophisticated tools not limited to specific types of application. There were, however, two main varieties, FORTRAN being the prime example of a high-level language for scientific computation, while COBOL became the standard language for commercial applications. With these languages came *compilers* — programs for translating the statements permitted in the language into the appropriate machine instructions for the specific machine, the so-called *object code*. The statements in the high-level language were the *source program*. (In theory, a program written in a high-level language should be *portable*, i.e. compiled and executed on any machine having a compiler for that language. In practice this is not always so.) Compiler-generated codes had over twice as many instructions as manually generated programs. To control the operation of the computer configuration with its various peripherals, application packages, and compilers, and to provide standard facilities for commercial data processing, such as file handling, programs known as *operating systems* were also provided with the computers. As these operating systems had to allow for many possible combinations of computer configuration, application programs, and compilers, they did not always use the computer very efficiently. Some operating systems themselves had hundreds of thousands of instructions, so they had to be kept on backing stores, such as magnetic tape or disks, with only those parts which were actually being used at a given time in core store (the so-called main store). The same applied to all the other software. There was, therefore, continuous transferring of program and data between the main store and the backing stores. All this insulating of the users from the technicalities of the computer greatly reduced the *throughput*, that is the amount of useful work done by the machine in a given time. It did, however, succeed splendidly in encouraging non-technical people to use the computers to do their data processing. As these users gathered experience and confidence they began to exploit the potential of electronic computers in applications requiring real-time operation. To do so they turned, quite naturally, to the suppliers who provided them with their large data-processing systems to meet these requirements as well. They could not have gone to the engineers developing the technical real-time systems anyway because the computers which these engineers were using were quite unsuitable. The maximum size of their main store was usually 32k short words. They had no large random-access backing stores (that is, disks or drums as opposed to tape) and the support software available with them was inadequate for the development of the extensive programs which were needed. To the commercial users these were mere *minicomputers* — adequate perhaps for those minor technical applications but not serious contenders for large-scale applications. The commercial users therefore settled down with their suppliers to develop real-time systems from scratch. They started off by coining a phrase to describe what they set out to achieve — *transaction processing*. This expressed the aim of having each transaction processed as it occurred, in contrast to batch processing where batches of transactions of the same kind were accumulated and processing postponed until there was a batch large enough to be processed. (Logically, transaction processing is not synonymous with real-time operation — in practice it largely is.)

For commercial data processing speed of computation was of secondary importance, the throughput of the computer configuration being limited by the speed of the peripherals. Real-time operation, having to meet the response times even under peak loads, does require high-speed processing. To increase the throughput of the computers the commercial users had to sacrifice their insulation from technicalities. The programs had to be written specifically for individual applications, mostly in *assembler*. (This is a language specific to a given computer in which, mostly, each statement corresponds to a machine instruction, so that assembler-written programs are as efficient as those written in machine language.) The splendid all-embracing operating systems had to go, to be replaced by operating systems or executives designed specially for the specific application. Even so, the systems sometimes included one or more minicomputers to do tasks which could be separated from the rest of the work and fitted into the limited main store of the minis. Mostly, these tasks were concerned with input, output, or transmission of data, taking advantage of the fact that the minicomputers often had better input-output facilities than commercial ones (see section 3.4). It also turned out that, for the type of processing for which they were designed, even the cheapest minis compared favorably with the commercial machines in processing speed (13). The minis to which input-output tasks were delegated became known as *front-end processors*.

The scale of some transaction-processing systems will be appreciated from a brief description of British Overseas Airways BOADICEA system. This system superseded a hard-wired seat-reservation system of the type described in the previous subsection. Its development began in the mid-sixties. The following description relates to the system as it was in 1972, by which time nearly 1000 man years had been spent on its development. (Since then, BOAC having merged with BEA, BOADICEA has given way to a more advanced system called BABS.) BOADICEA served 400 cities and airports on the five continents. Some 40 of these offices were linked directly into the system by means of terminals, the largest offices having up to 200 of them. All in all over 1500 terminals were connected to the system. A further 30 offices were linked directly into the system by means of printer keyboard sets.

The system maintained inventory records for the flights of British Airways and its pool partners for 11 months ahead. For all these flights records were maintained of individual passengers, with such items as ticket details, special meal and seat requests, and contact addresses or telephone numbers. (Contrast this with the mere 10 days worth of flight availability and status data only maintained by the hard-wired systems.) The system processed the itinerary for the whole journey, which could involve up to 20 or 30 flights, with perhaps over a dozen airlines. For this purpose the system also maintained availability and time-table information for hundreds of flights of other airlines. Bookings could also be made for hotels, tours, hire cars, etc. Tied in with the seat-reservation functions was the departure control function. This recorded that passengers checked in, took note of any special needs, such as special meals, and allocated seats as necessary. It would also prepare passenger lists and seat plans when required and forward these to other offices. The departure control function also accepted data on cargo and produced loading plans and information for trimming the aircraft. As the flight was closed a load sheet was produced automatically, together with any messages for other offices.

In addition to the passenger-services functions, BOADICEA also carried out flight functions. The flight-operations control function maintained a data base on the operational state of the airline in terms of flights, aircraft, and flight crews. This data base was used to control the operations of 65 aircraft and some 5000 crew. Flight-planning function calculated the optimum flight plans across the Atlantic based on weather forecasts transmitted directly from the U.K. meteorological office computer. BOADICEA also controlled the airline's world-wide telegraphic communications network as well as the special network which provided direct access from the terminals and printers into the computer. In 1972 over 700,000 messages a day were handled during the peak season.

In addition to all its operational functions BOADICEA was also used to provide training in a real-time mode. Departments with a need to train operators deposited suitable courses in the system. The courses were then available at any terminal at any time in a *conversational mode*, i.e. the trainee would be invited to carry out training exercises at the terminal, and the system would comment on what he did and issue further instructions. The computer complex on which the system was based is indicated in Fig. 1.3. The three system/360 model 65 computers each had 256 k *bytes* of core store (a byte is 8 bits) and its own control console. Total disk storage was about 250 Mbytes. There were also 18 magnetic tape units. Disk storage was used for all real-time operations. The data so captured was recorded on magnetic tape and subsequently used for a great many further *off-line* (i.e. non-real time) data-processing applications. The multiple interconnections between the processors and the switches and between the switches and the peripherals are an example of the system architecture known as *space diversity*. When a unit developed a fault the operational connections between the units would be changed over by means of the switches to remove the faulty unit and enable the system to continue operation. This was done manually within two or three minutes so that the system was operational for over 99% of the scheduled time. The data base was preserved by maintaining multiple copies. The telegraphic communications network controlled by BOADICEA was the world-wide network of BOAC and its associated airlines, operating mostly at 75 bits per second. It was also connected to the regional centers of SITA, the common international network of the airlines. The medium-speed network was specially designed for BOADICEA and connected the major offices directly into the system. Eleven lines operating at 2400 bits per second (the link to New York was actually triplicated, trebling capacity) served some 30 such centers by means of the multi-drop method. At each center one or more *concentrators* based on Argus 400B computers controlled up to 64 cathode-ray-tube terminals and eight printer keyboard sets. In addition to controlling the exchange of messages between these

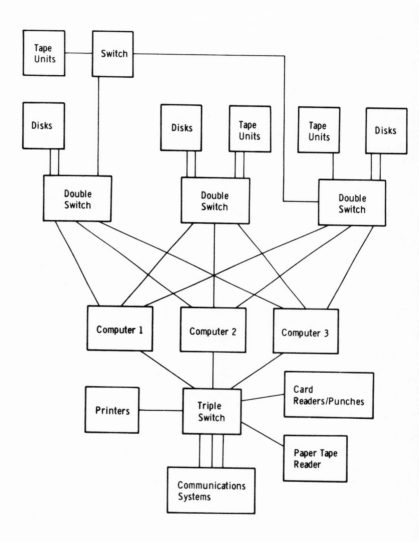

Fig. 1.3.   BOADICEA Central Computer Complex

terminals and the central computer complex the concentrators also provided a local processing capability (14). Offices with more than 64 terminals in them required multiple concentrators, while offices remote from the concentrators were connected to them by means of the keyboard printer sets.

The operation of the whole of the system was controlled by the ACP (Aircraft Control Program) operating system. This operating system was specially designed for high-activity airlines reservation systems and extended by BOAC to cover the communications facilities required in BOADICEA. It may be interesting to observe that based on this system BOAC in turn became a supplier of both program packages for system functions and complete seat-reservation and allied systems.

Transaction-processing systems were at first concerned largely with such highiy perishable commodities as airline seats or hotel beds. Then came applications requiring high-speed data retrieval, such as criminal data-retrieval systems for police forces. As transaction processing became more familiar it spread into many other areas of commercial data processing. Transaction-processing systems are by no means all large ones. Some have only a few terminals on a modest computer configuration.

Real-time systems were also developed for scientific and technical computation. Ideally scientists and technologists would have liked to have, without leaving their offices, unrestricted use of a computer large enough to contain programs for all the calculations they might require, and fast enough to provide the answers on the spot. The computer should also enable them to develop new programs, preferably in a scientific high-level language like FORTRAN or ALGOL. Individual scientists could neither afford nor load such a machine to more than a minute fraction of its capacity, even if they were using it continuously. The problem was solved by sharing out time on a large computer amongst a number of scientists. An experimental *time-sharing system* went into operation in Cambridge, Mass., in 1962 (15). It used one of the small minicomputers which had just become available (PDP 1) and had provision for five simultaneous users. The computers had 8k of core store, of which 4k was occupied by the executive which controlled the operation of the system, including input and output on the five typewriters, leaving 4k of main store for the user's program. The computer was backed by a drum which had 22 sectors of 4k words each. The user's program would be suspended and transferred from the main store to the backing store after being run for 140 μs, if it was found that it was waiting for an action by the user or it was held up waiting for output. At the same time the next program which was ready to run was transferred from the drum to the main store. The drum was specially modified to permit these simultaneous transfers. The computer was modified to provide a *privileged* mode of operation in addition to its normal mode. This mode was reserved for the executive program. Access to the 4 k of store reserved for the executive and input-output instructions would only be executed in privileged mode. Attempts at such access or instructions in normal mode, i.e. in a users program, would cause the program to be suspended and transferred to the drum and control transferred to the executive.

Large time-sharing systems offering their many users far more sophisticated facilities had to be based on large commercial machines. Such large time-sharing systems were made available to staffs of universities and research institutes in the second half of the sixties. Their use was then also made available to the general public on a commercial basis over the telephone network.

There is an essential difference between time-sharing systems and all the systems described earlier. The latter were all dedicated to the performance of a specific task and are in fact known as *dedicated* systems. In such systems the data-processing capacity is exploited as a means of achieving an objective which is usually a control or management function. In principle (but as has been seen not in practice) a dedicated system could be replaced by a hard-wired controlled system. In a time-sharing system, in contrast, the provision of data-processing capacity is itself the design objective. Some of this data-processing capacity has to be sacrificed for the control of the system itself, just as any organization has to devote some of its revenue to its own administration. The designer of a time-sharing system tries to keep this overhead to a minimum. Unlike the designer of a dedicated real-time system, the designer of a time-sharing system does not know in advance what the mix of the programs will be, nor what the load on the various resources such as central processor, disks, or printers will be. He can only try and balance the design so as to prevent any of these resources from becoming a bottleneck at some time or other. Time-sharing systems are covered in (16) and the relevant texts in the bibliography. This book is confined to dedicated real-time systems.

1.4. Big, Mini, Micro

To sell a commercial real-time system the salesman may have to convince the production manager that it will provide a solution to the production-control problem, or he may have to convince the financial manager that it will solve the stock-control problem. To do so he will have to suggest a method of controlling stock or production which required the use of a system made up of a computer configuration and programs, and which may well require further programs written by the customer himself. The production manager or financial director will probably know nothing about computers and will not be in the least bit interested in the word length or in how many microseconds the computer takes to add two numbers together. The product offered is a solution to a management problem, including a special tool. This tool, the computer, may represent some 20% to 30% of the price of the total product sold to a vice-president.

"Mini people on the other hand wear beards and sweaters and know about word-lengths and add-times . . . They expect to program in machine language and get inside the operating system as a matter of course. And they don't expect the computer manufacturer to hold their hand in any way. He sold them the machine and gave them a 'good luck' card and is now on his way selling another. They are the engineers who know what goes on under the bonnet while the big computer people think cars were made for driving, not for getting dirty under" (17).

As explained in the preceding subsection the "mini" tag was stuck on these computers at a time when they were in many respects much more limited than machines designed for commercial data processing. Inevitably perhaps the latter then became known as *big* computers. These names can no longer be justified by differences in the capabilities. Apart from the short word length, which most, but not all, minis have retained, the remaining differences are largely in the software. The operating systems of minicomputers are much more limited than those of the big machines. Minis have far fewer application packages and hardly any large-scale general utility programs such as, for instance, a general-purpose program for the management of a large data base. Also much of the software which is available comes from suppliers other than the mini makers themselves. The same applies to many peripherals. However, these remaining differences are disappearing rapidly. One which is not is price. If all that one requires is computing power supported by basic software for the development of programs, then such computing power may be between three and five times cheaper if bought as such, i.e. as a minicomputer. (Basic mini configurations of central processor and store only may be up to 30 times more cost effective than big machines (13).)

While minis may largely have caught up with big machines in performance, they are nevertheless products of a quite different nature. They are engineering components, while big computers (also called *mainframes*) are mostly business machines. Not surprisingly the companies making these two products also differ greatly. Big computer manufacturers are almost invariably companies which were large suppliers of business machines before computers came along. As and when they became convinced that suitable computers would become efficient business machines they took them aboard, marketing them in much the same way as they market their other products. It is instructive to reflect that large and highly skilled electronic companies which tried to penetrate this market failed to do so. The manufacturers of minis, on the other hand, evolved with the growth of their product. The average age, at the time of writing, of the six largest minicomputer suppliers is probably around 10 years. Mini suppliers are mostly smaller specialist companies in an intensely competitive market where products become obsolete in two to three years. To succeed in such a market place requires a rare combination of skills. A study of minicomputer manufacturers does in fact provide a highly instructive insight into the problem of economic exploitation of technological advances, but is outside the scope of this book.

The availability of low-cost minicomputers has made viable the business of supplying real-time systems to order. The suppliers of such systems are known as systems houses, and they often specialize in systems for certain ranges of applications. The systems house will agree with the customer on a specification for the system, will then design the system to meet the specification, buy in standard components, produce any special hardware or software that may be needed, build the system, and deliver it to the customer. With such tailor-made systems the knowledgeable customer has the advantage of getting precisely what he needs. To start with there was not much overlap between the systems houses and the big computer makers. In time full confrontation has developed, with the big computer makers competing in such traditionally technical areas as private branch telephone exchanges or on-ship radar collision-avoidance systems, while many systems houses are offering systems for commercial applications, both real time and batch processing.

The microprocessor chips mentioned in § 1.3.2 have made available a further level of do-it-yourself, in that they enable suitably qualified engineers to construct their own computers for their systems. With these microprocessor chips one does indeed have to design and make one's own computer. Further chips are required to first turn the microprocessor chip into a complete central processor. One then has to add store and whatever is required to communicate with the outside world. Furthermore, if a stand-alone microcomputer is required one will also need a box and a power supply, which may cost more than the electronics. By the time all this is done it may well have been cheaper to buy a mini, even if it means overkilling the processing required. The mini makers have helped see to this by reducing the prices of low-performance minis. The popular presentation of the microprocessor chip as a "computer on a chip" is therefore far from accurate. The main thrust of microprocessors is not in competition with minis but in the downward extension of the economic viability of computer control. Some examples of such applications have been mentioned at the end of § 1.3.2. The makers of both computers and systems are themselves major users of microprocessors. Computer makers use them in peripherals controllers, particularly display terminals. Some systems houses use them as the processors in small commercial systems. In all these applications the microprocessors are built into a host product.

Since microcomputer configurations are unlikely to have enough store for their support software their suppliers make this support software available on time-sharing systems. A program written in assembler or high-level language for a given microcomputer is then assembled or compiled on the machine of some time-sharing service and the resulting object code returned to the microprocessor user to be loaded into the microcomputer. This is known as *cross assembling* or *cross compilation*. Increasingly though, microcomputer makers also offer configurations with enough main store and low-cost backing store to enable customers to produce their programs on the microcomputer itself, as well as support software to assist in this task.

Microprocessors use semiconductor store, rather than core store, for cheapness. Cost is particularly low for store which, once written into, need only be read out subsequently. Such store is known as *ROS* or *ROM* (for *Read Only Store* or *Memory*) and is used for storing programs once they are fully *debugged* (i.e. all errors have been rectified) and proven (i.e. shown to do what they were supposed to do). Data is kept in store that can be both read and written into and is known for a historical reason as *RAM* (for *Random Access Memory*). With programs in RAM there is always the possibility that they may get overwritten or otherwise corrupted. Having them in ROM therefore has the further advantage of eliminating the need for an input device such as a paper-tape reader to reload damaged programs. Such an input device would have been bulkier and more expensive than the microcomputer itself, and would have frightened the customer of the host product into thinking that he was taking on a computer.

There is a close resemblance between the development of microprocessors and the development which the mini underwent in its day. Many of the first microprocessors were designed for manually operated calculators, had word lengths of 4 bits, and were capable of some 20,000 instructions per second. Since then the word length of some micros has grown to 16 bits and they have caught up in performance with the bottom end of mini computers. This upward extension of their performance capabilities is continuing. At first they were offered with no support software. More recent and powerful microprocessors do come with support software, including attempts at high-level language. Also, as their makers find out more about how their products are used, they add to the basic microprocessor chips further specially designed functional chips both for completing the basic chip into a full central processor and for *interfacing* it (i.e. connecting it to input and output devices). Microprocessors are therefore often bought as *chip sets*.

Computers differ from other bought-out components in that after a while the user often generates a major investment in a particular computer. This investment may consist of software written in languages specific to that machine, input-output devices designed to interface with it, sheer expertise in programming it and interfacing to it, and ownership of a more or less extensive configuration for program development. The value of this investment may amount to hundreds of thousands of dollars, and this means that a change to another computer would be prohibitively expensive. This phenomenon is known as *lock in*. Because of it computer makers try to make all their computers *compatible*, i.e. have the same set of instructions and the same interfaces. A customer is therefore usually locked into a particular manufacturer rather than a specific model. Lock in is so far not significant with microprocessors because software for them is on a much smaller scale. With further development of microprocessors this may change.

To summarize, technology or performance differences between big, mini, and microcomputers have proved to be transient ones in the past and are likely to prove so in the future. The essential differences are in the nature of the products, as the top part of Table 1.1. attempts to show. These differences boil down to the degree of do-it-yourself.

Table 1.1. Computer Suppliers, Products, and Customers

Maker	Product	Specification against which sold	Customer
Mainframe manufacturer	Big computer	Promise of solution to management problems	End user
Systems house	Tailor-made system	Performance specifica- tion of system (e.g. response times)	End user
Minicomputer manufacturer	Minicomputer	Performance specifica- tion of computer	OEM, end user
Semiconductor manufacturer	Microcomputer circuits, chip sets	Performance specifica- tion of individual integrated circuits	Mini-maker, OEM, manu- facturers of many other products
Peripheral manufacturer	Peripherals, maybe with interfaces	Performance specifica- tion of peripherals	Mini & micro makers, OEM, end user
Software house	Software	Specification of program	Mini & micro makers, OEM, end user
Add-on manufacturer	Add-on units	Performance specifica- tion of unit	OEM, end user

Table 1.1 also includes three categories of independent suppliers of other systems components. Programs from software houses are often general utility programs (e.g. universal payroll program or data-base man-

agement and access program) produced as a speculative venture. With these the software house often competes against a big computer maker on price/performance. Such software will tend to be written in a high-level language to make it portable to many computers with minimum modification. Software houses will also write software to order, both utility programs for a specific machine, such as a compiler for a given language for a particular machine, or programs for a specific application. The term *add-on* embraces main-store modules and peripherals designed to be plugged into and operate as part of designated computer configurations. (These units are also known as *plug compatibles*.) They mostly compete against peripherals supplied by the maker of the particular computer on price/performance, but may also be peripherals not available from the maker. (The latter is more likely to be the case with minicomputers.)

It is also convenient to distinguish between two types of computer customers. The term *end user* denotes the customer who actually ends up using the system. He may acquire the system either as a tailor-made one, or as a standard big computer, or he may build it himself; he may even run his system by buying time on a bureau machine. The customer who buys a mini or a micro to build it into a system which he then in turn sells to an end user is known as an OEM (Original Equipment Manufacturer). Minis are sold to either type of customer, the end-user customers for minis being either users who build their own systems or else people who buy them directly for their computer power as such, e.g. educational establishments. The mini maker often has different conditions of sale for his two types of customer, reflecting the fact that the end user will expect a higher degree of support. Also, the OEM may benefit from substantial quantity discounts, up to 50% in the limit.

The situation as summarized in Table 1.1 may well be affected by the advances in semiconductor technology. The tremendous advance in computer design described in the preceding section has been wholly dependent on the use of magnetic cores for computer main store, but cores are about to be ousted by semiconductor memory. At the time of writing computer makers are already offering a choice of semiconductor memory modules with a cycle time of 0.5 μs at substantially lower cost than core store with 1 μs cycle time. The significance of this is that it makes the semiconductor manufacturer a supplier of a computer component for which he did not until now compete.

Like a minicomputer, a microprocessor chip has its own special set of instructions. However, there are now on offer so-called *bit slices*, LSI circuits specially created for the design of central processors with any desired instruction set. Furthermore, some are fast enough to make the processors capable of performing up to several million instructions per second. Also, fast stores with cycle times of less than 100 ns are becoming available. This will make it possible to produce simple inexpensive mini-computers of straightforward design offering a performance which at present can only be achieved by sophisticated and expensive designs.

Another advance in semiconductor technology (*CCD*, for *Charge-Coupled Devices*) promises large-capacity stores to replace magnetic disks. These new stores should provide faster access to the data without the problems of rotating machinery. Here again it is a case of a semi-conductor product replacing something which until now exploited a different technology and has come from a different supplier. Not surprisingly, a movement towards vertical integration can already be discerned. Some computer manufacturers are moving downwards into semiconductor production. In the opposite direction some semiconductor manufacturers use their bit slices to produce minicomputers having the same instruction set as existing widely used minicomputers, which they then offer at low prices, without software support, largely to users locked into these machines. Other semiconductor manufacturers are moving upwards with their micro-processor chips by raising the level of support towards that offered by minicomputer manufacturers. The smaller mini makers, whose production quantities make it expensive for them to have custom integrated circuits designed for their instruction sets, are faced with a difficulty. They may solve it by turning into systems houses.

The bit slices also make it possible for systems houses locked into a given range of machines to design their own computers. This may not be competitive against large-volume production minicomputers on a straight computer-for-computer basis. It may, however, be financially beneficial where the systems house has to modify the standard bought-out machine to meet their needs, or where the computer is tightly integrated into the system. Again, such replacement of bought-out minis by machines built in-house is already taking place.

A further major force for change comes not from a technical development but from an educational one. In the sixties the spread of computers was very much a question of selling them to managements who, in the words of Fortune magazine, "do not know about computers but know about IBM". With knowledge gained and with the emergence of managers who have learned about computers at school, this is no longer quite so, and the preserves of the big computer makers are increasingly challenged by minicomputers and systems houses. All in all it would not be surprising to see an accelerating movement towards vertical integration, tougher competition, and a yet further shake-out of suppliers. Computers and computer systems will become still more cost-effective products in ever-growing markets. Microprocessor chips will probably replace minis as the fastest growth area. Their utilization in the downward extension area may result in possibly a fifty-fold unit-volume growth in the second half of the decade. Dollar-volume growth will, however, be much smaller. Even so microprocessors could greatly exceed minis in value by the end of the decade. Indeed, the impact of microprocessors may stop value growth in minis, in spite of continuing unit-volume growth. Big computers are so much more expensive that, even assuming modest growth, they could still represent a ten times bigger market than minis and micros together. All this depends on the distinctions between the three sectors still being meaningful by then.

1.5. The Future of Real-Time Systems

Real-time computer systems can be a highly effective means of optimizing the utilization of resources. The quest for a higher standard of living leads to the development of ever more sophisticated and hence ever more expensive machinery. Any significant improvement in the utilization of such machinery therefore results in major cost advantages. This applies not only to many kinds of productive capacity but also to the utilization of assets employed in the provision of services or amenities, such as transportation or theater performances.

In many cases a whole operation is only possible by virtue of the very rapid response achievable by automatic computer control. This, for example, is the case in many military applications. One such instance is the deployment of combat aircraft. Ground-to-air missiles are now capable of inflicting such a high casualty rate that in certain cases the use of combat aircraft is only feasible when the aircraft are equipped with means for jamming the missiles' radar. The control of the radar-jamming equipment requires response times in the microsecond region, which can only be achieved by means of fast airborne computers.

Many resources cannot be easily augmented by man. Room on our planet is one of these, as is the space around it. At one stage the air space over the so-called golden triangle (Boston-New York-Washington) became so congested that flying within this area turned into a gamble as to where and when one would end up. One of the objectives of an air-traffic-control system is improved utilization of the air space. Another objective is improved safety. A collision between two wide-bodied jets could be even more disastrous than a collision between two 1950 vintage airliners. A collision between two laden supertankers may have rather drastic consequences, as could the loss of control in a nuclear power station. Many real-time control systems are there to ensure acceptable safety levels.

While resources become scarcer and hence more expensive, the cost of real-time systems, on the other hand, is coming down. The cost of the electronic hardware is halved every two or three years. The cost of designing the system may be increasing, but is increasingly spread over a larger number of systems. The possible use of real-time systems to improve fuel economy of the private motor car, mentioned in § 1.3.2, provides a good example of these trends.

These factors are by no means limited to technical systems. Just as machinery is becoming ever more complex, so are management tasks, whether of an individual enterprise or over the economy as a whole. The majority of computer applications in this area are at present still of the batch-processing type. There are, however, several factors which make real-time systems increasingly more attractive in these applications as well. One is the increase in the cost of labor. Quite apart from cost, there are the problems of recruiting operatives and keeping them working happily on tasks which are by their nature repetitive and tedious. Thirdly, there are the delays and operational limitations inherent in batch processing. These features are illustrated by the way in which the use of computers in banks developed. Computerization was originally introduced to save labor, primarily to eliminate the problems of a large labor turnover among clerks engaged in routine tasks. Batch processing was used to start with; then, as it was realized that this did not provide a satisfactory level of service, there came the switch to real-time operation.

Over and above these factors, however, is the blatant inefficiency, as the use of computers spreads, of first translating data into a computer-suitable form and subsequently having the computer change it back into a form amenable to humans, who send it off to some other organization where it is manually handled and then again translated into a computer-amenable form for processing there. It is clearly much more efficient to have the computers transmit information, as and when required, directly to other computers. Much development work is in fact being devoted to the development of computer-controlled communications networks for transmission of data between computers. A group of computers interconnected in this way is referred to as a *computer network*. Not only does such a network allow the interchange of data, but also the sharing of processing resources such as programs (18,19).

Computer terminals to capture data at the point of sale, known as *point-of-sale (P.O.S.)* terminals are mushrooming. Once data on a transaction is so captured there is no technical reason why all the consequent financial transactions should not be completed between the various computer systems involved automatically without further human intervention. The combination of point-of-sale terminals and computer networks leads towards the so-called *cashless society* in which neither cash nor checks are needed. In the case of a small retailer, say, the terminals may well be connected to a computer at his bank. Assuming that data on all transactions is captured by the terminals, this then enables the bank to offer the retailer data-processing services, such as accounting or stock control. All this raises many operational, social, and legal problems. For instance, there has already been a case where a U.S. court has ruled that it is illegal for a bank to offer such data-processing services.

All in all the opportunities for the use of real-time systems and the benefits to be derived from such use are tremendous. Their growth is therefore more likely to accelerate than slow down. The great power of real-time systems implies, however, that they will have a major impact on our society and way of life. Their introduction and use must therefore be managed with careful forethought.

References

1. Weik, M.H. *A Survey of Domestic Electronic Digital Computing Systems,* p. 177. BRL Rep. No. 971; Aberdeen Proving Ground, Md., 1955.

2. *Ibid.,* p. 101.

3. Weik, M.H. *A Third Survey of Domestic Electronic Digital Computing Systems,* p. 876. BRL Rep. No. 1115. Aberdeen Proving Ground, Md., 1961.

4. Everett, R.R., Zraket, C.A., and Bennington, H.D. SAGE — A data-processing system for air defense. *Proc. Joint Eastern Computer Conf.,* 1957, pp. 148-55, 1957.

5. Powell, J.J. Mississippi Valley Gas Co. uses computer dispatching. *Chilton's Gas,* Sept. 1972.

6. Daigre, L.C., III, and Nieman, G.R. Computer control of ammonia plants. *Chem. Engng. Prog.,* pp. 50-3, Feb. 1974.

7. Notley, J.P.W. The computer as standard process control equipment. *Process Engng.* pp. 113-5, Sept. 1974.

8. Butler, J.L., and Mueller, J.J. A dual processor system for process control. *27th Annual Conf. of Instrument Society of America, New York,* Oct. 1972.

9. Nieman, G.R. Mini-systems in the processing plant. *Instrum. Control Syst.,* Feb., March 1974.

10. *Computer Networks,* p. 200. Infotech Information Ltd., Maidenhead, Berks, UK., 1971.

11. Morris, J.H., Patel, H., and Schwartz, M. Scamp microprocessor aims to replace mechanical logic. *Electronics* pp. 81-7. 18 Sept. 1975.

12. ITT's microprocessor programs washers and is adaptable to other appliances. *Electronics* Oct. 1975.

13. *Minicomputers,* pp. 403-17. Infotech Information Ltd., Maidenhead, Berks, UK, 1973.

14. *Computer Networks,* Infotech Information Ltd., Maidenhead, Berks, UK.

15. McCarthy, J., Boilen, S., Fredkin, E., and Licklider, J.C.R. A time-sharing debugging system for a small computer. *AFIPS Conf. Proc.,* V. 23, p. 51, 1963.

16. Wilkes, M.V. *Time-Sharing Computer Systems* (2nd edn.) Macdonald and Jane's. London, 1975.

17. Duncan, R. Mini-ways: what every big user ought to know, *Dataweek* 24 July 1974.

18. Roberts, L.C., and Wessler, B.D. Computer network development to achieve resource sharing, *AFIPS Conf. Proc.* 36, 543-9, 1970.

Deciding on
a System

2.1. The System as a Tool

Books on systems engineering define a system as "a set of objects with relationships between the objects and between their attributes" (1) or as "any set of objects related by some interaction" (2) or, more simply, as "a collection of interrelated parts" (3). Such a definition, by which "virtually anything can be a system" (3) is, however, by definition, no definition at all. It is more useful to consider some examples of the common usage of the word. We have systems of taxation, educational systems, systems of primary education, systems of classification, seat-reservation systems, and process-control systems. On the other hand, one does not refer to, say, the set of all teachers as a system, nor would one accept as a system of classification a method which is not valid for all the objects concerned. It is thus seen that *system* means a complete tool for the performance of an activity aimed at achieving a given purpose. The tool may be an abstract method or it may be a set of physical entities, in which case it may or may not comprise humans. Also, a system may well be part of a wider, more embracing, system, but even so it will comprise everything needed to pursue its part of the task.

Because systems are tools for the pursuance of a purpose they often come in hierarchies, so that one man's system is another man's component. For instance, the designer who combines matrices of ferrite cores with electronic circuitry and mechanical components into a complete tool for storing data within a digital computer will refer to his product as a memory system. To the designer of a digital computer, this memory is merely one of the components he works with, while to the designer of, say, an air-traffic-control system, the whole of the computer is just one component of his system. The air-traffic-control system is in turn a component of a country's air transportation system.

If a real-time system is a tool for performing an activity aimed at achieving a given purpose, then to be successful it has to be designed as such a tool. The many problems, frustrations, and, indeed, failures in the development of real-time systems are often presented as the inevitable penalties of pioneering technology. However, a study of the history of some disappointing systems shows that the prime cause usually lies not in technology but in the inadequacy of the preparatory analysis and in incomplete system specification. The seeds of failure had already been sewn before any engineering even started.

This chapter explains a method for ensuring that the real-time system will be designed as a tool for achieving the given purpose, indeed the optimal tool: first define precisely the overall objective, then decide the way of achieving it, and from this derive the specification of the real-time system (Fig. 2.1). All this is then optimised by comparative cost-benefit analyses, thus also providing the data for deciding whether it should be done at all.

2.2. Definition of Objective

Since the basic aim is to achieve a given purpose, this purpose must be precisely defined. It is a law of human behavior that any activity which has been going on long enough becomes a goal in itself, its original pur-

Fig. 2.1.   Objective to operational requirement.

pose forgotten. Consider, for example, Emerson's famous saying: "If a man builds a better mousetrap, the world will beat a path to his door". Here, building a better mousetrap became a goal in itself, whereas, as J.E. Arnold of M.I.T. pointed out, the true purpose was not necessarily to build a better mousetrap but to get rid of mice, whichever way this can best be done. He then went on to point out that the actual wording of the purpose had to be done with great care. Here, for instance, the purpose is to get rid of mice rather than to kill them; thus the true purpose would also be fulfilled if a means could be found to induce the mice to commit mass suicide by rushing into the sea like lemmings (4). If, on the other hand, the purpose is a new one, enthusiasm for it may confuse its true nature. "More up-to-date information on stocks" may sound a desirable enough purpose, but is it? What will you do with it? Reduce stocks? This then is your real purpose.

This, however, is still not enough. Suppose you achieve, say, a 5% reduction in stocks within a year, will this be something to be proud of or a miserable effort? The extent to which the purpose is to be achieved and the time within which this is to be accomplished both have to be quantified to know what one is really aiming for. One then has an *objective*. The quantification makes it possible to determine the benefits which will result from achieving the objective and also to monitor the extent to which it might be achieved, and thus, given the cost of achieving it, whether the objective is worthwhile. As will be seen in § 2.6, the answer to this question may not necessarily be restricted to yes or no. Quantification of cost and benefit may lead to a quantitative modification of the objective, should it in due course transpire that sights have been set either too high or too low. The quantification inherent in the definition of an objective also directly impacts on the next stage of our procedure; totally different methods may be appropriate depending on whether, say, a 10% or 90% reduction in mouse population, or in production costs, is to be achieved.

2.3. Design of an Operational Policy

Now that the objective has been defined, a way of achieving it has to be decided on. We shall refer to it as an *operational policy*. Working out the operational policy is a design problem. One starts by listing all the possible ways of achieving the objective. In order to encompass all of them, a technique such as brain-storming sessions may be used.

Equally, all the constraints which the operational policy must meet have to be listed. The constraints may be many and varied: political ones, such as the need for international agreement; social ones, such as problems with trade unions; economic, human, and technical constraints. It is clearly essential to be aware of all the constraints. It is equally important, however, not to assume constraints which are not really there. The radar field provides an example of a major breakthrough achieved by exploiting the absence of a constraint.

Radar was originally invented as a means for locating enemy aircraft. As it developed, it also became the main tool for the control of civil air traffic. However, the picture on a radar screen needs skilled interpretation, and even so it provides neither the height of an aircraft nor a means of identifying it. Meanwhile, it occurred to someone that the constraint applying to enemy aircraft, hell bent on avoiding detection, does not apply to co-operative aircraft, who are only too keen to be seen by the radar. This led to the idea of a new form of radar: instead of transmitting very powerful pulses in the hope that some of the energy in them will be reflected back to the radar, pairs of pulses of modest power, with specified time intervals between the pulses in a pair, are transmitted. Such a pair of pulses triggers off a so-called *transponder* in the aircraft to transmit a message which includes the identity of the aircraft and its height. This new form of radar is called *secondary radar,* while the original form is now known as *primary radar.* Secondary radar provides much more information, yet because it needs far less power it is much cheaper. After many years of delay while international agreement was being sought, it has now become the prime tool for air-traffic control.

Armed with the complete list of possibilities and constraints, the best overall approach to an operational policy is sought. This approach is then detailed to see what it will involve. When this is done, one may discover that the approach will not, in fact, work or that it raises serious difficulties. One then returns to the lists to look for an alternative overall approach. As with any design, a number of iterations will probably be needed before a satisfactory policy is achieved. Unless the operational policy is an extremely simple one, this design will consist of a pyramid of operations to be performed. The term *pyramid of ends and means* highlights the fact that in this pyramid an operation is an end at its own level while being a means to the level above it. For instance, to the pilot of an interceptor aircraft, effecting an interception is an end in itself, but to a battle commander the interception is only a means of winning the battle. As will be seen in Chapter 6, ends and means alternate in just the same way in the design of the real-time system, and this alternation determines both the way in which the design, whether of the operational policy or of the real-time system, is done and the manner in which it is subsequently implemented.

With any design one is designing simultaneously a way of operation and an organization for operating in this way. The fact that the design of the operational policy relies on human components means that all such human factors as motivation, control, measurement of performance, and training have to be provided for. The two decisive criteria for a design are whether it will work in an imperfect world beset with problems and whether it will be cheap enough to be worthwhile. Simplicity is the best way yet known of meeting these two criteria, and this applies at least as much to the design of a human organization as it does to other designs.

The time at which the operational policy will have to come into operation and the period during which it will be used are both determined by the quantification of the objective. The design of the new operational policy therefore has to envisage both how the transition to the new policy will be achieved by the required time and how it will function when implemented. All this must be based on the situation as it will be at the relevant times. In addition, the design may have to envisage changes to be introduced at given times to adapt to changes in the objective or to expected changes in operating conditions.

Think not that an operational policy is needed only for such major objectives as the defense of a country's air space. It is needed to achieve any objective, and anyone thinking that he is only out to improve the utilization of a chemical plant had better remember that the additional output will have to be sold. He should also bear in mind that people will have to be taught how to get the most out of the new control system and how to get it back into operation should it fail. People will also be needed to control the plant manually on these occasions, but using people as a standby for a machine, and for rare occasions at that, raises social, organizational, and psychological problems, not the least of which is that these people compete against a machine in a competition which they cannot win.

The operational policy, the analysis which has led to its design, and the method for implementing it must be fully and methodically recorded in a formal document. This will serve as the basic working document for the subsequent stages in our procedure, and the final version will be the guide and control document for the implementation of the operational policy. Furthermore, the very process of producing the document should go a long way towards ensuring that all aspects of the design are fully thought out, a rather desirable aim in a situation where any oversight may prove rather expensive later on.

2.4. Operational Specification of the System

2.4.1. *Allocation of Operations to the System*

Our procedure is concerned with those cases where the new operational policy appears to justify the use of a real-time system, and, indeed, one of the twin aims of the procedure is to quantify this justification. To do so we need to know what the system will have to do; that is, we have to decide which of the operations will be allocated to the system. The correct allocation of operations between the system and the human operators (which determines the so-called *man-machine interaction*) may be crucial for the success of the project. A major factor here is the additional load imposed on the operators by the very introduction of the system and the need to communicate with it. In the case of a production-control system, for instance, if the production operatives have to spend an appreciable amount of time and effort to feed information into the system some of the benefit expected from the system will be lost. In some cases the additional load thus generated may in fact outweigh the advantages which the operatives derive from the use of the system. There is the further consideration that the total load on the operatives, made up of the tasks they had to perform anyway and of the new additional load of communicating with the system, may exceed the capabilities of the operatives. Both these points are conveniently illustrated by the case history of an early experimental air-traffic-control system. This system was designed to superimpose upon the conventional radar display further information, such as position, identity, and height, derived by computer from primary and secondary radar. To communicate with this system, the air-traffic controllers were provided with two keyboards and a graphic input device. (The latter enables an operator to identify to the system a particular item on the display — see § 3.2.) The original design required the controllers to furnish the system with a large amount of imput data. Thus, for instance, when an aircraft took off from the airport where the system was installed, the controller had to identify the aircraft by means of his graphic input device, type in a number on one of his keyboards, and then inform the system that this was the flight number of that aircraft. Another example was the procedure for handing over an aircraft to the next controller; the original controller had to identify the aircraft to the system and then type in a request for such and such controller to take over. When they tried to use the new system, the controllers felt that the benefits afforded them by the system were outweighed by the extra work imposed on them. Furthermore, the extra work load left them no time for the task of controlling aircraft. The controllers decided to redesign the system, modifying the allocation of operations. For aircraft taking off they found that the flight number could be deduced by the system itself from data it already had. For the hand-over procedure use could be made of the fact that the boundaries between controllers were fixed; this made it possible to allocate to the system the operation of determining when and to whom a request for hand-over should be made. The receiving controller then just had to identify the particular aircraft with his graphic input device. This served as confirmation that he accepted responsibility for the aircraft, and the system then informed the original controller of this (6). With eight such modifications, the design became the prototype of a successful and widely used ATC system.

This example illustrates the point that the load imposed on the operators may be decisive for the success of the system, particularly where, as in the case of air-traffic controllers, the operators are also the users and their task requires quick decision making. Similar situations exist in the case of air defense systems and systems for the control of space vehicles or of sophisticated weapons, such as modern military aircraft. The ergonomic problems of man-machine interaction are now being investigated. Accounts of some investigations in this area are given elsewhere (7-15). The load on the operators will still be influenced by the form of the man-machine interface; some of the devices currently used for man-machine communications are described in Chapter 3.

2.4.2. Specification of System Outputs

Those of the functions allocated to the system will have to produce appropriate outputs, since such outputs are the only means by which the system can communicate the results to the outside world. These outputs may be commands to valves or relays, they may be analog quantities for the positioning of shafts, for instance, or they may be information displayed or printed. Whatever they are, they have to be analysed to determine what requirements they must satisfy. For each type of output these requirements have to be listed under the following headings.

(a) The information content. This states what functions of which parameters the output should represent. Care should be taken to specify only the information really required.

(b) The response time. If the output is one which is generated on command, this is the time interval between the demand for it and the moment it becomes available. If it follows automatically from a change in external circumstances detected by the system it is the time interval between the change and the resulting response.

(c) The freshness of the information. This specifies how up-to-date the information delivered must be.

(d) The form of output. This states whether the output has to be an electrical signal, mechanical movement, display of data, and so on. Whichever it is, all the parameters defining this form of signal are given, e.g. in the case of an electrical signal, the voltage level, impedance, rise time, etc.

(e) Accuracy of output. This should include not only accuracy in the usual sense, as in the case of analog signals, but also all the errors which could possibly be caused by malfunctions. An example of a specification of limits on system errors is given in the next section.

(f) The level of demand. As a minimum, the peak level of demand for each output has to be stated. If variations in demand level can be predicted, this information should be given as it may help to keep down the amount of processing power that will have to be provided in the system.

It is well worth considering whether increased response times can be accepted under conditions of peak demand. Consider, for instance, an airline seat-reservation system. It would be very nice if the response time could be guaranteed to remain always within, say, 5 seconds. However, if the specification is left at that, it would mean that the system would have to be designed with enough processing power to provide this response time even in the exceedingly rare event of every booking clerk at every terminal accessing the system at the same time. This may well be possible, but very expensive. It will therefore pay off to estimate the magnitude and duration of peak demands that are likely to arise. One may then find, for instance, that a response time of, say, up to 10 seconds will be acceptable when more than one-third of all the terminals are accessing the system simultaneously, and that a limit of, say, 20 seconds will be acceptable when over two-thirds of the terminals load the system simultaneously. In applications where occasional increases of response time are acceptable, specification of the maximum response time as a function of demand may result in a very considerable saving in cost.

Then there will be the instances where the system develops a fault. Systems can now be designed to provide a maximum response time of, say, 15 seconds even under fault conditions. Again, however, such a system would cost very much more than a system which allowed a response time of, say, 5 minutes once in so many months. Acceptance of eventual system non-availability for, say, 3 hours once a year may allow a still cheaper system. (The fare stages in the technology for ensuring the specified response times under fault conditions are indicated in § 3.5.)

2.4.3. Input Possibilities

To generate the specified outputs the system will require appropriate input data. The data-capture capability within the system is a responsibility of the system designers. Providing for the capture of the data, however, is an operational consideration. The starting point here is to determine all the parameters on which the specified outputs depend. This in turn determines the required input data. Sources where this data may be captured have to be considered together with any constraints on the data-capture operation, whether the data is captured by sensors measuring process parameters or whether it is fed in by human operators.

2.4.4. Running Aspects

In addition to inputs and outputs there are many other aspects of running the system which have to be considered and planned for, such as the following.

(a) How it will be accommodated: what would be the optimum location for the system and what space can be allocated to it? Will it be possible to provide facilities like air conditioning or security of access?

(b) How it will be administered: the system may be intended to assist in performing just one activity in which case it will have a single user within the organization. Should this user be responsible for the running of the system? Where the system may be intended to assist with a number of activities it has to be decided how it would fit in the overall organization and also whether users will be charged according to use. In any event, consideration has to be given to the build-up of the team running the system, how it will be staffed, and how the staff will fit in the organization as a whole.

(c) How it will be maintained: it is necessary to determine the limit of the facilities which it will be possible to provide for the maintenance of the system, since the level of such facilities has a direct impact on the way the system will have to be designed.

(d) How it will be secured: ways and means have to be prepared to ensure security of the system. The considerations here extend from factors outside the system which may affect the system availability, e.g. fire, sabotage, and, in the case of some systems, enemy action, to security of the data and programs and on to the prevention of fraud either from within the organization or through unauthorized access to it from outside. Then there are the problems of arranging insurance against the various risks in the system. System security is a rapidly developing subject of increasing importance (see e.g. 16-19).

(e) How performance will be monitored: the envisaged use of the system and real life will inevitably turn out to differ. In order to assess these deviations and to find out how they have arisen, ways and means to measure performance and to determine costs will be needed. These have to be prepared in advance.

2.4.5. Implementation and Enhancement Aspects

The steady use of the system as envisaged in the preceding three subsections will not just happen by itself overnight. The method devised for implementing the new operational policy has to include plans for the introduction of the new system into service. This entails working out solutions to problems such as the following.

(a) How the system will be prepared for: This includes the education of the future users of the system to accept and to use the system to the fullest possible advantage, the training of operators, preparation of accommodation for staff and for the system, and the provision of any accessories which may be required.

(b) How it will be tested for acceptance: When the system is delivered it becomes necessary to determine within a comparatively short period whether the system does, in fact, perform to the specification against which it has been supplied. Since it is by no means easy to test all the functions of the system under all conceivable circumstances which may arise, plans must be carefully worked out well in advance to provide for the most comprehensive testing which is possible within an acceptable period of time and which will still prove adequate to determine whether the new system should be accepted as meeting the specification.

(c) How it will assume its tasks: An overall plan must be prepared for the orderly transfer of the various tasks to the new system to avoid upheavals on the one hand, and long, expensive, parallel running on the other hand. Special problems arise in the case of on-going activities, like telephone exchanges for instance, which must continue without a break during change-over. Such a smooth transition may require special facilities to be designed into the system for this purpose.

(d) How it will be adapted: One needs to consider what aspects of the operational policy may have to be modified so as to foresee what adaption may be necessary in the system during its life. In many cases the best course is to start out with initial usage at a given level and an advance plan for more extensive usage requiring expansion of the system at a later stage. The system then has to be designed for such expansion. Eventually the operational policy will be changed, necessitating replacement of the system. Plans have to be made for doing this smoothly and economically.

2.4.6. The Need for the Operational Specification

Hopefully a complete picture of how the new system will be used has been built up in this manner. This picture of the future has to be complete in two senses: it has to be exhaustive in embracing all the aspects, and every aspect has to be fully and realistically thought out. Any sloppy or wishful thinking will be shown up as such during implementation. This picture of how the system will be used will be referred to as the *operational specification*. It has to be fully documented both as an aid in achieving completeness in the two senses mentioned and because it is the main control document for subsequent implementation and use.

The derivation of an exhaustive operational specification is certainly no mean task, requiring detached analytical thinking and decision taking — surely the two most demanding intellectual pursuits. No wonder then that this task is shunned and every possible excuse advanced for its avoidance. The most frequent excuse is lack of time, the argument being that the time scale of the project does not allow it. There is a wealth of bitter experience to demonstrate just how self-defeating this argument is. Quite a number of complex systems in various countries have been undertaken without a thorough operational specification. The deficiencies in the operational specification were being realized while the systems were still being designed or implemented, resulting in incessant requests for modification. This in turn repeatedly delayed completion, so that implementation appeared to go on for ever. In some instances the situation became serious enough for the matter to be raised in the legislative assemblies of the countries concerned. This in turn has prompted a number of technical journalists to produce articles explaining the supposedly technical reasons for the delay, ranging from the choice of an inappropriate computer to the use of an ill-suited high-level language. The simple truth, however, perhaps too simple for some tastes, is that *it takes a very long time to design a system if nobody knows what it has to do.* Another common excuse for evading the preparation of the operational requirement is to say that, because there is not enough experience in the use of such systems on which to base a realistic operational requirement, a preliminary phase of trial operation with an experimental system is required. There are undoubtedly instances where this is so, but this does not eliminate the need for an operational specification; it merely renders its preparation more difficult. The trial operation has to be carefully planned to allow the evaluation of various modes of system usage in so far as these can be envisaged. From this the requirements on the system will be determined in the way described in the next section. Without an exhaustive operational specification there is no way of ensuring that the system will be adequate to evaluate all the alternative modes of operation whose evaluation will eventually be found desirable. More serious even than the consequent loss of time and money is the possible danger of being saddled with an unsatisfactory mode of operation for many years to come.

A study by the British Central Electricity Generating Board has shown that deficiencies in design lead to problems and delays in the implementation stage which cost up to a hundred times more than it would have cost to solve the problem at the design stage (20). This, surely, is just as true for the design of an operational policy as it is for the design of a power station, or any piece of machinery.

2.5. Operational Requirement

2.5.1. Why an Operational Requirement

Once it has been established what the system has to do, this information has to be given to the people who will design it. All this information is contained in, or is derivable from, the operational specification. It is, however, not much use giving the operational specification on its own to the designers. Even if the designers happen to understand the language of the operational people, they will find in the operational specification much that is not of direct interest to them, while many of the things which are required of the system are only implied in the operational specification. A document is therefore needed which will set out explicitly everything which is required of the system, and only these requirements. This document is the interface between the operational people who will use the system and the system designers. It is couched in a language common to both, which is the functional performance required of the system and the operational constraints on it. It is known as the *operational requirement*. This section explains how this document is prepared.

2.5.2. Outputs Required

Many of the outputs from the system will already have been analysed and defined during the derivation of the operational specification. However, the further aspects considered in §§ 2.4.3 and 2.4.4 will show the need for additional outputs. For instance, the need to monitor the performance of the system may demand the output of information on how heavily various parts of the system are loaded. Outputs may also be required for logging faults and malfunctions. If it is planned to charge users on the basis of the amount of use of the system, information may have to be output for this purpose. The security arrangements may demand an output whenever an attempt at unauthorized access to the system is made. The operational requirement has to provide full information on all the outputs from the system under the headings explained in § 2.4.2.

2.5.3. System Availability and Integrity

The extent to which outputs are always delivered within the specified response times is the measure of system availability. Even if outputs are delivered within their response times, they may still be erroneous. System integrity is the extent to which the outputs, when available within their response times, are within the specified accuracy. In a system with adequate processing capacity to meet peak demand, failures of outputs to meet response times will be due to faults. If, for example, a telephone exchange has adequate capacity for its load but breaks down, on average, for two hours in 40 years, it has an availability of 0.999994 or 99.994%. If, further, 0.1% of outputs do not achieve the specified accuracy (e.g. calls are misconnected or disconnected before release) system integrity, within its availability, will be 99.9%. By specifying the response times and accuracies the operational requirement therefore also implicity defines the required levels of system availability and the required level of system integrity. It is system availability and integrity, rather than reliability which concern the user. Reliability is an engineering concept considered by the system designers in achieving the specified availability and integrity, given the level of maintenance that can be provided for the system (see § 2.5.5). How this can best be done should be left to the system designers. The operational requirement therefore makes no stipulations as to the reliability of individual system components.

It is sometimes more convenient to state the required availability and integrity explicitly. Some examples of such requirements for a hypothetical telephone exchange are as follows.

Service to individual subscribers. Exchange faults of any kind, including those dealt with below, should not cause any one subscriber to suffer loss of incoming and/or outgoing services for longer than 10 minutes more often than once in 10 years on average.

Service to groups of subscribers. Exchange faults which cause more than 10% of the subscribers on an exchange, or 400 subscribers, whichever is the less, to suffer loss of incoming and/or outgoing service for longer than 10 minutes should not occur more often than once in 20 years on average.

Exchange breakdowns. Exchange breakdowns shall not involve loss of incoming or outgoing service, or both, to more than half the subscribers, or more than half the trunk and junction circuits on the exchange: (a) for longer than 20 minutes more often than 50 times a year; (b) for longer than 15 seconds more often than 12 times a year; (c) for longer than 2 minutes more than once a year; (d) for longer than 5 minutes more often than once in 20 years; (e) for longer than 10 minutes more often than once in 50 years.

Call failures — premature release and inadequate transmissions. The requirement is that the probability of an established call encountering inadequate transmission, premature breakdown, excessive crosstalk, or double connection within a given exchange should not be worse than 1 in 10,000.

Metering. The requirements for overall accuracy of the metering system are as follows: the probability of recording one unit too many or too few must not exceed 1 in 10,000.

These requirements have to be given for all the functions to be performed by the system. Observe that all the requirements are stated on a purely operational basis, without in any way restricting the system designers as to the method by which these requirements are to be achieved. It may also be worth noting in passing that such levels of availability and integrity are now probably achievable even without on-site maintenance, with computer-controlled telephone exchanges, and at a cost competitive with that of electromechanical exchanges, given a large enough production run to cover the design costs.

2.5.4. Input Sources

The operational requirement has to provide full data on all the possible sources where the required input data may be captured. At some of these sources data-capture sensors may already exist, but as these may not be suitable for a real-time system, the data on the sources themselves should be included. For each source the data and the form in which it is available there have to be stated, together with the constraints which will have to be observed when capturing data from this source.

In order to enable the system designers to decide whether they will be able to utilize any sensors which may already exist, data on these sensors should be given under the following headings:

(a) Form and format of the data. This gives the physical form of the data, e.g. mechanical or electrical signals, and the data content of the signals.
(b) Normal and peak rates. The normal rate at which data is delivered by the sensor has to be stated. If data may sometimes arrive at higher

rates, the incidence and duration of such periods, together with the peak rate on these occasions, have to be given.

(c) Freshness of the data. This states the time difference between the actual situation and the data on it from the sensor.

(d) Accuracy of the data. This is the percentage by which the output from the sensor may differ from the true value of the data to be captured.

(e) Interface. A full specification of the output interface of the sensor should be provided.

(f) Reliability of the sensor. Full data on the effects of possible faults and on their incidence has to be given.

The specifications of the inputs and the outputs taken together determine the amount of processing the system will have to do to produce the outputs within the specified response times from the available inputs. This is often referred to as the *traffic* through the system.

2.5.5. Constraints

The operational specification has to be carefully scrutinized in order to deduce from it all the constraints which the system will have to meet, and the important point here is to ensure that all the constraints are identified.

In many cases cost is a decisive factor. A quantification of the benefits, as discussed in the next section, together with preliminary estimates of the cost of introducing and running the system should provide an indication of the maximum acceptable cost for the system itself. Sometimes other constraints, such as the availability of finance, may determine the maximum acceptable cost. In any case it is highly desirable that this should be stated in the operational requirement; not only may this save a great deal of wasted effort if a system as required cannot be produced within the stated cost, but also a cost limit has been found to be a remarkably effective way of prodding designers to come up with new ideas for more cost-effective systems.

Just as a system may be unacceptable if it costs too much, it may also be totally futile unless it can be in service by a given date. The operational policy has a time scale attached to it. If the system cannot be there when it is required, the new operational policy cannot be implemented as envisaged and has to be reconsidered. The need for the system as specified is thus eliminated altogether (although a requirement for another system may arise when a new operational policy is worked out). The required delivery time is therefore an essential part of the operational requirement. Furthermore, as will be seen in the next section, the value of the benefits deriving from the system may depend on when it goes into service, so that the limit of acceptable cost may have to be specified as a function of the delivery date. A number of constraints on the system will emerge from the considerations in §§ 2.4.4 and 2.4.5. The accommodation available may limit weight or size; the electricity supply available has to be specified, including information on transients as these may cause malfunctions in the system. The level of maintenance which can be made available should be stated, e.g. whether the maintenance personnel will be capable of actually repairing faults, or merely of replacing complete modules, or indeed whether any maintenance personnel will be available on site. The method chosen to ensure systems security also imposes constraints, e.g. that access must be refused if the rules for access are not fulfilled (as when the correct password is not supplied to the system).

2.5.6. Implementation, Maintenance, and Enhancement Requirements

The operational requirement must include a full specification of the acceptance tests. This must include, for each test, the performance level accepted as satisfactory. As will be seen in Chapter 7, these tests play a key role in contractual arrangements.

In addition to the system itself, there are other things which the system designers will have to provide. These may include facilities for training or the actual training of user personnel. The supplier may be required to undertake maintenance or part of it, even if it is only the supply of spares for a specified period. Invariably, he will have to supply documentation. All these requirements have to be fully specified.

Various system features may be required by the implementation and enhancement plans. An example of such a feature is the requirement that the introduction and proving of a new system function should not interfere with the already established operations of the system. The adaptability features needed in the system as mentioned in § 2.4.5(d) have to be stated. For instance, an air-traffic-control system has to be adaptable to changes in the route structure. There may be a requirement for the application software to be written in a specified problem-oriented language to make it easier for users, who might perhaps be chemists rather than programmers, to introduce modifications. Modifications may increase the load on the system. To allow for this additional processing load, a given percentage of spare processing capacity may be specified. Any planned enhancements have to be analysed and specified in the same way as the base functions. Depending on the planning status of the enhancements it may be right to specify them separately, subsequently doing a separate cost-benefit analysis for them.

2.5.7. The Operational Requirement as the Definition of the System

The operational requirement as outlined in this section is the definition of the system. Like all definitions it must be complete, consistent, and irreducible. If a system is duly delivered which fully meets the operational requirement but is subsequently found not to be a satisfactory tool for the job, then those who formulated the requirement will have only themselves to blame. To ensure that the operational requirement is complete it is necessary to go over the whole of the operational specification time and again to check that all the implications of the envisaged use are fully reflected in the operational requirement and that all the requirements are fully defined. Consistency in our case embraces two aspects. One is the possibility of deriving all the outputs as specified from the available inputs. One is not concerned here about how this will be done but whether it is at all possible. It has happened that information has been called for that could not possibly be deduced from the input data. The other aspect is the consistency of all the requirements. It is well worth searching thoroughly through the whole of the operational requirement for any inconsistency. Such a search may, for instance, show up that the acceptance tests check a given output to an accuracy different from that specified.

The requirement for irreducibility is complementary to that for completeness. Just as the operational requirement must include everything demanded by the operational specification, it must not contain anything that is not actually needed. This applies just as much to stipulations as to how the system should be designed. Typical instances of such stipulations are the designation of the computer to be used or the laying down of the method by which the required availability will be achieved. Every requirement is potentially a further demand or constraint on the system designers, probably increasing the cost. System features which are not essential for the operational specification but which are nevertheless beneficial should be stated as options and their subsequent cost-benefit analysis separated from the analysis for the basic system.

2.5.8. *User Responsibility for Operational Requirement*

The four stages of the process of deriving the operational requirements for a real-time system as a tool for achieving an objective are summarized in Fig. 2.1. The potential users of a real-time system are the only people with the knowledge needed to carry out this process. As against this they may feel a lack of knowledge of real-time system technology. This has led to the invention of the so-called feasibility study — a process whereby a joint study by the users and system designers is supposed to determine whether, and if so how, it is feasible to use a real-time system to assist in carrying out a given task. All very well, but how can you tell whether a real-time system can assist with a task unless you know first what the task is? Unfortunately, the very setting up of such a joint study makes the users feel that they need not design an operational policy, or even define their objective, for how can you do so if you do not know what is feasible? Feasibility studies therefore tend to lack both a solid starting point and a clear method for their execution, which explains why so many of them have been unsatisfactory.

Another approach often used to overcome the lack of real-time-system knowledge is to hire engineers, quite likely frustrated system designers, to prepare the operational requirement. This means, firstly, passing on to the engineers a task which only the operational people are really in a position to do; secondly, engineers are the wrong people for this task, as they are specially trained to determine how to make things, not to decide what is required. Experienced system designers can spot an operational requirement prepared by such engineers straight away: it is a document in two parts, the first of which fails to specify what the system has to do while the second part proposes a part of an impossible design.

The lack of knowledge of real-time-system technology may, in fact, be an advantage, since attempts to look ahead to the design of the system may cause requirements to be bent to technology. Also, looking ahead to possible designs while still formulating the requirement means that design is being started while the specification of the product is only partly completed. This is dangerous when designing anything, because it may cause the design to be optimized for part of the requirement, to the detriment of the optimization of the design as a whole. Furthermore, with such a rapidly developing technology as that of real-time systems, it is by no means certain that it is a good thing to seek information about detailed technical possibilities. There are cases on record of genuine requirements being dropped because the operational people were told, correctly at the time, that no means existed to meet these requirements. Nobody told them when such means were invented while they were still working out the operational requirement.

There are many reasons why the operational requirement arrived at is unlikely to be the optimum one, and a lack of technical knowledge may or may not be one of them. However, what has to be optimized is the overall solution, from objective to real-time system, and the way to do it is described in the next section.

2.6. Optimization by Cost-Benefit Analysis

2.6.1. Cost-Benefit Analysis

It is now necessary to find out whether a real-time system meeting the operational requirement is technically feasible and if so how much it will cost. Should it turn out that the system as required is not technically feasible, this still does not mean that the objective is not achievable, nor does it necessarily mean that the operational policy as designed cannot be implemented, as will be seen in § 2.6.2. If a real-time system as required is technically feasible, the designers will provide a *functional specification* of such a system. This document sets out what the system will do to meet the users' requirements. Where the operational requirement gives possible sources of input data with limits of the load which may be imposed on these sources, the functional specification states which of the possible sources will actually be used and what the interfaces will be. Where the one document quotes maximum response times and minima of availability and integrity, the other one specifies the response times and levels of integrity and availability which will be achieved. While the user states the maximum maintenance level and maximum cost acceptable to him, the designer sets out the maintenance method and quotes his price. The functional specification does not set out *how* the system works. This is of no real interest to the user. His interest is in *what* the system will do for him, and to this end he thoroughly checks the functional specification against the operational requirement to ensure that the former does in fact fully satisfy the latter. If this is found to be so, it becomes possible to compile an estimate of the total cost of implementing the operational policy. To ensure that this will in fact be the total cost, it is necessary to scrutinize the description of the operational policy (see § 2.3) and the operational specification and to cost everything that will be needed to bring the operational policy into existence and to keep it going. *The cost of acquiring the real-time system is only part of the total cost.*

The benefits resulting from the achievement of the objective also have to be carefully quantified. The quantification of the benefits rests solidly on the fact that the objective has been quantified to start with. The benefit of achieving, say a 20% reduction in stocks can be assessed without much difficulty. It may be more difficult to quantify the benefits in the case where a real-time system is used to enhance the output from a chemical plant. In this case changes in the marketing strategy may be needed to derive the full benefit from a new product mix having a greater proportion of higher-grade products. The benefits of reduced fuel consumption with the consequent reduction in the cost of getting rid of waste heat will also have to be quantified. It may be still more complicated to estimate the saving which will result from reducing the need for additional roads by improving the flow of traffic through existing roads by computer control. The quantification of the benefits may be helped by data, where available (see e.g. 21) on similar applications, provided due allowance is made for the fact that no two cases are quite alike. This still leaves many social and military applications which are not directly quantifiable in money terms. In such cases the process has to be reversed: given the cost of achieving the objective, one has to decide, given one's social priorities, whether the cost would be justified. Quantification of the cost and benefits is rarely an easy task (see e.g. 22), but is one which must nevertheless be done. Appropriate accounting techniques then have to be applied to these estimates to determine the profitability. The task, however, is not yet complete.

2.6.2. *The Need for Optimization of the Operational Policy*

The cost-benefit analysis may show that achieving the stated objective will not in fact be profitable. There are also the instances where it is not technically feasible to design a system meeting the operational requirements. In either of these cases it does not mean that the objective is not achievable or, indeed, profitably achievable. Nor, indeed, does it necessarily mean that the objective is not profitably achievable by the operational policy as designed. Frequently the only thing that may need modifying is the allocation of operations between the real-time system and the human operators. The cost-benefit analysis may show that operations allocated to human operators can be more economically performed automatically, or conversely that operations allocated to the system cannot be performed automatically given the state of technology or that they are more economically performed by hand. If so, only the operational specification will need modification, not the operational policy.

In other cases modifications to the operational policy may be required, or even another policy altogether, if the objective is to be achieved at all. It is also possible that feasibility may be achieved by modifying the quantification of the objective. For instance, the objective might have been to absorb the expected increase in traffic without any addition to the road network and without any increase in journey times. It may be found that this is not a feasible objective but that it is perfectly feasible to halve the amount of additional roads that would have been required without a road-traffic-control system.

All the above considerations are still pertinent to an operational policy which is both feasible and profitable. Suggestions for improving the objective or the operational policy may result from the submission of so-called non-compliant proposals. These are functional specifications which do not comply with the operational requirement, but for which it is claimed either that they will make achieving the objective or the operational policy feasible where otherwise they are not, or that they will be more profitable than compliant functional specifications. At one extreme the non-compliance may be limited to a constraint in the operational requirement which is alleged to be unnecessary. If a thorough check shows that the constraint does not in fact follow from the operational specification, such a non-compliant proposal can be accepted without the need to modify anything. At the other extreme the justification for the non-compliance may be based on a change in the objective. The time element may be a major factor in such instances. In the process-control field, for instance, a case may well arise where it can be shown that a 30% increase in output can be obtained from existing plant by the use of a real-time control system. A non-compliant proposal in a case like this may be for an off-the-shelf control system giving only, say, 20% increase in output. Such a system will almost certainly be much cheaper than a specially designed one. Furthermore, the total benefit over a given period may in fact be greater with the off-the-shelf system simply because it could be in service much sooner. The cost-benefit analysis could therefore show the off-the-shelf system a better investment on both of these counts. It is not only the cash-flow considerations which make the benefit time dependent; this can also be brought about by competitive factors. It is said that the first airline to introduce a seat-reservation system experienced quite a marked increase in its market share, as the traveling public quickly discovered that the probability of suffering a postponement due to over-booking was smaller for that particular airline. Airlines who then followed suit did not experience quite as marked an increase in their market share.

It is thus seen that, irrespective of whether the real-time system arrived at is feasible and whether the overall solution (comprising objective, operational policy, operational specifications, and real-time system) is profitable, one still needs to determine the optimum overall solution. The method of doing this is described in the next section.

2.6.3. Optimization

The aim of the optimization is to find the most profitable overall solution. Insofar as various possible solutions start out with different objectives, these objectives differ in their quantification, the nature of the objective remaining the same. To compare the profitability of various solutions the whole of the process described so far, including the promulgation of further operational requirements right down to the cost-benefit analysis, has to be repeated for every solution to be evaluated. The optimization process is shown schematically in Fig. 2.2. Time being limited, these repetitions can only be done in outline. What has been learned through the first execution of the complete process should provide data for judgment as to which are the most promising solutions and also the basis for assumptions as to what the results would have been if parts of the work had been done in detail. Where solutions differ substantially, inferences may be impossible and part of the process may have to be done in detail. There may be more than one operational policy for achieving a given objective which needs investigating. Similarly, one may have to compare various operational specifications possible with an operational policy. Solutions may therefore contain branches. There can be no branching from the operational specification since the operational requirement is uniquely determined by the operational specification. There may be more than one functional specification satisfying the operational requirement (including, possibly, specifications based on the use of a bureau machine — this is now possible for real-time systems). It does not matter which of these is assumed for a cost-benefit analysis unless the prices quoted differ enough to make a significant difference to the total cost. The question then arises as to which is the cheapest specification which is still credible enough to be relied on. This is discussed in § 7.2.

With each outline repetition of the procedure a better insight is obtained as to which solutions are the more promising ones. Also, as information on various possibilities accumulates, the outline repetitions are done more quickly. In this sense the process is iterative and hopefully it converges to the optimum overall solution. When it is considered that this has been achieved, this solution needs to be fully detailed, with every stage re-done as a whole. Think not that because only limited modifications have been introduced into, say, an operational specification, the rest of it will remain valid. At each stage the design is so tightly knit that even a single modification can, and does, have unsuspected ramifications. There have been cases where these ramifications were not discovered until it was too late to do anything but find some way of making the solution work at all, rendering the solution less cost effective than other solutions considered at the time. Once the validity of the optimum

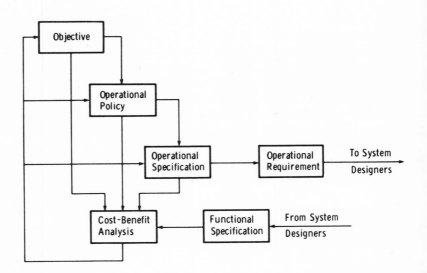

Fig. 2.2.   Optimization process.

solution is fully confirmed a cost-benefit analysis for it is there by the very way the work has been done. In deciding whether the profitability is high enough to justify the investment, allowance has to be made for the margins of uncertainty in the various estimates.

The whole of the procedure described in this chapter is the responsibility of the potential users. Close co-operation with the real-time systems designers is needed, but this co-operation must be limited to information on what is feasible and how much it will cost. To go beyond that leads to a free-for-all in which the real-time system designers tell the users all about their job while the users engage in real-time-system design. A most interesting time is had by all, with decisions taken on the basis of something said in a meeting, ending up with a piecemeal solution which is never checked as a whole and with no one responsible for it. The definition of a camel as a horse designed by a committee is unfair to camels; the camel, as a design, works.

2.7. Use of Consultants

An organization which makes electric motors or sells seats on aircraft, while knowing all about its business, may nevertheless lack the analytical skill needed for the self-examination of its policies or whatever it is that makes some people good designers. Nor may the acquisition of such expertise be justified for a one-off task, for, even if a decision is taken to install a real-time system, the expertise needed at the implementation phase is not quite the same as for the decision phase. The temporary employment of consultants needs to be considered. Our concern here is specifically with the use of consultants to carry out the procedure described in this chapter. The possible use of consultants for the implementation phase will be discussed in Chapter 7.

The difficulty with consultants is that they can be used or misused and, accordingly, they may be a boon or a disaster. The considerations here are much the same as with most management assignments, namely, the choice of the right person and adequate definition of the task, responsibility, and authority. With consultants, it is necessary to realize at the outset that they may be employed in either of two distinct roles: as temporary managers or as educators. Where our procedure is seen strictly as a one-off task, the right thing may be to use the consultant as a temporary executive. In this case the objective, and of course a time scale for the task, must first be agreed by the management of the organization. The consultant then has to learn enough about the operation of the company to be able to work out the operational policy. The consultant clearly has to extract information from and explain things to many executives within the organization. He may be greatly helped in this if one or more of the permanent employees of the company are seconded to work for him. If the size of the task warrants it, the consultant may bring assistants with him. He will then head a mixed team combining permanent employees, with their knowledge of the organization and its work, and his assistants with their special expertise. The responsibility of the consultant working as a temporary executive is the same as it would have been if he were in fact an executive of the organization; he has to produce his recommendation by the agreed date and it has got to be the right one. It is up to him to accept or reject forecasts from the marketing department, for instance.

Alternatively, it may be felt right to build up within the organization some measure of expertise in this type of task. Nevertheless, the future outlook for this type of work may not be substantial enough either to justify or attract an expert of the appropriate caliber on a permanent basis. In this case, a consultant may be brought in on a temporary basis in his educational role. If so, an executive from within the organization is charged with the overall responsibility for the task. The responsibility of the consultant is to ensure throughout, and thus be in a position to confirm at the conclusion, that the methodology has been correctly applied throughout. This being so, the consultant supervises the work in much the same manner as a university professor supervises a team of research students, i.e. suggesting lines of enquiry, ensuring exhaustiveness, pointing out relevant prior work, and so on. In this role the consultant cannot ensure that input data for the procedure, such as sales forecasts, is correct. He can, and must, ensure that this data is obtained with the right questions asked.

The situation within the organization needs to be assessed to decide in which of the two roles, if any, the consultant should be used. It is only too common to put the consultant firmly between the two stools. The next problem is that of finding a suitable consultant. Professional societies provide lists, but it should be appreciated that inclusion in such a list is more likely to signify respectability than possession of a specific expertise. Suitability for the task may have to be determined in an interview. This will depend on which of the two roles has been decided on. If the consultant is to act as educator, his quality as teacher may be as important as the breadth of his experience, for a really good teacher does not merely teach people but makes them learn by themselves, thus possibly producing a better job than if he had done it all himself. The candidate consultant should be asked to explain some of the work he has done and how he proposes to go about the task for which he is being considered. If after the interview the interviewer feels that he has learned a great deal in the course of the interview, then the consultant most probably is a good teacher. It should also be possible to judge from the interview the extent of his experience and the quality of his thinking ability. If the consultant is to act as a temporary executive, he should be evaluated as such. An exposition of previous work and explanation of the approach he proposes to adopt for the work under discussion should provide a very useful basis for the candidate's evaluation for either role. A candidate to be wary of is one who throws around technical buzz-words. If a person cannot explain his work without the private jargon of his particular profession the question must necessarily arise as to whether he himself understands what he is talking about. Furthermore, whichever of the two roles the consultant will have, an ability to communicate effectively with people from other disciplines is essential.

Information on the consultant's work from previous customers should be very useful. When evaluating such information, it is important to distinguish between hard facts and impressions created by the consultant on other people. There are consultants who have reached the top of their profession mostly on the basis of the impression they create. Allied with this is the problem of the eminent figurehead consultant and his assistants. When such a consultant over-commits himself, the work may in the event be done by an assistant who is not quite up to it and under inadequate supervision.

2.8. Summary

The trigger for an investigation into the possible use of real-time systems may come from a variety of sources, not least from a salesman for such systems. Whatever the trigger, however, it is essential to go back and start from the beginning, which is: "What, how much, and by when, is to be achieved?" The answer provides the *objective*. The next question is: "How can it best be done?" To answer this one needs to envisage in advance a way in which the organization will operate which will achieve the objective. This way of operating has to be envisaged in its entirety in order to ensure that it will work and that it will in fact achieve the objective. When this is done, one has an *operational policy*. The operational policy may require the use of certain tools. If so, envisaging how the tools will be used provides an *operational specification* for each of these tools. It may be that one or more of the tools look like being real-time systems, in which case it will be possible to deduce from the operational specification precisely what the capabilities of the real-time system or systems will have to be and what constraints they will have to meet, thus obtaining an *operational requirement.*

The operational requirement is given to one or more experts in the design of such systems. If they can provide the required system they will furnish a functional specification defining just what it will do, setting out how it will meet the constraints and quoting the price. You are now in a position to prepare a complete cost-benefit analysis for the whole enterprise to see whether the investment would be profitable enough to go ahead with. However, even if it all looks very promising, there may be still better ways of doing it, some of them based perhaps on modifications to the objective. Sometimes the system designers may suggest alternatives which they would claim are better for you. For any alternative solutions which you feel should be considered, you have to re-do, at least in outline, all the stages of the procedure in which it differs. When you have found what seems to be the best solution, it has to be taken through all the stages of the procedure in detail to check carefully that you have thought of everything and got it right. When you are satisfied that this is so, you will be left with a full description of your operational policy, complete operational specification and operational requirement, your chosen functional specification, and a thorough cost-benefit analysis. You will now be able to see whether your investment should be profitable enough to go ahead with.

All this will, of course, take time, which you may feel you cannot afford. However, can you afford the loss of time and money which will inevitably result if you do not determine in advance just what it is that you are setting out to achieve and how you are going to achieve it? Can you honestly believe that overall it will not take very much longer and not cost incomparably more if you do not know precisely what needs to be done, so that you have to keep on asking those implementing your policies or supplying the tools for them to modify and modify again what they have done, as you come to realize what you should have asked them to do in the first place? Will they ever complete their work under such circumstances? If they do, will it work and, even if it does work, will it achieve what is needed?

The procedure set out in this chapter calls only for what both good managers and good designers have always done. Deciding on an investment in a real-time system is not substantially different from other investment decisions. It is therefore surprising to find that so many hard-headed managers who would have had a realistic cost-benefit analysis done as a matter of course for any other major investment decision went bankrupt by computerization. Enthusiastic but not very experienced system designers undertook to deliver quickly and cheaply real-time systems that would do efficiently anything that might be asked of them, while potential users accepted that the magic of computers would solve all their problems without them even having to define what these problems were. The ensuing disasters brought the whole use of computers into disrepute. This is a major loss, for real-time systems are an extremely powerful tool for management and control. They will not, however, do the management for you. Indeed, precisely because they are such a powerful tool they must be competently managed.

References

1. Hall, A.D. *A Methodology for System Engineering*, p. 60. Van Nostrand, Princeton, NJ, 1962.

2. Motil, J. *Digital Systems Fundamentals*, p. 2. McGraw-Hill, New York, 1972.

3. Waters, S.J. *Introduction to Computer System Design*. NCC Publications, Manchester, UK, 1974.

4. *Ibid.*, p. 94.

5. Grindley, K., and Humble, J. *The Effective Computer*. McGraw-Hill, New York, 1973.

6. Freedman, A.L. Man-machine interaction as a fundamental aspect of overall system design. *Proc. Conf. Computers — Systems and Technology, 1972*. Institution of Electronic and Radio Engineers, London, 1972.

7. Phatak, A., and Kleinman, D. Current status of models for the human operator as a controller and decision maker in manned aerospace systems.

   Proc. AGARD Avionics Panel Meeting No. 24, 1972. AGARD, Neuilly-sur-Seine, France.

8. Bisseret, A. Memoire operationnelle et structure du travail. *Bull. Psychol.*, *24*, 280, 1970-71.

9. Sperandio, J.C. Variation of operator's strategies and regulating effects on workload. *Ergonomics 14* (5), 571-7, 1971.

10. Bisseret, A. Analysis of mental processes involved in air traffic control. *Ergonomics 14* (5), 565-70, 1971.

11. *Publications Concernant les Etudes Psychologiques sur le Controle de la Navigation Aerienne (Orly).* Equipe Psycho Au CENA, Orly Aerogares, France.

12. Neviss, J.L., and Johnson, I.S. Man's role in integrated control and information systems. *Proc. AGARD Avionics Panel Meeting No. 24, 1972.* AGARD, Neuilly-sur-Seine, France.

13. Gerber, C.R. Space station information systems requirements — a case history of man-machine system definition. See 7.

14. Chubb, G.P. Monte Sarlo simulation of degraded man-michine performance. See 7.

15. Premselaar, S.J., and Frearson, D.E. Man-machine considerations in the development of a cockpit for an advanced tactical fighter. See 7.

16. Hamilton, P. *Computer Security.* Cassell/Associated Business Programmes Ltd., London, 1972.

17. *Where Next for Computer Security.* NCC Publications, Manchester, UK, 1974.

18. Chadwick, B., Farr, M., and Wong, K.K. *Security for Computer Systems.* NCC Publications, Manchester, UK, 1974.

19. Gibbons, T.K. *Integrity and Recovery in Real Time Systems.* NCC Publications, Manchester, UK, and Hayden, New York, 1976.

20. Fishlock, D. Bid to minimize delays in power station construction. *Financial Times*, London, p. 36, 20 Feb. 1976.

21. Summersbee, S. (ed.) *Computer Case Histories.* Machinery Publishing Co., London, 1970.

22. *Economic Evaluation of Computer Based Systems,* NCC Publications, Manchester, UK, 1971.

System Components
and Architecture

3.1. Introduction

This chapter is a survey of the equipment used in real-time systems and of the ways in which it may be combined to perform the required tasks. The general considerations for the choice of input and output equipment and the methods for their physical connection to the computer are briefly surveyed to start with. An account of the devices available for implementation of man-machine interfaces follows. The methods for transferring the input data from the input equipment into the computer and the processed results from the computer to the output equipment are then described. Some aspects of computer architecture are pointed out in § 3.6, and an overview of the configurations in which computers are used in real-time systems is given in § 3.7.

3.2. Input-Output Equipment

A real-time system captures data and delivers processed information on demand. The information delivered is either presented to human operators or it is used to modify the environment directly. Information for human operators is mostly printed out or presented on electromechanical or electronic display devices, but may also be provided as aural messages. Information which acts on the environment does so through appropriate transducers, such as shaft-positioning devices, or by controlling valves or switches. The capture of input data is also accomplished by means of appropriate transducers. These transducers are therefore the means by which a real-time system communicates with the outside world. The transducers employed in real-time systems range all the way from large, complex radars costing millions of dollars to little light bulbs. It would, therefore, not be profitable to survey the various transducers in a work which is not dedicated to a particular application. There are, however, a number of system-design considerations, which apply to all transducers, aimed at ensuring that the transducers are capable of performing their function as system components. The most basic question for an input transducer is: Does it provide the data which has to be captured? If the output from, say, a temperature-measuring device also depends on other parameters there is a problem. Similarly it has to be ascertained that an output transducer has the capabilities required for the task, e.g. that a controller is capable of operating the valve it has to control. If the transducer displays information to a human operator, does it provide the required levels of brightness and legibility? If an input transducer does provide the correct data, does it do so with the required accuracy? How often will the data displayed on a cathode-ray tube have to be refreshed to provide a flicker-free display? Then there are problems of the delay through the transducer, particularly in the case of output transducers controlling mechanical devices where, for instance, the time that it will require a controller to move a valve to the specified position may well be a major design factor.

Once suitable transducers have been found there is still a long way to go before the data provided by them is safely tucked away within the computer. Many real-time systems operate in a largely analog environment. Even when suitable transducers are available for converting analog parameters into electrical signals, the output from the transducers may well be in the microvolt region and accompanied by a great deal of noise. Amplification and filtering methods have been developed to overcome these problems. One then comes up against a basic discrepancy between the analog environment and digital systems in that a digital computer is inherently unable to handle analog quantities. Analog parameters have to be converted into a series of numbers representing the values of the analog parameters at given points in time. This process is known as *sampling*. Well-documented mathematical laws determine the minimum frequency of sampling (see, e.g., 1-3). To overcome the further problem that the analog parameter may be changing even while it is being sampled, special sample-and-hold circuits have been designed. There is a variety of commercial products for the actual conversion of the analog value into a digital number; these are known as *A-D converters.*

Often a great many analog parameters have to be sampled, and in such a case the economically attractive solution is the use of a single amplifier and A-D converter with the analog sources successively connected to the amplifier. This is known as *low-level multiplexing,* and multiplexers for such application are commercially available. Attractive as this arrangement is economically, many problems have to be overcome to achieve satisfactory low-level multiplexing. To the noise generated by the data sources and transducers is now added the noise picked up by the lines (4). The switching raises further problems such as loading of the transducers, switching transients, and settling times. The common amplifier becomes a problem when different parameters require different amplifications. In this case the computer can sometimes be used to control the amplification. The same applies to filtering, if a common filter is used.

If the outputs from the transducers are amplified before being multiplexed into an A-D converter one has *high-level multiplexing.* In any case the number of channels that may be multiplexed is limited by the required resolution, i.e. the number of digital increments into which the total range of the analog variable is subdivided. The higher the required resolution, the smaller the number of channels that can be multiplexed.

Even when the data to be captured is digital or has been converted into digital form this is by no means the end of the problem. Input data to be captured is usually there and available for capture only for a limited period. This period is known as the *survival time* of the data. The effective survival time can be lengthened by transferring the data to an intermediate store where it is held until it can be transferred to the computer. This is known as *staticizing.* There is, however, a limit on the maximum time for which data may be staticized; this limit is set by the arrival of new data from the same source. Storage may be provided to accommodate data from one or more sources for a period longer than the survival time before calling on the computer to accept the data. Such temporary storage is known as *buffering.* In some cases buffering is essential because it cannot be guaranteed that the computer will be able to accept the data within the survival time. Buffering normally involves an economic penalty. Whether or not it also adds to the overall system response time depends on the particular application. Thus, for instance, there is clearly no increase in response time when a buffer store is used to accumulate a message which arrives in successive parts which are no use to the computer until the complete message is there. It should, however, be noted that the buffer store has now acquired some data-processing capability, in that it can string the parts together and can also recognize the beginning and end of the message. In practice any buffer store will have some data-processing capability. This capability may in some cases be so extensive as to make the buffer store a special-purpose processor. Such local processing of the data before transferring it to the computer is often referred to as *pre-processing*. Just how much should be done in the buffer store and how much should be left to the computer is one of the design considerations discussed in Chapter 6.

If the transducer provides digital data, so-called interface circuitry is usually required to match it to the staticizers or buffer store, if any. Interface circuitry is sometimes also needed at the output of the A-D converters. Then there is the interface to the computer itself. This interface differs from the other ones in that it not only shapes the electrical signals to the specified levels and durations but also interchanges control signals with the computer. Some of these control signals will identify the interface demanding attention, while in other cases they may specify the store location into which the data is to be deposited. Most modern computers provide acknowledgment signals when the action requested by an interface has been carried out and in turn expect such signals from the interface. This is known as a *handshake* procedure.

The output chains are governed by analogous considerations. Here again it is possible to time share the converters, this time digital to analog (or D-A), by the use of sample-and-hold circuits which preserve the value of the analog voltage produced by the D-A converter until the next conversion of that parameter.

The word "interface" is sometimes also used more loosely to describe the whole of the equipment chain between the transducer and the computer, and the task of designing this chain is then referred to as "interfacing" (5,6).

Since the delays through the whole of the input chain form part of the system response time, as do the delays in the output chain, they are an important factor in the system design. The degradation of the accuracy through the input and ouput chains and the degree of reliability of the equipment in these chains also have to be allowed for in meeting the relevant parts of the overall system specification.

The input and output chains are even longer and more complex when the transducers are in one place and the computer in another one so that the data has to be transmitted between them. A whole new set of design considerations arises in such a situation, such as the optimum transmission means, coding of the data for transmission, methods of error detection and correction, the concentration of data from a number of sources at an intermediate point for bulk transmission, and pre-processing at various stages and localities. There is an extensive literature on all these aspects of systems design (7-13).

It is interesting to observe the reciprocal relationship between data transmission and computers. Data transmission serves computers in many real-time systems, while on the other hand computers serve data transmission as the controlling elements in data-transmission systems — some of them for transmitting data between computers (14,15).

3.3. Transducers for Man-Machine Interface

The transducers employed in real-time systems are application dependent. There are, however, some transducers which are common to a great many applications — those which are used for the man-machine interface.

Cathode-ray tubes (CRT's) are currently the most widely used means for displaying computer-generated information, whether graphics or alphanumeric characters. So far most displays are monochrome, but the use of color is increasing (e.g., 16). A special two-color tube for the display of computer-generated information has also been developed (17). Known as the *Penetron* it has two layers of phosphor, usually a green one on the face of the tube with a red one behind it. As the accelerating potential of the tube, and with it the speed of the electrons, is increased, the color changes from red to green. Changing the accelerating potential is a comparatively slow process so that there is an advantage in writing the data to be displayed in different colors in turn. The Penetron does not seem to have achieved wide usage. The same applies to the so-called *rear-port projection* tubes. These are CRT's with optical projectors built into the rear. The idea is that semi-static information is projected optically, with the dynamic information projected electronically. Precise alignment of the two projections presents a problem.

CRT's are bulky devices with a short average lifetime, and in the case of systems in a hostile environment require careful and hence expensive mounting. For the display of small numbers of alphanumeric characters they can now be replaced by *light-emitting diodes* or *liquid crystals*. The latter have the characteristic that they can be switched from a light-transmitting state to a light-reflecting state by changing the potential across them. They therefore have the advantage of requiring very little power. A more general replacement for CRT's are plasma panels (18). These are glass panels containing a large number of small gas-filled cells. Each of the cells can be ionized by a suitable addressing mechanism and will then emit light. High-brilliance television-raster-type displays with optical projection systems are probably the most widely used device for *large-screen* or *conference-type displays* (e.g., 19). The *eidophor* has been used for many years without gaining wide acceptance (20,21). A new method for semistatic displays relies on a laser beam punching holes in a thin metal film (22).

The first and simplest devices for enabling the operator to communicate with the system were switches and push-buttons. Signals from the system to the operator lit up lamps or sounded audible alarms. An extension of the push-button is the keyboard. In systems where the operators are not typists the keys of alphanumeric keyboards are often arranged in alphabetical order rather than the normal typewriter layout; it is, however, not certain that this is in fact preferable.

The problem with alphanumeric keyboards is that a large number of depressions may be required for any one message, thus imposing a heavy load on the operator. This is particularly undesirable if the operator also has other tasks to perform. The load on the operator can be reduced by the use of so-called *function keyboards*, on which single keys represent complete messages calling for the execution of a given system function. A function keyboard does, however, lose much of its attraction if it contains too many keys. The number of keys may be greatly reduced by taking advantage of the fact that there is usually only a limited selection of messages that the operator may transmit to the system at a given stage in the use of the system. It should, therefore, be possible to get away with a comparatively small number of keys if the computer is programmed to assign to each key one of the messages which may be required at the particular juncture and provided that there is some way by which the functions assigned to the keys can be communicated to the operator. This is known as a *program function keyboard* presumably shortened from programmed function keyboard.

The program function keyboard has the further advantage that it relieves the operator from having to remember what has to go into the message and in what order, thus greatly reducing the training needed. Consider, for instance, a real-time stock-control system. To start with the keys represent the list of services provided by the system. If the user depresses, say, the key indicating a stock-level enquiry, he will then be asked to depress one of two keys depending on whether he does or does not know the code of the particular item he is interested in. If he indicates that he knows the code of that item, the keys will be given alphanumeric designations to enable him to type in the code. If he does not know the code he will be taken through a sequence of questions, each with its choice of answers with each answer assigned to a key, which will lead him to identify the relevant component to the system.

In spite of their obvious advantages program function keyboards are not widely used or even known. This may be due to the difficulties of physical implementation. Light bulbs controlled by the computer to illuminate alternative legends for each key have been tried but found rather limited. The CRT offers a means of displaying the legends but this means that the keys now have to be provided on the face of the CRT. One way of doing this, known as *touch wire*, is to embed a number of short pieces of wire in the implosion screen in front of the CRT. These short pieces of wire are connected to electronic circuitry which detects which of them has been touched by the operator. An alternative device, the *Digitatron* (17), has eight light-beam sources along, say, the right-hand edge of the CRT with eight photocells opposite them along the left-hand edge of the CRT. Similarly, there are eight light-beam sources along, say, the upper edge of the CRT with eight photocells opposite them. The user's finger at any one of the 64 beam intersection points will interrupt two of the 16 light beams. Neither of these implementations of a program function keyboard has achieved large-scale production. Similar designs using infrared light beams across the face of a plasma panel with up to 320 beam intersections are now becoming available (23,24). Another implementation of a program function keyboard consists simply of a CRT screen with a number of buttons alongside the screen, the operator pressing the buttons against the function or item required. This has become known as *menu-picking*.

When a system displays graphic information some means is usually required to enable the operator to designate any point on the display. This is referred to as a graphic input device. The best known of these is the widely used *light pen* or *light gun* which operates by detecting when the electron beam hits the phosphor at the spot at which the *light pen* is pointed. Because a knowledge of the timing of the writing is required the interfacing software for a light pen is fairly complex. Another graphic input device is the *rand tablet* (e.g. 25). A pattern of electromagnetic radiation is generated over the working surface by means of flat coils underneath it. The position of a pen with a small sensing coil in its tip is determined by special circuitry from the magnitude and phase of the currents induced in the coil. The position of the pen relative to the data on the graphic display is indicated by a special symbol on the display. When this symbol has been moved to the required position by moving the pen the operator identifies it to the system by pressing down the pen.

A lack of robustness and the need for a cable and for the operator to pick up and hold a pen, make the light pen and rand tablet unsuitable for military and similar systems. Such systems use mostly joy-sticks or rolling balls. As with the rand tablet, the operator uses these devices to move a special, sometimes pulsating, symbol on the CRT. With the joy-stick the spot is moved either by moving the stick, or, in the case of the so-called force-controlled joy-stick, by the pressure exerted on it. The rolling ball is in fact a billiard ball, largely embedded in the operator's console. The special spot on the CRT is moved as the operator rolls the exposed part of the ball.

A graphic input device developed by the National Research Council of Canada is available commercially (26). This method employs 4-MHz elastic surface waves generated by transducers located along two adjacent edges of a rectangular glass plate. The two wavefronts are thus at right angles to each other. If the surface is touched the waves are reflected from the point of contact, and this is detected by the transducers which are alternately switched between transmitting and receiving circuits. The co-ordinates of the touched points are determined by measuring the time lapse between the transmitted and reflected waves.

A graphic input device intended for written input is based on work done at the British National Physical Laboratory (27,28). It has two resistive films with a gap between them. A piece of paper is placed over the films and the pressure of, say, a ball-point pen when writing on the paper establishes contact between the two films. The co-ordinates of the point of contact are determined by means of an electrical gradient applied alternately and orthogonally to the two films (29).

A detailed account of computer graphics is given elsewhere (30). No method is as yet available which enables the system to recognize more than a very limited range of spoken messages. Audio communication in the reverse direction is, however, available, mainly by means of messages assembled by the system out of pre-recorded words.

3.4. Direct Memory Access

As mentioned in Chapter 1 direct memory access (DMA) is an input-output method by which data is deposited into or extracted from the store of a computer. To implement this feature some special circuitry is provided which checks during every store cycle whether any peripheral operating by DMA is requesting access. If so, a signal is sent out to the peripheral that it has been granted access to the store. On receipt of this signal the control circuitry of the device presents to the store an address into which the data is to be deposited or from which it is to be read out, a word of data if one is to be written into the store and some control signals, e.g. to inform the store whether data is to be read out or written into the store. Direct memory access has the great advantage that no time is wasted on switching between computation and input-output operation. In fact, the central processor can carry on computing for as long as it does not require access to the store. Analysis of some programs has shown that even with a store-limited computer (i.e. one in which the speed of the store is largely the limiting factor) the central processor requires the use of the store for only about two-thirds of the time. One may therefore expect computation to go on for about one-third of the time taken up by DMA. Another very important advantage of DMA is its fast response time — usually several microseconds maximum. However, in some computers it may be significantly longer, so this is a point to be checked when this response time is critical.

Not all minicomputers have a DMA feature as described above. In these machines direct memory access is performed instead by the CPU acting as an intermediary between the peripheral and the store. In this case the time for the transfer of one word is longer than a store cycle and no overlap of computation and DMA is possible. Even so, this is quite adequate for most applications. There are, however, some applications, particularly those involving the driving of displays, for which such computers are unsuitable. Where it is necessary to distinguish between these two implementations of DMA, the one not involving the central processor is referred to as true DMA or *cycle stealing*.

The penalty for the use of DMA is that the peripheral has to present a store address as well as a highway for the data together with various control signals. With 16-bit words, a similar number of wires for the address, and some further wires for the control signals, some 40 wires are required. These are known as the *DMA bus* and the various peripherals which may request DMA will all be connected to it. In some

designs, known as *multiplexed buses*, the same wires are used in turn
for the address and the data. More than one input-output device may
request access at the same time. This then has to be granted in accordance
with a pre-determined priority. With one method for doing this individual
wires carry the requests for DMA and priority circuitry within the central
processor decides which of the devices should be granted access. With
another method the requests from all the devices are put onto a single
wire. The signal granting access to the store then also goes out on a single
wire. This great signal is hogged by the first device requesting access in
that it stops the signal from propagating further. With this method the
relative priorities of the devices are determined by their physical position
on the bus. This is an example of a *true-priority method*, which actually
does rank the peripherals by their priorities. The danger with true priority
is that repeated requests from one or more peripherals will greatly lengthen
the DMA response time for peripherals of lower priority. It is then up
to the system designer to ensure adequate response times by limiting the
demands from individual peripherals. Where the requests are conveyed on
individual wires the computer designer has the choice of providing either
true-priority of so-called *round-robin* arbitration logic. With the latter
the input-output devices are strobed in cyclic succession to see whether
any of them requests access. Even though the strobing may be done at a
few nanoseconds per device there are nevertheless applications for which
a round-robin is unsatisfactory.

Some computers will only allow alternate cycles to be used for DMA
in order to prevent it monopolizing the machine. Such a computer may be
unsuitable for applications where a higher instantaneous peak rate of DMA
than that possible with this limitation may be needed for short periods.

Since the central processor does itself interchange data with the store
in just the same way as do the peripherals, this can also be done over the
DMA bus. Except for store cycles reserved for the central processor, if
any, the latter has a lower priority than any of the peripherals. In such a
design the store modules are also connected to the DMA bus. The store
modules then have to be able to recognize addresses in the ranges allocated to them.

The DMA provides the basic facility for transferring a single word
between the store and peripherals. Mostly, however, such transfers involve
whole blocks of work. The transfer of a block is achieved by a combination of special hardware and software. The latter is usually known as a
device handler or *driver*. The special hardware is called *DMA interface
unit, selector channel*, or *block multiplexer*. The handler sets up the start-

ing address of the block of data in the store, the number of words to be transferred, and, where relevant, the address within the peripheral to or from which data has to be transferred. The transfer then proceeds autonomously with the DMA interface unit counting the words transferred, carrying out the successive single-word DMA transfers, and producing an interrupt (see next section) when the transfer is complete or when a problem arises, such as parity error or other malfunction. Both the DMA interface unit and the control circuitry of the peripheral (known as the *controller*) contain a so-called status register in which information on malfunctions and on the operational state of the peripheral is kept. This enables the handler to check whether a peripheral is free, acquire its use, and check that it is operating correctly. The handler also has to provide for the various actions consequent on all these possible situations. In some designs the DMA interface unit and the controller form a single unit which is connected directly to the DMA bus. When a system is made up of a computer and peripherals from the same manufacturer (or plug-compatible units) all this is taken care of by the manufacturer. If a system contains other peripherals, special hardware will have to be designed. This may be designed to be connected directly to the bus or it may be designed to interface with a DMA unit supplied by the manufacturer. Special handlers will also have to be written and the system designer is then responsible for ensuring that all the peripherals will gain access within adequate response times.

An extension of the DMA feature provides some processing of the data during the DMA transfer. An example is to read a word from the store, increment or decrement it by one, and write it back into the store. Another one is to read out a word, shift it 1 bit to the right and return it to the store, thus extracting only 1 bit during each DMA. In performing such extended DMA accesses (or *auto-I-O* as this is sometimes known) the processing facilities within the CPU are utilized under the control of the DMA circuitry (31). Very few computers offer this feature and even so it is rarely utilized, possibly because system designers find it simpler to provide such processing by special hardware within the peripheral controller without having to delve into the innards of the central processor.

3.5. Interrupts and Polling

Peripherals with a longer survival time and a slower data rate are usually dealt with by interrupts. Interrupts are also generated by peripherals operating by direct memory access on the completion of the transfer of a data block, when an error is discovered, such as the failure of a parity check, in the case of hardware malfunctions, and when special conditions arise such as the detection of a character of special significance. The design of some computers also provides a facility, coveted by programmers, for setting up interrupts by software.

The interrupt mechanism operates in principle as follows. Just prior to the completion of each instruction a check is made to see whether there are any requests for interrupts. If so, three problems arise: Which devices are demanding service, which of these (if there be more than one) should be serviced first, and where is the program for servicing that device? The simplest arrangement for dealing with these three problems is that used in some of the cheapest minicomputers. Hardware is provided to detect the fact that a request for an interrupt has arisen. When this happens, control is transferred to a fixed location, a record of where the program has been interrupted being kept in another fixed location. A subroutine is then entered which checks, in turn, hardware indicators on the peripherals in order of their priority. On finding the first of these which is set, the program jumps to the location where the program for servicing that device starts. It is the responsibility of the service program to preserve the contents of accumulator and index registers that it needs to use and to restore the contents on termination of the service program. Such a search by software can be a time-consuming process. To eliminate the software search, hardware for finding the call with the highest priority is available, optionally, on most minicomputers. Once the search for the request with the highest priority is done automatically the subroutine jump to the service program for the particular peripheral can also be automated. This is known as *hardware vectoring*. In some computers this is fully automatic, while in others the address of the appropriate service routine is forced into an index register leaving it to the software to decide whether or not to execute a subroutine jump to this address. In some computers the automatic subroutine jump also automatically stows away the contents of one or more of the program-accessible registers. In other computers, particularly those with a large number of registers, stowage is left to the service routine. In some multi-register machines the whole set of program-accessible registers is duplicated, with automatic switching from one set to another one when an interrupt is entered.

The parameter which is basically of interest to the system designer is the total interrupt overhead, which is the sum total of the times needed to jump to the service routine and to resume the interrupted program on the completion of the routine. The first of these two should be taken as the time from the moment the program is interrupted to the moment the service routine is in a position to perform its first instruction, following the stowage of any registers it may need to use if this is not automatic. The time for returning to the interrupted program is similarly defined. With hardware priority determination and hardware vectoring, the interrupt overhead on current designs ranges from microseconds to tens of microseconds. Just where it is within this range is probably only of consequence in applications with very many interrupts.

In considering the response to requests for interrupts, a distinction has to be made between priorities and *priority levels*. If a peripheral operating in the interrupt mode has a higher priority than another one, its request will be granted if both are calling at the same time but not if the service program for the peripheral with the lower priority is already running. If, on the other hand, a peripheral is of a higher priority level than another one, then its request will be granted even if this means interrupting the program for the peripheral with the lower priority level. Chapter 4 goes into the problems caused by multilevel interrupts and explains how the software may be organized to avoid the need for such interrupts. Nevertheless, many computers do provide hardware for such a facility. Also, some designs use the DMA bus for servicing of interrupts as well. In one design (32) this is done as follows. Four interrupt request lines are added to the bus. Peripherals are connected to these lines according to their level of priority. Just before the end of each instruction, the four lines are examined. If a request is present on any of them, but there is no DMA request, a bus grant signal is sent out on a line corresponding to the highest priority on which there is a request. This grant signal is again hogged by the first peripheral on that line so that it does not propagate beyond it. The peripheral which has thus acquired the use of the bus then sends to the CPU a word containing the starting address of the service program for that peripheral. Appropriate circuitry within the CPU causes a subroutine jump to this address.

An alternative way of achieving both request arbitration and priority levels for interrupts is provided in some computers by means of an input-output interrupt mask. A special instruction transfers the mask into an interrupt masking register in which each bit is associated with a peripheral. The order in the register determines priorities. Only interrupts for which there is a 1 in the associated bit position in the mask are accepted. This dynamic method provides the equivalent of being able to change priority levels under software control; it simply determines which interrupts will be accepted at any stage of operation. It is particularly attractive in systems performing more than one task.

Big computers do not usually provide hardware vectoring for peripherals as this might be too technical for their users. Once a request is detected control passes to the operating system which sorts it all out by software. This means that the overhead can be up to several hundreds of microseconds. This is one reason for the use of minicomputers as front-end processors to big computers to service peripherals. This high overhead of switching on interrupts may also have been the reason for the invention of *polling*, which is simply a bulk interrupt. With this method a request for an interrupt is generated by a real-time clock. The service program then interrogates a group of peripherals, or all the peripherals, to see whether any of them require servicing. This "don't call me, I'll call you" method will only work if the interval between successive pollings is less than the shortest survival time. Polling is therefore best suited for dealing with peripherals having equal survival times.

Teleprinters, keyboards, paper-tape readers, or punches are typically devices served by interrupts or polling, while drums, disks, and magnetic tapes are served by DMA. In a given system there may, however, be intermediate devices which will be served by one method or the other, depending on overall system considerations. For a peripheral which delivers data in bits or characters the choice ranges all the way from using an interrupt for each bit or character to the provision of a buffer which accumulates one word's worth of data and then deposits it into the store by direct memory access. Which would be the optimum arrangement in a given system depends on such considerations as the number and speed of peripherals involved, and on the comparative costs of buffers, computers of various speeds, and of optional equipment for reducing the interrupt overheads.

3.6. Developments in Computer Architecture

Most computers perform a single instruction on a single item of data at the time and are known as *SISD* machines. To speed up operation some computers start executing the following instruction or instructions before the current one is finished. This is known as *pipelining*. Until the advent of semiconductor stores central processors have been faster than the stores available at the time. One way of increasing the speed of the store is to interleave the operation of a number of store modules, typically two or four. Another method exploits the fact that at any point in the processing only comparatively small parts of the store are actually used. Some 1 or 2 k words of fast store are therefore interposed between the main store and the central processor. With a cycle time, typically, in the 100-ns region, the *cache* store, as it is known, is sometimes divided into two parts, in effect, for program and data respectively. Transfers between the main and the cache stores are automatic, and various algorithms are used to obtain as high a hit rate as possible, this is the percentage of occasions on which the word addressed will in fact be found in the cache store. With the price of semiconductor store falling rapidly all these complications will become unnecessary, and simple, inexpensive computers capable of one or two million instructions per second should become available.

On many minis and micros the multiply and divide instructions are still an option, and there are many applications which get by quite happily without them. A number of instruction formats of varying lengths is a common feature on all types of computers. The fact that a given segment of program ranges over only a part of the store means that there may be room to increase the efficiency with which instructions are packed by suppressing some of the address bits. With their mostly short word lengths, minis do so extensively, with several bits in the instruction indicating how the *effective address* is to be constructed. The several ways of doing this are known as *address modes*.

The original design of many minis provided addressing for only 32 k or 64 k words. In many designs the addressing range is extended by *memory-management* units which map, under software control, segments of store within the original addressing range onto store segments outside that range. This introduces a certain amount of inconvenience. In one case at least the problem has been solved by adding some longer instruction formats with more bits for the address.

None of the order codes of the more widely used computers has emerged as particularly efficient. Computers do, however, differ by the degree of store protection which they offer, usually as an option, and this may be important for some real-time applications. The simplest form is known as *foreground/background*. In this case the store is divided into two parts, any processing task having access to one or the other part. This has been designed to allow the utilization of time left over from the main application, possibly a real-time one, for other work, without the latter

possibly interfering with the former. Sometimes a number of levels is provided with programs at any one level having access to storage assigned to
its own, or lower, levels but not to storage assigned to a higher level. With
the *lock-and-key* method the store is divided into fixed-size segments and
a fixed number of keys is provided. Programs are assigned keys and the
store segments locks, access depending on the key corresponding to the
lock. There is a master key (e.g. for the control program) which will open
any lock as well as the possibility of leaving store segments unlocked. It is
also possible to limit access to reading only. A more flexible method is that
of *base* and *limit registers*, which specify the limits of a segment or segments accessible to any program. A more powerful extension of this
method are the capabilities described in § 4.3.6.

A good example of the way in which design is influenced by the state
of the available technology is the spread of microprogramming (33). With
this technique the successive patterns of control pulses required to take a
computer through the successive stages of the execution of the instruction
are stored in a so-called *matrix* or *control store*. To take the machine
through the sequence of stages required for the execution of a given instruction the appropriate pulse patterns are read out from the matrix.
Each such pattern is referred to as a line, while the successive stages are
usually called *microsteps*. The succession of patterns needed for a machine
instruction set is known as a *microprogram*.

Microprogramming is nearly as old as modern computers, going back
to 1951 and 1953 (34-36). Until the early seventies, however, it was not
widely used. Several microsteps are required to implement a single machine
instruction; microprogramming therefore requires a very fast read-only
memory. As such memories were not economically available, microprogramming was not a very cost-effective design technique. With the emergence of cheap, very fast read-only memories it is now tending to become
the standard technique for designing the control unit of a computer.

Whether their computer is a microprogrammed one or not makes no
difference to most computer users. It does, however, make a great deal
of difference to anyone building computers on a small scale. The advantage of microprogramming is that it concentrates the equipment required
to implement the instruction set in one comparatively small part of the
machine — the microprogramming matrix. It therefore makes it possible
for a user designing his own computer to buy himself a ready-made
machine, or standard parts for it, and then give it whichever instruction set
he requires. One may well do this when locked into an obsolete machine.

A feature easily provided on microprogrammed machines is one enabling the user to extend the instruction set. Although this *extracode* feature is available on some minis and micros (e.g., 37,38) it is not widely used, presumably because of the problems it raises, as explained in § 4.3.7.

With the microprogramming matrix, or part of it, in a read-write memory, the instruction set may be changed at will. This is known as *dynamic microprogramming* or *writable control store*. This sounds rather exciting, but the practical applications are few and far between. One is the evaluation of various instruction sets when a machine is being designed. It has been proposed that a multiprocessing system (see § 3.7.4) be built with dynamically microprogrammed processors which would enable processors of one type to be changed into ones of another type to accommodate variations in the load mix (39). By and large, however, dynamic microprogramming is, so far, a solution in search of a problem.

There are, however, two areas where microprogramming may have a major impact on computer design. One is *high-level language computers*. On reflection today's instruction sets can be seen to be a historical accident. They are derived from the hand calculators which were in use before automatic computers became available. The high cost, at the time, of the control equipment required to implement the order code, together with the way computers were then used, led to the transfer to automatic computers of the basic arithmetic functions available on hand-operated calculators, with the addition only of various jump and indexing instructions which were essential for automatic operation. With programs increasingly written in high-level languages and current microprogramming technology making it practical to design computers to operate directly in such languages, a great deal of work is being done in this area (e.g., 40,41). A machine operating in BASIC is commercially available (42). The commercial future of such machines depends greatly on whether it will become evident that the cost of producing software for a high-level-language machine is significantly lower than the cost of producing software for machines with our present instruction sets.

The other area of possible impact is operating systems, as microprogramming makes it practicable to build modules of the operating system into the hardware, increasing the speed of operation (e.g., 43). One commercially available machine has already gone along this path (44), and one may well see optional plug-in hardware modules of operating systems in future designs.

Single Instruction Multiple Data (SIMD) machines mostly have the data stored in an array of several hundred rows, each several hundred to several thousand bits long. Each row has its own 1-bit arithmetic unit. The basic mode of operation is to read out successive columns and to operate on all the bits in them. Arithmetic and logical operations are thus performed on hundreds of variable length fields simultaneously. Such machines are also known as *associative processors* because they have the long-sought-after ability of locating data by its content without needing an address. Many papers have been published showing that tasks such as sorting or the detection of collisions between aircraft in flight can be done several hundred times faster than on an SISD computer (e.g., 45,53). In practice the gain in speed is usually much smaller as the programmers of single-stream computers exploit *ad hoc* possibilities of optimizing their programs. Then there are the system tasks which do not lend themselves to parallel processing. Practical architectures therefore combine processors of the two types, with the SIMD machine acting as a special processor for those tasks which require parallel processing (54,55). In such systems the single-stream, or *sequential*, processors and the peripherals access the associative array or arrays by rows, or parts of rows. These arrays are therefore also described as *orthogonal stores*. High-level languages for SIMD machines are being developed (56,57).

It has taken a long time for SIMD machines to come into commercial use. The problem has been to find an application where the parts requiring parallel processing were extensive enough to justify the cost. It appears that some SIMD computers are now in use for such applications. Mostly they involve digital image processing for map making, in one instance for the Large Area Crop Inventory Experiment (58). This is a joint project by the US Department of Agriculture and two other agencies aimed at the improvement of crop forecasting.

Multiple Instruction Multiple Data (MIMD) machines are few, being large, expensive, specially designed machines. A review of innovative computer architecture with a very useful bibliography has been given elsewhere (59).

3.7. Some System Architectures

3.7.1. Systems with Single Computers

Simple real-time systems consist of input-output equipment, a single computer, and the interface between the two. The single computer may be quite an extensive configuration. In addition to a central processor, store modules, and backing stores, it may also contain special-purpose processors, such as the fast-Fourier-transform computers which are now available as add-on devices. Nevertheless, since there is only one central processor, a fault in it will stop the operation of the system.

Some systems have a *by-pass mode* of operation, in that they contain a hard-wired control unit which takes over in the case of a computer failure and provides a rudimentary service. A single computer system can be designed to have, to some extent at least, the ability to continue to operate when the fault is not in the central processor. Unless there is some redundant hardware, tasks will have to be shed and the operation will be degraded. The provision of graceful degradation considerably complicates the design. Also, it does not provide a complete solution since it does not help in the case of a fault in the central processor. It is therefore rare in single-computer systems.

The system will remain inoperative, or degraded, until the fault is repaired. With a 24 hours a day on-site repair capability and a spares holding which includes spares for every one of the replaceable modules which make up the computer, the mean time to repair can be brought down to about an hour or two. Such an arrangement, however, costs money and also comes up against some other problems. In the case of a modest computer configuration, there may be no more than a couple of faults a year. What does the maintenance man do in between? In many cases the solution may be to train people who are on site anyway for other purposes to maintain the computer. Also, in these days of a complete central processor on a board, most boards and other replaceable units are of different types. An exhaustive spare holding therefore implies near complete duplication of the computer equipment, leading up to the consideration of a duplicate computer. This, however, involves a great deal more than just duplication of the computer equipment, as discussed in the next section.

The availability situation in a system with a single computer is very much one of "you pays your money and you takes your choice". What is the best choice depends primarily on how much a lower mean time to repair is worth to the system user.

3.7.2. Multi-Computer Configurations

The size and characteristics of the data-processing load may be such that the work is best divided between a number of computers. It may be that part of the processing is best suited for a commercial computer, possibly because of the availability of existing software, while the other part, because it requires very fast response times, may be best done on real-time computers. In some cases separate data-processing tasks are required in geographically separate locations.

Another reason for using multi-computer complexes may be to enhance system availability. This is most easily achieved in those cases where

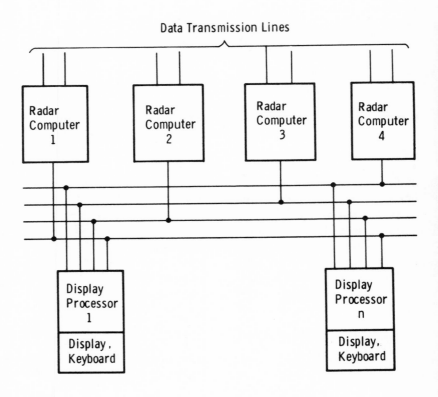

Fig. 3.1.   Radar processing and display system.

the system as a whole contains multiple, alternative paths; an example of such a system is shown in Fig. 3.1, which shows a hypothetical simplified air-traffic-control system which obtains its data primarily from four radar services. The latter are combined primary and secondary radars with special-purpose computers, known as *plot extractors*, on each radar site. The outputs from the plot extractors normally produce a message giving the position, height, and identity of the aircraft every time a radar echo from an aircraft is detected. These messages are transmitted to the control center on duplicated 7200 bit/s transmission lines. The data provided by each radar service is processed separately in the radar-processing computers to provide a file for each aircraft. The air-traffic controllers are provided with computer-controlled displays. (For some mysterious reason a computer controlling a display is always called a display processor.) By means of messages to his display processor each controller selects a radar service, and defines the portion of the air space he is interested in and the items of information he wants displayed. The task of the display processors is to accept the controllers' messages and to process the information to provide the required presentation.

The availability requirements for this system were as follows. Data from at least two out of the four radar services had to be available for at least 999,999 hours out of a million and the availability of a display position had to be better than 0.995. It turns out that the average failure rate of the basic 32k minicomputer is 200 faults in a million hours, with the same fault rate for the assembly of interfaces and other items of special equipment per radar service. This gives a mean time between failures of 2500 h and a mean time to repair of 2.5 h (assuming 24 hours on-site repair facilities). The availability of a radar-processing chain is thus $\frac{2500}{2500 + 2.5} = 0.999$ so that the availability of at least two radars is in fact 0.999999.

Considering a display position, one finds the expected number of failures per million hours as follows:

minicomputer, 24k words	170
display control unit	280
display module	200
keyboards and other equipment	250
	900

This gives an MTBF of 1111 h and, with the mean time to repair again 2.5 h, the availability is:

$$\frac{1111}{1111 + 2.5} = 0.998$$

i.e. well above the requirement.

The design just outlined is an example of *distributed processing*. By distributing the processing load between a number of computers the specified availability has been achieved. This approach has also made possible the use of minicomputers rather than big computers. If the processing load had been concentrated in one or two computers, big computers would have been required, at a much higher total cost, in spite of the inefficiency of having the same program in all the display processors.

The advent of low-cost microprocessors has given a major impetus to work on distributed processing. Much of this, however, is misguided. Firstly, there is the confusion between the price of a microprocessor chip set and the cost of a microprocessor made up of it, referred to in Chapter 1. The effort needed to turn the one into the other may be a positive advantage at a university, where projects are sought for research students, but not elsewhere. Secondly, some of the new enthusiasts for distributed processing may overlook the extent to which the applicability of distributed processing is application dependent. The system just outlined lent itself naturally to distributed processing, but it is a far cry from this to attempts at working out a general method for distributing the processing between an army of microprocessors. Furthermore, these efforts are likely to be overtaken by the rapidly increasing speed of operation of microprocessors.

With systems which lend themselves naturally to distributed processing and designs where this is taken advantage of, it may still be possible and worthwhile to have manual or automatic reconfigurations in that they may be designed so that another computer or computers take over the task, or part of it, of a computer which fails. This approach has been adopted in the design of a telephone exchange (60).

The situation is totally different in systems like, say, the BOADICEA system outlined in Chapter 1 with its central data base. In systems like these reconfiguration is essential for operation to continue. If reconfiguration is manual, breaks in service of up to several minutes may have to be accepted. An advantage of multi-computer systems with manual reconfiguration is that they can be built up of standard or semistandard hardware modules. Some computer ranges even contain peripherals which enable one computer to interchange blocks of data with the store of another computer, as if that store were, say, a disk. Where reconfiguration in a multi-computer system is automatic, specially designed hardware may be needed to achieve the required level of fault detection. Whether reconfiguration is manual or automatic there are all the problems of recovery of operation and preservation or reconstitution of the data base discussed in Chapter 5.

A higher level of system availability may be achieved by the use of three computers with majority voting between them. In this case there is the choice of having the three machines clock synchronized or not. With clock synchronization there is an element which is common to all three machines with the possibility of overall failure if a fault develops in this element. With non-synchronized machines, on the other hand, complications arise in the operating system because comparisons between the three machines can only take place when all three have the results ready for comparison. This will not necessarily happen at the same time in the three computers. It is, for instance, possible that one of the three computers, and only one, will reject an input because a transient fault in that machine will make it decide that the input is invalid and request a resubmission of that input. With methods currently available of designing small items of equipment with enough redundancy at the circuit level to ensure that a fault in the hardware will not result in a malfunction, there may be an advantage in having the three computers synchronized.

A half-way house in which the central processors are triplicated with majority voting between them, while error correction is employed in the store, has been adopted for the T200 telex exchange outlined in § 5.6.4.

3.7.3. Multi-Port Store

An extensive single-computer configuration leads to inefficient use of hardware. Such a configuration may contain many peripheral stores and peripheral devices and yet only one operation can take place at any one time. This represents a very severe limitation, which may limit the throughput to a fraction of the potential throughput of all the modules together. This has led to the development of multi-port stores. A simple example of a system utilizing a multi-port store is shown in Fig. 3.2. Here the whole of the data base used in the processing task needed to be displayed. This data base was kept in store module 2 while the program and all other data were in store module 1. The load due to the processing task on the interface between the central processor and store module 1 was some 60%, while the load on the interface to store module 2 was negligible. The load on the interface between the display drive and store module 2, on the other hand, could go up to a peak of virtually 100%. This did not imply that all available store cycles were used, as the display drive did not use more than two successive store cycles. Given the maximum operating speed of the display drive, however, all the available time was used up, at peak load, to achieve the required refresh rate. One might claim that by exploiting multi-port store the computer could be loaded to 160%.

Multi-port store requires that each store module has *arbitration logic* (also known as priority circuitry). Alternatively, one may consider that in this case a DMA bus is associated with each store module, instead of there being one bus for the whole of the computer configuration. Several minicomputers with multi-port stores are commercially available (46,61, 62). Multi-port stores are also available for some minis as special products. These may not always be as satisfactory as *ab initio* designs. The problems of possible conflicts in access to data files are no different from those in single-processor configurations with single-ported store and no special features are required to overcome them. Observe, however, that, while

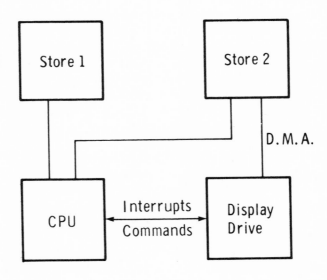

Fig. 3.2. Application of multi-port store.

the DMA buses are now associated with the store modules, the interrupts remain associated with the processors and peripheral controllers. A combined bus for DMA and interrupts may therefore not be efficient with multi-ported store.

3.7.4. Multi-processor Configurations

In this book *multi-processor* configurations will be defined as configurations with more than one central processor sharing multi-ported store modules in which the processors can address individual words. The central processors may also have their own *private* or *local stores*. One can distinguish five levels of operation of multi-processor configurations. The least degree of interaction between processors occurs in *allocated static* configurations. In this case the processors are allotted specific tasks and the peripherals are connected accordingly. This is not very different from a multi-computer configuration. The common store is then usually merely a means for the transfer of data between one processor and another one and is therefore often described as a *postbox*. The use of a common store does, however, require a lock-out facility which will enable one processor to lock-out other ones from a data file which it is in the process of modifying. This can be achieved by purely software means in that the processors may come to an agreement between them through an interchange of messages to hand over a store segment to one processor only for a certain time. It is, however, much more efficient to provide a hardware facility for this purpose. This usually takes the form of a *test-and-set instruction*. This operates as follows. A fixed bit, often known as a flag bit or semaphore, within the address specified by the instruction is examined and if found to be 0 is set to 1. If it is found to be already 1 a change of condition will occur in the testing processor which can be detected by a suitable instruction, or else a jump or skip will result. The crucial point is that this examination and eventual setting of the flag bit takes place within a single store cycle to prevent another processor getting in between the examination and the eventual setting.

An allocated static system does not provide any advantages for expandability or availability. Expandability may, however, be provided for if the system is capable of expansion by the addition of central processors and other modules. Such an expansion may well involve a re-allocation of tasks between the processors. This level may be defined as a *statically re-allocatable* system. To provide enhanced availability it may be enough to have a *manual dynamically re-allocatable* system in which, in the case of a fault, the faulty module is manually switched out of the system and the tasks re-allocated between the remaining modules. This is the multiprocessor counterpart of multi-computer configurations like those in BOADICEA. The problem here is that it may take longer to determine the faulty module than to pinpoint the faulty computer. This problem is overcome in an *automatic dynamically re-allocatable* system where fault detection and reconfiguration are automatic — at the cost of special hardware and software for fault detection, hardware reconfiguration under software control, and recovery of operation.

In a *non-allocated* system tasks are not allocated, each processor picking up the next task in the queue, whichever this happens to be. It is at this level that there has to be a single operating system for the whole system with all the problems this raises, as explained in Chapter 5. Another major problem with non-allocated systems is *store contention*. This refers to the delays arising from processors contending for access to the same store module. The degree of this inefficiency is highly application dependent, but in some cases unpublished studies have shown that it is such as to set the effective limit at three central processors. Yet another problem with non-allocated systems is the acceptance of interrupts. Since there is no allocation of tasks, any processor may have to pick up any interrupt. With both dynamically allocated and non-allocated systems there is often a severe cabling problem in providing sufficient flexibility of interconnection (63). Minicomputers designed for multiprocessor configurations are now becoming available (64).

The US Navy Advanced Avionic Digital Computer (43,65,66) aims in part at statically re-allocatable systems. The air-traffic control system outlined in § 5.6.4 is essentially a dynamically re-allocatable one. It does have a single operating system, but this operating system is normally run by only one of the central processors which then allocates tasks to another one, with a third one mostly on stand-by. A non-allocated system, called *Pluribus*, has been designed for the ARPA data-communications network (15,67).

As a general proposition it may be argued that an automatic dynamically re-allocatable system seems capable of achieving as much as a non-allocated system without the special problems of the latter. However, the optimum choice of system architecture is too highly application dependent for such generalizations to be of much use. This is neatly illustrated by the ingeniously simple solutions of the problems of non-allocated systems evolved in the Pluribus design, but which may not suit other applications. Like any other designer, the professional designer of real-time systems therefore requires a wide knowledge of various designs to assist him in selecting the architectures to consider in detail as possibly the most cost-effective ones for his application. The real-time system designer, however, has the special problem of finding out how designs have turned out in practice, which may be rather different from what has been envisaged at the beginning. Computer people are rather good at describing the designs they are about to implement, but less forthcoming with accounts of subsequent developments.

References

1. Gordon, B.M., and Seaver, D.H. Insight into sampled data theories. *Systems* 2, (1) 30-34, Jan. 1974.

2. Jury, E.I. *Sampled-Data Control Systems*. John Wiley, New York.

3. Ragazzini and Franklin. Sampled-Data Control Systems. McGraw-Hill, New York.

4. Nakasone, R.T. How to solve noise problems of D-C transducers on long lines. *ISA J*. Nov. 1959.

5. Paker, Y., Cain, C., and Morse, P. (eds.) *Minicomputer Interfacing*. Miniconsult, London, 1973.

6. Cluley, J. *Computer Interfacing and On-Line Operation*. Crane, Russak, New York, 1975.

7. Martin, J. *Telecommunications and the Computer*. Prentice-Hall, Englewood Cliffs, NJ, 1969.

8. Martin, J. *Teleprocessing Network Organization*. Prentice-Hall, Englewood Cliffs, NJ, 1970.

9. Martin, J. *Future Development in Telecommunications*. Prentice-Hall, Englewood Cliffs, NJ, 1971.

10. Martin, J. *Introduction to Teleprocessing*. Prentice-Hall, Englewood Cliffs, NJ, 1972.

11. Martin, J. *Systems Analysis for Data Transmission*, Prentice-Hall, Englewood Cliffs, NJ, 1973.

12. *Handbook of Data Communications.* NCC, Manchester, UK, 1975.

13. Wilkes, M.V. Communication Using a Digital Ring. *Proc. PACNET Symposium Sendai. Aug. 75.* Res. Centre Applied Info. Sciences. Tohoku University. 2-1-1 Katahira, Sendai, 980, Japan.

14. Davies, W.D., and Barber, D.L.A. *Communication Networks for Computers.* John Wiley, London, 197

15. Ornstein, S.M., and Walden, D.C. The evolution of a high performance modular packet-switch. *Proc. Int. Conf. on Communications, San Francisco,* 1975.

16. *VT31 Color Graphics Display System.* Digital Equipment Corp., Maynard, Mass.

17. *Image Tubes and Devices.* Thomson-C.S.F. Paris.

18. *Digivue User Manual 512-60,* Ref. UM501. Owens Illinois, Toledo, Ohio.

19. *Solid State Color Mammoth Projector.* Pye TVT Ltd., Cambridge, UK.

20. Bauman, E. The Fischer large screen projection system (Eidophor). *J. Soc. Motion Picture TV Engrs, 60,* 351, 1953.

21. Good, W.E. A new approach to colour television display and colour selection using a sealed light valve. *Proc. Nat. Electronics Conf., 24,* 771-3, 1968.

22. *Large Screen Display.* Librascope Division, Singer Corp., Glendale, Calif.

23. *Technical Specification for the Model 27 Touch Panel.* Magnavox Co., Fort Wayne, Ind.

24. *Plessey Touch Input Device.* Plessey Co., Addlestone, Surrey, UK.

25. *User's Manual, GT50 Graphical Tablets.* Computek Inc., Cambridge, Mass.

26. *TSD — Touch Sensitive Digitiser, Direct Man to Computer Interface.* Instronics Ltd., Ottawa, Ontario.

27. Pogbee, P.J., and Parks, J.R. Applications of a low cost graphical input tablet. *Information Processing 71.* North-Holland, Amsterdam, 1972.

28. Day, A.M., Parks, J.R., and Pogbee, P.J. On-line written input to computers. *Proc. Conf. Machine Perception of Patterns and Pictures.* Institute of Physics and Physical Society, London.

29. *Datapad.* Quest Automation Ltd., Stapehill, Wimborne, Dorset, UK.

30. Walker, B.S., Gurd, J.R., and Drawneek, E.A. *Interactive Computer Graphics*. Crane, Russak, New York, 1975.

31. *16 Bit Series Reference Manual, Publ. No. 29-398*, pp. 100-5. Interdata Corp., Oceanport, NJ, 1974.

32. *PDPII, Peripherals Handbook*, pp. 5-11 - 5-38. Digital Equipment Corp., Maynard, Mass. 1974.

33. Husson, S.S. *Microprogramming Principles and Practice*. Prentice-Hall, Englewood Cliffs, NJ, 1970.

34. Wilkes, M.V. The best way to design an automatic calculating machine. *Manchester University Computer Inaugural Con.*, p. 16, 1951.

35. Wilkes, M.V., and Stringer, J.B. Microprogramming and the design of the control circuits in an electronic digital computer. *Proc. Camb. Phil. Soc.* 49, 230, 1953.

36. Wilkes, M.V., Renwick, W., and Wheeler, D.J. The design of a control unit of an electronic digital computer. *Proc. Instn. Elec. Engrs. 105*, 121, 1958.

37. *Model 8/32 Micro Instruction Reference Manual, No. 29-438*. Interdata Corp., Oceanport, NJ.

38. *MCP-1600 Microprocessor*. Western Digital Corp., Newport Beach, Calif.

39. Reigel, E.W., Faber, V., and Fisher, N.A. The interpreter — a microprogrammable building block system. *AFIPS SJCC*, p. 705, 1972.

40. Shapiro, M.D. A SNOBOL machine: a higher-level language processor in a conventional hardware framework. *IEEE 1972 Computer Soc. Int. Conf.* Institute of Electrical and Electronic Engineers, New York, 1972.

41. Merwin, R.E., and Broca, F.R. Direct microprogrammed execution of the intermediate text from a high-level language compiler. *Computer Languages*, vol. 1, pp. 17-28. Pergamon Press, Oxford, UK, 1975.

42. *General Product Guide to 2200 Computer*. Wang Laboratories, Tewksbury, Mass.

43. Berg, R.O., and Thurber, K.J. A hardware executive control for the advanced avionic digital computer system. *Naecon 71 Record*.

44. *GEC 4080 Technical Description*. GEC Computers Ltd., Borehamwood Herts., UK.

45. Eddey, E.E., and Meilander, W.C. Application of an associative proces-

sor to aircraft tracking. *Proc. Sagamore Conf. on Parallel Processing*, 1974.

46. Gilmore, P.A. Matrix computations on an associative processor. *Proc. Sagamore Conf. on Parallel Processing*, pp. 272-90, 1974.

47. Prentice, B.W. Implementation of the AWACS passive tracking algorithms on a Goodyear STARAN. *Proc. Sagamore Conf. on Parallel Processing*, 1974.

48. Reddaway, S. D.A.P. − a distributed array processor. *Proc. 1st Annual Symp. on Computer Architecture*, pp. 61-5. *Computer Archit. News, 2*, (4), 1973.

49. Malik, R. Minicomputer army may fight the weather. *New Scientist*, 13 Sept. 1973.

50. F.A.A. Univac enhancing ARTS-3 systems. *Aviation Week Space Technology*, p. 48, 1972.

51. Higbie, L.C. The OMEN computers: associative array processors. *Proc. IEEE Computer Soc., Int. Conf.* Institute of Electrical and Electronic Engineers, New York, 1972.

52. Thurber, K.J., and Berg, R.O. Applications of associative processors. *Computer Design, 10*, (11), 103-10, 1971.

53. Defiore, C. Fast sorting. *Proc. AFIPS Conf.* p. 47, 1970.

54. Boyd, H.N. An associative processor architecture for air traffic control. *Proc. Sagamore Conf. on Parallel Processing*, 1974.

55. Rudolph, J.A. A production implementation of an associative array processor − STARAN. *Fall Joint Computer Conf.* pp. 229-41, 1972.

56. Larson, A., and Remick, H. An extended COBOL language for associative array processors. *ACM/NASA Conf. on Programming Languages and Compilers for Parallel and Vector Machines*. New York, 1975.

57. Vineberg, M.B. Implementation of a higher-level language on an array machine, *Proc. IEEE. Computer Soc. Int. Conf.* Institute of Electrical and Electronic Engineers, New York, 1972.

58. *Staran Newsletter*, 20 May 1975. Goodyear Aerospace Corp., Akron, Ohio.

59. Newton, R.S. *A review of innovative computer architecture*. Technical Note No. 784, Royal Radar Establishment. Malvern, Worcs, UK.

60. Adelaar, H.H. The 10-C system, a stored program controlled reed switching system. *IEEE Trans. Commun. Technol.* pp. 333-39, June, 1967.

61. *Argus 700 System Reference Manual.* Ferranti Ltd., Wythenshawe, Manchester, UK.

62. *Modular One Outline System Specification.* Computer Technology Ltd., Hemel Hempstead, Herts, UK.

63. Thurber, K.J., Jensen, E.D., Jack, L.A., Kinney, L.L., Patton, P.C,, and Anderson, L.C. A systematic approach to the design of digital bussing structures. *AFIPS Conf. Proc.*, vol. 41, pt. II, pp. 719, 1972.

64. *Honeywell Level 6 Minicomputers.* Honeywell Information Systems, Waltham, Mass.

65. Entner, R.S. *Advanced Avionic Digital Computer Development Program Rep. No. 9.* Naval Air System, Washington, D.C. Code AIR-5333F4, 1971.

66. Entner, R.S. The advanced avionic digital computer. *Parallel Processor Systems, Technologies, and Applications.* Spartan Books, New York, 1970.

67. Heart, F.E., Ornstein, S.M., Crowther, W.R., and Barker, W.B. *A New Minicomputer/Multiprocessor for the ARPA Network.* Bolt, Beranek & Newman, Cambridge, Mass.

Processing
the Data

4.1. The Nature of Data Processing

This chapter is concerned with the actual handling of data within the computer, as opposed to the considerations of the type of data, equipment, and system management involved, which are dealt with in other chapters. Section 3.3 has discussed the hardware and software combinations for capturing data and transforming it into a wholly software form, as well as means of communicating results. Therefore this chapter deals with purely software matters — software engineering principles which may help in the successful realization of operational systems.

We have an almost perfect manifestation of a theoretically pure environment and can pre-arrange all the consequential actions, knowing they will be carried out under complete control, without any outside influences, and all the results can be completely predicted. There seem to be very few instances in nature where such a controlled environment exists as that for handling data in digital computers. To realize this may help a software designer to overcome that "boggling" stage where one can feel there is going to be so much happening, arriving, going wrong, and piling up in the computer with so many asynchronous possibilities, undefined situations, and unknowns in seven or eight dimensions that one does not know how to decide where to start sorting it all out and beginning to design. To know that one has control and to have the confidence that it will work exactly as planned is some asset.

The systems designer has to consider all aspects of a system. The software designer, however, has the starting point "the computer". Assuming for the present purpose that the shape of the computer configuration has been decided, this starting point is different in different cases. It could be an empty computer, several empty computers, or maybe a computer system already containing an operating system, just an executive or some other software. The need is to recognize what the starting point is and to understand fully the framework which has been or will be bought or provided. While the framework may need some changes, once firm it is at least defined and one area of possible confusion is removed.

A second and major area to be tackled is the randomness of the external world, to remove the uncertainty which arises from independent timing relationships in real-time data, in fact to "freeze in time" or "*staticize*" the situation while the data is processed so that each function can be performed on consistent information. In third-generation minicomputers only one function can be carried on at any instant by a CPU. The basic point made here is that it considerably simplifies real-time software if the software designer decides rather dogmatically the scheduling order of these functions, rather than allowing the system so much flexibility to respond to real-time traffic that certain patterns, extreme or special-case situations not envisaged at design time could cause blockage or faults. One does not want to have the system driven by the occurrence of data, but rather to have a system driven from within, yet capable of handling as wide a range of traffic patterns as the specification demands — a *defined* range, which excludes the possibility of the system straining and possibly failing to meet unexpected situations. Such a system is much more impervious to real-time effects from a peak-loading point of view. The consequence of this is that as little as possible of the software should be interrupt driven; rather, the real-time data should be captured as dynamically as necessary, but then staticized and buffered ready for processing when scheduled. Figure 4.1 illustrates this separation of real-time events from the main data processing.

It further simplifies design if the scheduling of programs to perform different functions is as sequential as possible and arranged so as to minimize the need to break off one function to perform more urgent tasks. Multi-level programming is undesirable because organizational software overheads are increased and also more special data situations are possible. A system with fewest possible levels of activity is more impervious to real-time effects caused by the varying time relationships of data.

We discuss these real-time aspects later in this chapter but now return in more detail to the staticizing of input and output to give the software designer a cleaner environment for the application functions.

Whether data arrive by interrupt or by computer-initiated transfer, once control has been given to the receiver program, this program moves the data from an external hardware register into the computer itself. Quite often a lot of information is lost at this stage: the context or time relationship with other events or even the channel of arrival. Labeling of data is one answer; another is to have dedicated receiver programs for each type of channel rather than commonized routines. It is better if the system design relies just on the data rather than the circumstances in which it is received. It may be that much of the arriving data can be discarded and only the useful fields retained. Some validity checking and filtering may be efficient at the receiver stage, but generally it is preferable to do only the very minimal work in the real-time routines, especially if these are in interrupt mode or other high program level, leaving message checking and so on until after the data has been staticized. This means that the receiver programs, and similarly the transmitter programs for output, should be really short, typically just a few instructions, even less for some machines or for direct-memory-access (DMA) transfers, and should just handle the signaling and possibly overall message format parts of the protocol. It is found to be very rare indeed to require an instantaneous

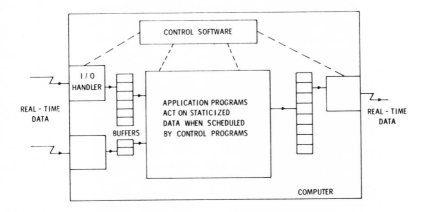

Fig. 4.1. Separation of most software from immediate real time.

response to an input. By staticizing at the earliest opportunity, not only can most of the software run in less severe real time, but both it and the interfaces can be of more simple design and easier to check out.

Once the data are safely stored, the goods are under cover, as it were, and the necessary checking and manipulating functions can be carried out with less interference from outside events. These programs are not triggered when the data thinks it appropriate, but according to the predefined scheduling rules. Such a system is more impervious to real-time noise on data and to interference between real-time events.

A common exception can be made with advantage. When individual pieces of data arrive, which together make up a whole message to be processed as one unit, the individual bits, fields, etc., can be associated in real time with the rest of that message and some functions such as software parity checking, field counting, and so on carried out by the receiver before their immediate context is lost, because this can save a later waste of CPU time. Better still, such frequent short operations may be best carried out in special-purpose hardware or by special microprogrammed instruction, because the cost may be small in relation to producing the equivalent software. It also gives the software designer a cleaner environment and allows extra power in hand in CPU time. It is better engineering. In some cases, where there are many fast data lines, it is essential, otherwise the CPU spends all its time handling standard signaling requirements. This is considered in § 6.3.3.

Where a minicomputer is used as a front end to a larger computer, we have a scaled-up version of this approach. The special equipment is relieving the main computer of the most time-urgent events so that it can press on with whatever is the current task in hand without being continually interrupted. Where there are not too many lines and where there are several transmission speeds, message formats, and so on, a front-end transmission-handling minicomputer may be more appropriate than a multiplexer and can carry out more involved message checking if necessary. The aim is always to reduce the consideration which the main programs have to give to the immediacy, noise, and time sequence of real-time events, and to transforming the information between a transmission mode and a form for processing.

It may be helpful then to think of the transformation from, say, a series of signals or even characters spread out in time into a tidy byte or message staticized in store, for this shows the line we are trying to draw between real-time event handling and the processing of the data. Where these are seen as distinct asynchronous parts of the computer function, the design of each part can be so much simpler.

The actual mechanisms for the hardware-software conversion of data have been discussed in Chapter 3, and we have now considered the use of these from the software designers' point of view in a general way. Some applications may dictate the input-output method to be used for a particular channel, but a preference has been expressed for polling the channels so that the CPU is not driven by external real-time events. Polling may be driven by an external clock but is more ordered than if driven by interrupt on data arrival.

Another distinction one can make is between the arrival of data and the knowledge by the software that data are ready to be processed, because the main programs are only relevant when a message has been received, not during its arrival. Where economic, therefore, good use can be made of a direct-memory-access facility for actually getting the data efficiently in or out of the computer, combined either with polling the buffers or with setting flags on interrupt to indicate that data is ready for processing or has been transmitted.

Much of the foregoing suggests very small input-output routines of an application-independent nature. They are much more related to the equipment hardware than to any particular processing function. A further benefit arises since these routines may be available from the computer manufacturer, perhaps even as hardware, or can at least be used again in similar systems even if the applications are different. There is then the temptation to consider them as part of a general-purpose operating system or real-time supervisor. We return to this consideration in the next chapter, but suggest here that these I-O routines give the applications program designer a more stable and predictable environment for processing, being thus sheltered from immediate real time.

Leaving aside the transformation of data into and out of the computer between the real-time world and the processing function, we now turn to the data processing itself. This can be considered in a number of typical stages, considering first the point of view of the data. Data received is checked for legality, in type of message and message content for that type. It is then checked for validity in the current system context. Only then should processing functions be carried out, manipulating the data and acting upon it in the light of its own content and related data already stored in the computer. The results may need to be checked for feasibility before using them to update the stored data, for further processing to

produce output data, or to start another function. The output data can be
checked and left convenient for the transmitting routines to transform
back into the real-time environment. All this main processing is done in
the ideal environment, protected from other events.

In dedicated systems the range of message types is well defined.
Routine checking is straightforward; it is necessary to ensure that the data
which may have come from a manual, noisy, or faulty source cannot corrupt the system. If the data are wrong then the wrong results will inevitably be obtained, but the system can protect itself from data which could
cause errors in adjacent data or in program function. In other words the
processing function must be impervious to whatever data are hurled at
it — it must continue to function, rejecting faulty data and where necessary
advising the operator or other parts of the system of this rejection. In all
cases the action to be taken if certain data fail any of the tests must be
defined.

4.2. Processes

4.2.1. Processes and Tasks

While the designer and programmer are interested in the function or program that is to be performed, the user is interested in data and results.
Consider, therefore, programs as transformation *processes* on data and
the need to run a program on a particular set of data as a *task*. So, when
a process is scheduled to operate on particular data, the management function or control software is allocating various system resources to the
task; storage space, CPU time, the use of the process or program, and
possibly other equipment resources. This is the philosophy taken by
Dijkstra in the 'THE' multi-programming system. (1)

Such a system is most efficient if tasks are not interrupted but run
until they are complete. Moreover, it is attractive to allocate to a task when
it starts all the resources it will or may need to complete the process. The
considerations are very similar in a real-time system to those for batch
and multi-programmed systems. Although such a straightforward method
is efficient for each task, it is not necessarily efficient for a mix of tasks.
For instance, while one task is waiting for a slow device such as a disk,
another task could be making progress. However, just as for multi-programming systems, it is often still found desirable in real-time systems
for a task to run until it is held up and also that some resources, such as a

printer, CPU or transmission line, storage area, or a particular file, should be allocated to a task throughout its work to ensure by simple rules that it cannot get held up. To resort to complex optimizing and highly dynamic allocation does itself require considerable storage and processing power which may aggravate the very situation it is trying so cleverly to ease. A simple resource-allocation system leaves more time and room for the actual job. Also it can be well understood by the programming team who thereby gain confidence, make fewer mistakes, and can more quickly identify sources of error.

Because some tasks may take longer to execute than others can wait, some method of breaking off is necessary. The multi-programming method of letting a task run until it has to wait for a device or other resource may not be satisfactory. To rule that tasks must themselves break off after a certain running time imposes a constraint and relies on the programmer, but maybe this is acceptable. It is called *self-suspension*.

Because we are considering dedicated systems, the software designer knows what kind of programs there are and either of the two methods above may be perfectly satisfactory in many cases. It is most annoying to see simple methods passed over because they are not of general or academic use. For specific projects the main criteria are that the system shall work well and be economic. We are suggesting that in many ways both these aims are likely to be met by keeping to rather simple principles, not necessarily sophisticated ones. The designer can take advantage of knowing the nature of the particular system.

Some disciplinary rules are generally considered good engineering practice. The very identification of individual processes as stages in processing the data for any particular application is itself a voluntary discipline. From this arise the concepts of modular programs, a range of available subroutines, rules for the boundaries between processes, routines, etc., and constraints on the structure and use of stored data. We discuss some of these aspects in § 4, but here consider the implications and discipline of programming processes to run as tasks on data more from philosophical points of view than as a set of advocated rules. Although the control programs and not the data drive the system, the tasks run are appropriate to the data. Each data packet is processed as necessary. This approach is known as *transaction processing*. Each program function is called a *process*. The need to run a process on particular data is called a *task*. So it is tasks that are scheduled, not programs.

Fig. 4.2 shows how task data is stored, its position being kept as a pointer. The control programs decide which task to run next and pass control to the appropriate process, with the pointer value. If the task-data areas are in a contiguous queue, the separate pointers are not needed.

4.2.2. Stages of a Process

The purpose of a task is to produce some resultant data either for immediate output or for storing as new or updated information for later use. All efforts therefore are towards this end.

Called by control programs to run a task, a process routine is to that extent a slave; it may be called in varying circumstances and possibly without knowledge of other processing in hand. An assigned system resource, a process needs to be self-sufficient and able to execute its task with only the assistance of the utility routines. It is useful to consider the task as the active all-important aspect and the application program which forms the process as a disinterested operator which can be relied on to execute its function mechanically in a repetitive way as required. So tasks are set up

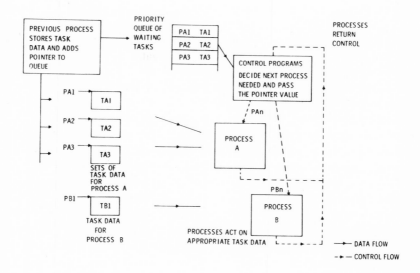

Fig. 4.2. Controlled running of processes to service queued task data.

each time in the same way, and the process performs the fixed logical operation on each piece of data presented to yield the consequential product.

Just as in any automatic machine it helps if parts are pre-oriented, so a process is simpler if task data is arranged in a fixed format. A workspace may be set up for a task, containing the starting data and with space for the intermediate and final results of the task, the parameters always occupying the same relative positions in the workspaces of all tasks for a process. Data only remain in workspaces for the duration of the task.

We consider a process in two main parts: the organizational part and the function or algorithm part. The first gets the data ready in the workspace, then the algorithm operates on this data to perform the appropriate function, and lastly the organizational part of the process is used to store or pass on results.

If a process can *gather* together all the necessary data at the start of a process and output or store away all the resultant data at the end of the process, the actual function part of the program can be simpler and more rugged. The function is simplified because it is not encumbered with complex addressing structures to access indexed files. The process is more robust if data are gathered, checked, and fully worked on before writing any results away, for if there is any data fault, ambiguity, or out-of-range result, the task can be terminated before any partial results have affected stored data. Moreover, the data once gathered into the workspace cannot be changed during the task by other processes which may share the same main data files, so each process can work on consistent data in its own workspace (see § 4.3.5). In some cases the overhead penalty of gathering may be too great, but others may be more efficient than if data files were accessed by indexing throughout the process. If the function works only on data in the workspace and does not access files, then functions and files can be independently designed and changed. Also programs are easier to write and test with fewer index registers active. Indeed it may be possible to use a simpler processor altogether.

Of course, many processes will still need to access files during the function because they may not know at the outset which records in the files are needed if these depend on the task-data values. However, one can still aim at the preparatory part of the process going as far as possible to help provide data in a way that will be the most convenient for the function.

Figure 4.2 shows task-data areas. If a process moves the task data into the workspace for the process, following the data-gathering suggestion, then the function does not have to work relative to the pointer value for the task-data area. The designer decides whether it is worth moving the task data into the process workspace. Another possibility is to use the task-data area as the workspace for that task. The area must then have space for intermediate and final results. This latter method, where workspaces are associated with each task rather than with a process, is necessary where there is any kind of parallel processing with more than one similar task active at any time.

The designer's decision as to what data to move from main data files into workspaces is influenced by the indexing efficiency of the programming language used. Whereas with symbolic and higher-level languages it is very easy during a process to refer to field data, arrays, and so on, the real-time programmer should know how the operating system and compiled code make the file access. It could be most unfortunate if repeated disk accesses were made for the same data, and preferable if that data were stored in a workspace after the first access. This suggests a whole record could be transferred from a disk to the workspace rather than each field when required.

Lastly, two more advantages of workspaces arise through having all the data for a task or process stored in a contiguous and easily identified area. It makes for easier program debugging if the initial data and intermediate and final results are all grouped together, and it also helps a process to hand to a subroutine or to another process for a further task in a convenient and direct way.

Having discussed the organizational part of a process, we look at the part which actually does the useful function. The actual function part of an application process does the logical transformation on the data for its tasks; the rest of the work is receiving, checking, manipulating, and storing the data — the organizational part. The mathematical method chosen to carry out a particular function is sometimes called the *algorithm*. There may be several algorithms or ways to make a certain transformation, and sometimes the specification of the function allows the programmer to make the choice. Here is one of the areas where the constraints of real time need to be known by the application programmer, for otherwise the function chosen may be unnecessarily accurate or use an algorithm that is too slow. So the programmer needs to know not only the consideration he must give to the amount of storage used by the function, its data, and its workspaces, but also the acceptable duration of a task using the process.

This may be determined by the response time required or by the through-put, the maximum traffic capacity, which must be catered for. We discuss this distinction and its effects on the choice of algorithm in §4.4. For the present we have considered the separation of the main function from the organizational parts of the program for a process.

There is another important link in the chain of processing yet to dis-cuss. How does one know what tasks are required to be performed on any particular data? It may be that data on a certain channel always requires certain tasks, or it may be that the appropriate tasks depend on the data itself. An initial task can assess the data to decide into what category they fall and arrange for the appropriate tasks to be called, otherwise the live data, always subject to error, might call unfeasible combinations of tasks. The same reasoning applies at all decision points, that the choices are pre-specified and a selection is made from these rather than constructing from the data a possibly unspecified choice leading down a non-existent path. These choices and the pre-specified processing paths for each choice can be listed and defined in pre-stored tables. The live data are assessed and the relevant choice is made. The corresponding process-ing tasks are then carried out, not as specified in the data, but as set out in the pre-stored table entry appropriate to that choice. This is illus-trated in Fig. 4.3. Such a *table-driven* technique is not only more ro-bust in action than a data-driven method but can also be more easily tested. If data do not fall into one of a finite range of types an error will be detected and appropriate action taken. Also the processes for each of the types of data can be methodically tested prior to running external tests. In dedicated real-time systems the range of types of data is usually small enough for this table-driven approach to be efficient in store and in run-ning time. The table content helps in the checking that the programmed actions will match the specification, but, if later changes in the processing algorithm for certain types of data are required or if new types of data are to be processed, the necessary changes are more easily made to the table than to the existing logic and are less likely to interfere with existing procedures.

It may be that the type of data received cannot be fully identified on arrival but will need some processes to be run first on a coarsely iden-tified type and then further assessment made on the result. So a number of decisions may have to be taken at different stages. This makes the table structure more involved as more levels of fragmented tables are required. The boundaries between logical decisions on data during a process and the fineness of the choice of data types, as well as the number and level of tables and the detail of their contents, must be carefully considered for each application. Greatest benefit occurs where it is easy to identify data types, but, even for wide ranges of types, extensive use of the table-driven technique can simplify programming of processes, giving, as in other areas where simplification is possible, cleaner, more efficient software which is quickly produced, checked, and modified and more robust.

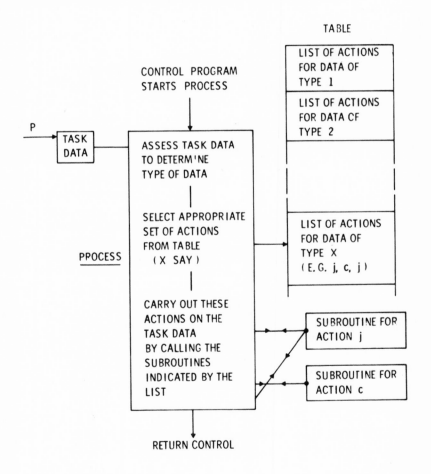

Fig. 4.3.   Table-driven process.

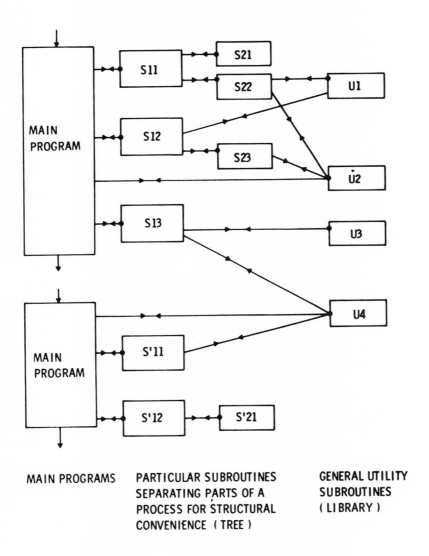

Fig. 4.4. Two reasons for subroutines — general utility and special.

Not surprisingly, much of this discussion on various aspects of processes is just as applicable to any software as to real-time systems. One would expect this where real-time programs are sheltered as far as possible from real-time events and operate in staticized situations.

4.2.3. Subroutines

Subroutines are beautiful. Each carries out a defined operation or function which is required at several points in the software. At whichever point it is used it carries out identically the same function on the data which are current at that point. The more often a subroutine is used, the greater its benefit in terms of store saving, for a subroutine only has to be stored once in a system yet contains instructions which can be used at many points in the software logic. Normally a subroutine is called at some point in a program, carries out its operation, and returns control to that same point in the calling program. While it is quite possible for a subroutine to decide from the data that return should be to another program, this is bad engineering and is not advocated.

A subroutine should not have too many alternative branches to cater for different data, but neither should the calling program spend undue overhead preparing data in order to use a standard subroutine. This means the exact boundaries of a subroutine function have to be carefully defined when the subroutine is designed so as to give the greatest benefit to store saving with least troublesome demands on programs which call it. In particular it is considered bad practice for a calling program to have to prepare special flags in the data to tell a subroutine which alternative path to follow, or to have to decipher results returned by the subroutine. The dilemma may be eased by using several levels of subroutines where one may call another in nested fashion. The subroutines ultimately called in this way may be of more general or more specific nature than the calling routine: more general if they perform a small task that is often needed in different circumstances, and more specific if they are only used when the calling subroutine or program has made the choice of alternative path. The general subroutines are like utilities; the more specific ones are like outer branches in a tree structure. The difference is shown in Fig. 4.4. In either case control returns to the root calling program via the levels used in the nested calling sequence.

Besides saving store, the use of subroutines helps to organize a process. Distinct areas can be seen, designed, tested, or changed with less effect on others with the same kinds of benefits in economic software as achieved by using distinct processes.

One danger of using subroutines which may be called by many processes, yet which can relinquish control by being interrupted or suspended to await further data, is that they may need to be protected against use by other tasks meanwhile. Such complexity is undesirable, and suspendable subroutines are best not shared between independent processes.

Whenever subroutines are called and again when they return control to the calling program, time is spent in changing the contents of the active registers (the accumulators, index registers, and sequence control register) to their previous values. While this can be done by software instructions, it is quicker if this standard operation can be done by the CPU hardware. It would be expensive to provide hardware registers to cater for many levels of nested subroutines, so some manufacturers provide a *stack* feature. This stores the active register values in a reserved store area when a subroutine is called and keeps a pointer to the last set stored. On exiting a subroutine, the register values are automatically replaced by the last set of values stored. Thus, on a last-in-first-out principle, the time penalty of using nested subroutines instead of direct code is reduced. The "pushdown" stack feature also encourages the orderly return out of a nested structure to the original point in the calling program. Where such standard operations are provided by the computer hardware they are not only faster but also prevent the occurrence of some possible software errors.

4.2.4. Re-entrancy

A process may work on a particular store area, assuming the task data is correctly positioned and leaving results in a fixed area. In this case, processes must be sequential and one task finished before another can be started. Just as on a production line, however, one can arrange that a similar task is started before another is finished. Such a process is said to be *re-entrant*. For a machine a task is just a different workspace; for the process it is just another workspace in store. The process needs a pointer to the relevant workspace for each task and must act on the data relative to this pointer. Where there is more than one CPU, two similar tasks can be performed simultaneously using the same instructions in core for the process. Obviously for re-entrant programs instructions must not change during execution and any data, loop counters, and so on must be stored in the workspace associated with each task as there can be no workspace associated with the process itself.

It is attractive to be able to start each task at the earliest moment, but just as on a production line so with software processes it is the slowest stage which determines the throughput in the steady state. Rather, therefore, than to insist on re-entrancy to try to force highest throughput it is more important to concentrate on speeding the slowest stage. Whereas a production line may have several successive machine tools, if the computer configuration has only one CPU there is less advantage in having re-entrant processes.

Re-entrancy has many overheads. First and foremost a variable number of workspaces may be required for a re-entrant process, and if these would not all be needed to store data for a one-task-at-a-time process (sequential process) then there may be a high store penalty. There are also store and running overheads which vary with the type of computer hardware: for such things as setting the data pointer for each task and recording which tasks are waiting, active, or completed, for deciding with which task a given disk read must be associated, whether a task is now free to run, and so on. So the whole situation is more dynamic both in store requirements and in relative events, and if there is a fault it is harder to know what data is at what stage and how to recover. Moreover it is difficult to ensure a program really is re-entrant and to link it satisfactorily with sequential processes and devices which are not re-entrant. Often there are better, more efficient ways of organizing the processing than to demand re-entrant programs.

The situation is different, however, where a parallel or multi-processing facility is provided by the computer configuration. If the hardware has more than one processing unit, then the same process or program can be simultaneously used for more than one task with possible advantage, particularly where the process is one of the slower ones in a production-line kind of sequence. Dijkstra's operating system conceives the same piece of code being given as a *resource* to any number of tasks at once, just as processing units are assigned to tasks as resources by the operating system. In such a case of multi-processing one would currently be considering a large computer configuration with sophisticated control programs, and the overheads cited for re-entrancy are not so significant as in a smaller system. Parallel processing essentially requires the same process to operate simultaneously on several sets of data.

Even if re-entrancy is not actually used, some of the attributes of re-entrant programs are nevertheless considered good and desirable practice in real-time applications. These are ones which do not have high overhead and which do not introduce new time variables. Such a code or program can be regarded as assignable to a task irrespective of other events and with confidence that the process can disinterestedly handle one set of data just as if it were one of many, keeping the effects of data clear of all programs and other active data. It can easily resume the task after waiting for slow devices, utility routines, or other devices. Sometimes it is useful to work relative to a data pointer set up by a calling program, even for non-re-entrant programs. One point in particular is that a program should never modify itself, for instance to arrange exits from loops or to set branch switches in advance, even if these are left unchanged at the end of the process; it is bad practice and an area where clever tricks are often regretted. Let the code always remain as it was loaded, separate from variable data both physically and in concept. It is equally abhorrent to try to execute real-time data which have been received — a less useful ability of the general-purpose computer. In many ways, then, the robustness of a process which would be demanded for re-entrancy is desirable for real-time use, but the increase in overheads and in the complexity of control programs may be avoided if the programs are used as a single-stream process.

4.3. Real-Time Aspects

This section deals with software design parameters that arise in real-time systems. The basic feature of real-time systems is their ability to operate continuously or whenever necessary so as to receive data and produce related output within a time that is normally short compared with the overall system of which the computer forms a part.

4.3.1. Response Time

The time between the event calling for a result and the output is called the *response time*. For the kind of systems we are considering, a typical response time might be a few seconds or less. It may be that steady input of certain data does not require any output until a request is made, so response time is not necessarily the time between receiving information and passing it on in processed form; the data might be stored meanwhile.

Because the designer is interested in meeting a required response time economically, the time taken for processing or running time must be carefully assessed at the analysis stage to ensure that the design can react promptly enough.

4.3.2. Throughput

There is a distinction between response and throughput constraints. Because most real-time systems must operate continually, the design must be able to process the highest traffic rate. To meet this *throughput* may place greater or lesser demands on the processing speed than that for meeting the response to any individual input. There must never arise such a build-up of work to do that any output is unavailable within the response time. It may be quite acceptable for the system capacity to be below that for processing an instantaneous peak input rate so long as the maximum quantity of input which can arrive during a period equal to the response time can be processed before the end of a further such period. That is to say, the peak input rate can be averaged over a period of approximately the response time, and the capacity of the system must be able to process this level of traffic.

From these two different considerations of response and of throughput, the maximum allowed running time is calculated for each type of task. Considerations for providing adequate response are discussed in § 5.2.1. To provide adequate capacity, the running times for each process multiplied by the number of essential tasks for the process in a given period of the heaviest traffic conditions of the specification must not exceed in sum the length of that period. The calculation must take account of the number of processors and the time required between tasks — the control software overheads. Normally a figure is calculated for each process being the percentage of the total processor time required. In this way a predicted total loading figure for the processor in heaviest traffic conditions is derived. The processor is only one resource, and similar figures are required for the use of disks, printers, and so on. As discussed later in this section, the use of these resources can be optimized to ensure that the most-needed resource can be active on useful work all the time, not waiting for another. The calculations will show whether the system tends to be CPU bound or perhaps disk bound.

4.3.3. Survival Time

Sometimes data have to be acted upon in a period shorter than the system response time in order that it should not be lost or to obtain the necessary accuracy. For example, as mentioned in Chapter 3, characters received over a fast data line must be accepted from the input register before they are overwritten by subsequent characters, or a device may need to be examined very frequently to determine its status or value at well-defined times. In these cases there is a short internal response time for a certain activity, but it is not necessary to perform all the resultant processing within this time. In the examples, characters can be stored in a multi-character buffer to await processing as a message at more leisure, or when a device is found to have a certain status the time can be noted and a task set up scheduling a process to run later. The important constraint is to catch or provide data at the required instant, irrespective of the time at which they are processed, but within a fine tolerance called the *survival time* beyond which the data would be lost or not valid. At the beginning of this chapter we suggested that as much of the processing task as possible should be insulated against such fast real-time events. The kind of buffering mentioned considerably eases the constraints on design, for one piece of data does not have to be fully processed before the next is received. That is to say the response time is not made unnecessarily short; it can be longer than the survival time of a particular piece of data.

4.3.4. Buffering

A *buffer* is a store area where several sets of similar data may be temporarily stored to await later processing. Several messages can be queued in a buffer as they arrive, allowing the processing to be done asynchronously, when convenient, smoothing out instantaneous and short-term demands for processing. Normally a buffer is a *cyclic queue,* messages being processed in the order they arrive and new messages being added to overwrite the areas used by earlier messages. These individual message areas may be either consecutive in physical store or chained in some way. In either case, the buffer has associated pointers to indicate the next area available for filling and the next messages to be processed.

The length of a buffer can be determined from the maximum input rate, the slowest allowed response, and the process duration. Preferably, permanently assigned buffer areas can be large enough for the worst cases.

Where there is a wide spread of input rate, dynamic allocation of buffer space may be necessary. When input is randomly received from many independent devices, then buffers might have to be designed to the most probable maximum input rate. In either case, the action in the event of full buffers must of course be defined.

4.3.5. Simultaneous Tasks

It would be very nice if the processing to service one event could be completed before the next event, but often this cannot be economically achieved. The next best thing would be to complete the processing for one event, to complete one task, before commencing work for another event, the new task having to wait. However, where several different processes are involved, maybe to handle tasks arising from quite independent external events, it may be more difficult to arrange that only one task is active at a time. To meet different response times for different types of event or while waiting for a further event (such as completion of a disk read), it may be necessary to start a task before another is complete. In these cases, of *simultaneous tasks*, a new set of problems can arise. They also arise in multi-processing systems, where tasks are deliberately made simultaneous, and in the special case of re-entrant processes.

If simultaneous tasks refer to the same data and one or more of them can modify this data, then, if there are variable time relationships between the tasks, it cannot be reliably predicted whether one task will read data which have or have not yet been modified by another. Worse still some data may have been modified and other data not, so a task might act on inconsistent information. We have suggested earlier in this chapter that processes should gather all the data they need at the outset and also deposit results only at the end. This is not always possible or economic, and even then does not logically protect fully against this effect of interacting simultaneous tasks.

One can see that if the data in question, whether in a file or not, are regarded as a resource needed by the process to run a task, it may be possible to ensure that the resource is only allocated to one task at a time, solving the problem. There are two levels at which resources can be allocated, either by control programs before a task is activated, or by allocating on a first-come-first-served basis during the running of tasks, unlucky tasks having to wait (suspend) until the resource is free. In the first method the data resource is regarded like other more physical resources and the control program, knowing what is presently allocated, can select the next task to activate and avoid the data-sharing problem in the same way as an operating system in a batch-processing environment would avoid scheduling two programs both requiring, say, a printer. However, there are two main penalties: the control program must know what data the process may need to run the task, and, if tasks could share many files, the result could be virtually the same as only having one active task, which as discussed before may not be sufficient.

In the first-come-first-served method, a task has to ask if a resource is free and if so reserve it, or otherwise the task has to wait. Two undesirable things can happen with this method. The first is that one task may examine an unused resource and find it free, but, before it can reserve it, another task may have examined it and also found it free. So both tasks will proceed, to possible conflict. A solution is for one task to make the assessment and reservation for a resource while other tasks are prevented from doing so. A crude way is temporarily to halt other tasks, inhibit interrupts, examine some kind of status flag for the resource and if it is not set as reserved to reserve it, and then to remove the inhibition on other tasks and proceed (if the resource was free). One wants to remove the inhibition as soon as possible and certainly within the shortest time tolerance for any task in the system which might have been inhibited. If many separate data accesses are made these overheads become high. A more efficient way, if available, is to carry out the lockout, examination, setting, and the resumption in one operation. In some computers this is provided by a *test-and-set* instruction, of the kind described in Chapter 3. A flag can be read and set to reserved status in the same uninterruptible operation, such as a single store cycle. The effect is to set the flag and provide the original contents for the task to assess. If the flag is then found to have been previously set, indicating the resource was reserved, then the task can wait, but if previously free the task can proceed knowing the flag is now set. In either case the flag is left set. When the resource is no longer needed, the flag can be simply cleared. Where a test-and-set instruction is not available the cruder method may be used, locking out other tasks by inhibiting all interrupts for instance or all higher-level activities. In either case it is not necessary to stop other tasks while the resource is used, only while the flag is assessed, and one relies on all programmers to observe the discipline of testing flags before using resources which could, if shared, upset tasks using their processes. Dijkstra called these special flags *sema-phores*. Essential for multi-processing, we see the test-and-set facility is very useful in single-processor applications.

The other undesirable thing that can happen in the first-come-first-served method is that one task holding resource A may have to wait for resource B which is held by another task, and then, if the second task wants resource A neither task can proceed. Dijkstra called this situation the *deadly embrace*. Here is another reason for allocating resources at or near the outset of a task, and also for releasing them as soon as possible. It is nevertheless up to the software designer to ensure such mutual lock-out situations cannot arise either by arranging that no such patterns of currently scheduled tasks could occur, or by demanding that such resources must be allocated at the outset.

4.3.6. Protection

In a complex system with many different processes, one may wish to im-pose more than disciplines of programming to ensure that some processes cannot interfere with others, or that some tasks cannot access another's data. It may be necessary to protect certain programs and data from others either momentarily or, for non-interactive processes, more permanently. In time sharing, as opposed to multi-access systems, processes are unable to access another user's program or data if programs are compiled or run relative to a *base register*. If each user has a different base register, the users are spatially separated. A limit register restricts the upper level of addressing. In a *swapping* system, where only one user's program is in core at once, the same base register may be used; in this case the users are separated in time. It is helpful if computers selected for such applica-tions do have base and limit hardware registers, and ones which can be set during running by the control program before a task is started. Some designers prefer not even to trust application programmers with the ability to set or play with such registers or to do other things allowed only to control programs. This means that control programs have to act in a privileged mode to set the registers, yet another feature then required of the hardware. While one realizes program faults do occur, the chance of deliberate abuse of privilege might be thought small, especially in dedicated systems where programs usually have more thorough examination than in others. Nevertheless, there are advocates of the privileged or executive mode. For other reasons, a special higher level may be desirable for control programs, for example to regain control from a program found to have overrun its time.

In *multi-access systems*, where the several users are interactive and use the same data, we have seen the need for flags or resource allocation to protect data. Base and limit registers could also be used for this purpose to define the allowed and protected data areas just as they can define the allowed program-access area. So the control programs or allocation stages have to set up for a task a series of base and limit pairs for data and program areas. Moreover, one may want to restrict the type of access in a certain area, so as not to overwrite the allowed program, not to execute data, or not to alter certain data but only read it. Therefore each area needs to have a base, limit, and type defined. Furthermore, different processes may be allowed to make different types of access on the same area, so these type definitions for each area need to be stored for each process.

This forms a list of *"capabilities"* for the process. Each capability states what area can be accessed and whether the contents can be read, modified, or executed by that program. The programmers or system builder program set up a capability table for each process. During running the control programs set up in hardware registers pointers to the appropriate table before activating a task which is then constrained to run within those *capabilities* (2); attempts at execution or access outside these constraints are detected as errors by the processor hardware. All this can become a complex mechanism to create and set up; it also requires considerable computer hardware and imposes an overhead in running time. It can catch some infrequent software errors and some errors due to unusual data patterns, but it does demand that the mechanism itself has been correctly set up and it may still not detect errors due to faulty computer hardware, so even these lengths cannot guarantee that program or data cannot get corrupted. Careful analysis of the cost and benefit should be undertaken before such special features are demanded. It may be that a more straightforward design can give adequate performance more economically; it may even give more reliable performance.

4.3.7. Running Time

In the above considerations of response time and traffic rate we have said that buffering allows the maximum traffic for processing to be reduced to the maximum peak rate averaged over a period of the order of response time. So now one knows the processing rates required of the system and the maximum running times for each process if the computer only had to handle one type of traffic. Many dedicated systems are like this and there is no need to go to complex designs for scheduling the tasks, but where the traffic mix demands different combinations of process to be run for different types of input and output, the division of processing time among processes may need more careful planning, and allowance must also be made for the running time of the control programs. The scheduling does not have to be so flexible in a dedicated system as in a general system, and the designer may do well not to throw away the knowledge of the traffic mix when designing the method of allocating running time and priorities to processes or scheduling tasks. We return to these considerations in Chapter 5 and assume for the present that the maximum permitted running time for a process to execute a task has been determined. One then has to ensure that the algorithm to be chosen for the process can run within this time. This includes the organizational parts of the work as well as the main functions of the process. Looking at each process in this way, one may happily find that there is plenty of time available; one has more confidence than to insist on the shortest running time just in case a high processing load should ever arise, because one knows for certain what is the worst case for which the system is designed and positively what action is being taken in cases worse than this. It may turn out that storage is the scarce resource; this balance between storage required and running time for a process is considered in the next section.

In dedicated systems as well as many other systems it is often found that the running time of a process is largely spent in doing certain operations within the function repetitively, many times for each task. This is usually the area worth concentrating on if it is necessary to reduce running time. This optimization can be carried out at many levels. The lowest level is that of the individual instructions. One can use instructions so that an operation, such as a search for a matching field, can be carried out at each iteration in the least number of instruction accesses. For dedicated systems one might even choose the computer on the basis of certain instructions in the set, for example auto-incrementing an index register. In a computer with read-only-memory facility certain frequently used instructions can be microprogrammed in to execute faster than if a series of standard instructions were used. There are penalties in this, for programs relying on special instruction sets are less portable to other systems, and also one might invent special instructions which gave rise to curious effects at execution, sometimes difficult to identify in changing real-time environments, which may be due to unforeseen hardware effects where such instructions have not been tested, proven, documented, and supported by manufacturers. One could regret clever tricks here but the facility can be ideal for fast-repeated operations in dedicated systems.

One kind of area where particular processors in a system have specific tasks is in the performing of special functions, functions for which they are designed and dedicated. Examples of such special functions are input-output processing, code coversion, running control programs, fast data acquisition, multiplexers, display processors, associative retrieval, mass-processing devices, and processors for special mathematical routines such as Fourier analysis. These special microprocessors, even if programmed, can be regarded as special-purpose hardware devices running either relatively slowly in parallel with the processes in the main processor(s) just like a disk controller or in series like a hardware multiplier. Such devices can earn their keep in continuous utilization as components in dedicated systems by relieving pressure on processing time in the main processors and so allow some of the simplifications we have proposed for real-time software.

The next level of software running-time optimization is to arrange for the repetitive part of the operation to be as small as possible, maybe by organizing the data and index registers in the best way before the tight loop is entered so that the loop is as short as possible.

There may be ways of optimizing searches or other parts of the algorithm giving worthwhile savings. Naturally these depend on the exact application. It helps if data is organized to benefit the most time-critical processes. Some algorithms might only be long for certain values of data, so testing the value early in the algorithm may enable a long operation to be avoided where it proves unnecessary, reducing average running time. The algorithm can be examined for accuracy to ensure valuable time is not unnecessarily wasted in working to too many decimal places or to too many terms in a polynomial.

Sometimes much more significant than these detailed considerations is the resource which has most effect on the total running time of a typical task. Examining where the running time is spent, perhaps with the help of a time-base diagram such as Fig. 4.5, may show ways of improving performance. If there are repeated disk accesses for a task it is unlikely that optimizing individual logical operations will have as significant an effect as reducing the number of accesses and, for instance, bringing a whole record into main store at the outset of a task rather than field by field when required. Two tasks, queued up for the same process, could be scheduled to be run consecutively as one if this could halve the number of disk accesses and allow two tasks to be processed almost as fast as one. Then the control programs are really scheduling a process rather than a single task, and the process runs until no more queued data is waiting for it. This may give worthwhile savings in overheads.

4.3.8. Suspending Tasks

Very often a process is not processor-bound, but limited by waiting for data transfers to complete, for instance from disk. The programmer should know when the transfers occur, but when using high-level languages or

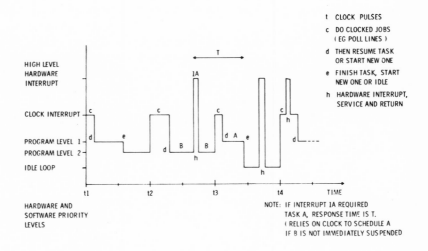

Fig. 4.5. An example of a time-base diagram showing ways in which CPU time will be allocated.

powerful operating systems this may not be the case because such transfers are deliberately made transparent to the programmer. If the control programs do not do it automatically, the programmer can arrange for the process to *suspend* a task instead of waiting. That is to say, the process leaves data in the task workspace and begins another task or exits to the control programs. When the transfer is complete, the task must be flagged to be rescheduled. The transferred data must be associated with the appropriate task. This sort of suspension gives the simultaneous task problems already discussed and also increases the organizational running time overhead.

When a task is suspended, one might decide not to start another similar task until the first is complete because the overheads of managing the simultaneous tasks and the re-entrant process might be greater than the processor time saved. Unless processes are very long with only a few disk accesses, the simple single-task approach is preferred. The spare processor time could, however, be used to advance dissimilar tasks provided the suspended tasks can resume soon enough after their transfers are complete that their overall elapsed times are still within the required response. The decision will depend on whether the system is disk bound or CPU bound. In other words it depends on the application and one does not look for a general solution — it might be far from optimum for the particular case.

A simple approach may prove not only cheaper to program and store, but also faster to run, giving altogether better performance in small dedicated systems. We do not pass comment here on the economics of full-blown operating systems with optimized disk queues and so on, found in systems with unpredictable job mixes, except to point out that such systems are generally found to be not just flexible, but also large and expensive.

When the processor time has to be divided among different processes for different types of data received, the various response times have to be considered. If an urgent task could not wait for another to complete, then one must suspend the lower-priority task. Where processes are not independent, we have expressed preference for this suspension to be done at planned points rather than for the lower task to be randomly interrupted. This means tasks should regularly suspend themselves within a time period which allows more urgent tasks to meet their response time and be able to resume without conflict. In dedicated systems all required response times and maximum traffic rates are known and actual running times are estimated at the design stage. Therefore the software designer knows how often and how long each process might be suspended, so he can calculate the longest elapsed duration from start to finish of a task in the worst case. This, plus any queueing time for task data, must not exceed the response time required of the process. If tasks do suspend themselves instead of continuing till interrupted, a multi-level system is reduced to a single-level system in which all possible situations between interdependent tasks can be seen or predicted and catered for. Processes suspend in a tidy, protected way at known, convenient points.

Once these real-time considerations have been taken into account for a system and any software disciplines set down, the actual programming and testing of individual processes can be carried out without the programmer having to consider the possibly confusing dimensions of the unpredictable real-time world or having to be aware of other processes in the system.

4.4. Storage and Data Organization

The previous section dealt with real-time aspects. The content of the present section has been separated from those because, once they have been considered, the arrangement of data for storage and use by processes is separated from real time, and the considerations are those of efficient running and use of store. That is to say, we can now forget about interrupts, response times, multi-level actions, and a general feeling of being pushed about by events and chasing the most urgent jobs. We are still concerned with achieving the designed running time for each process and with sharing out the available storage just as in any efficient multi-programming system.

4.4.1. Storage Allocation

Consider first a single-level storage system, that is, the only storage is directly addressable, such as magnetic core store. Its size may be limited by cost or technical constraints such as physical space, addressing range, and so on, so the designer will need an efficient, economic use of store. In dedicated systems the job mix for the application is known; the full set of programs and data files is drawn up. For each of the processes there may be a range of possible algorithms which satisfy the running-time constraints. For each of the main data files the number of records is known, but the same information can be organized in files in many different ways. The structure chosen for each file may not alter the storage it needs, but can greatly affect the running time of the processes. Therefore one can select a file organization to suit the most time-critical processes by ensuring the data are organized in a way that is easiest for them to access, for example by retrieval parameter or by sequential access.

Taking the most urgent processes, there may be little choice of algorithm; the code is optimized to fastest response or greatest throughput. Although these are two different criteria they have the same need for short running time. For less urgent processes one has a wider choice, perhaps using slower procedures that take up very little store — a further advantage in removing as much of the system as possible from the fastest real-time areas and the dictates of short survival times, and declutching into less urgent internal areas. Knowing that the designed running times are fast enough the designer does not have to seek the shortest possible processing times from every process.

As well as the choice of algorithm, there is a choice of language in which the program for a process is written. This is discussed in the next section.

Eventually a *storage map* can be drawn up, showing the full set of on-line programs and data simultaneously in store, with size estimates for each. If they add up to more than the store available, the software designer must ensure additional store is obtained or reduce the specification until the software will fit in. He should resist trying to squeeze everything in. Ample store allows the programs to be more comfortable and to keep the clean shape we have been discussing, rather than being pruned down to fit, leaving them with not quite such a robust algorithm, with less accuracy, checking, or even less capacity, because a squeeze on store can cause increased running time. Tight packing gives less scope for changes and extensions. Moreover, the cost of ownership will be higher if the software has been squeezed up into a nasty knot one dare not touch.

Storage costs for minicomputers have fallen continuously and dramatically, whereas software costs have risen continuously with labor costs. While there have been some advances in software techniques, they have failed altogether to match advances in hardware technology, and now the cost of one instruction word of software is typically something like ten times the cost of the main storage it occupies. For single systems in all sorts of dedicated real-time applications it is common, indeed usual, to find the software has cost more than the hardware. To provide more store does not mean there will be even more of the costly software but rather the software can be more simple minded and straightforward, perhaps in a high-level language, thus reducing design, testing, and commissioning costs. A manager who controls the budget for both software and hardware expenditure for a system may find a definite advantage in buying more store and hiring fewer programmers.

This does not mean to say a programmer should be able to meander through core; there is an economic balance point. It is worth considerable thought early on in design to save substantial amounts of program. One looks back at some software and finds areas that can be stripped out altogether leaving the system better, cleaner, and simpler. Such savings are worthwhile. One tries to avoid the expense and delay of rewriting programs just to save a few instructions so that all the software will fit in.

Where there are to be large numbers of the same system produced, the balance between hardware and software costs is altered. It needs to be decided, before design, over how many systems the software is to be spread, budgeting appropriately for custom tailoring and a "policy of continual product enhancement". In some cases, such as avionics systems, store really is at a premium, and the expense and snags of tight coding may, sadly, be unavoidable.

Whatever storage is provided, estimates for each separate program are required, and some contingency has to be allowed for the inaccuracy of these estimates as well as some deliberate provision for changes and extensions. One does not forget the control programs, the data files, workspaces, buffers, and so on, and one may wish to allow room to fit in permanently some recovery and small diagnostic routines. Nevertheless in dedicated systems one can make rather accurate store estimates.

Even in single-level storage systems there are the possibilities of either fully dedicated store or dynamically allocated store. In the first case, areas of store for fixed buffers and workspaces are assigned to each process at system building time and may not be used for other purposes. Therefore each variable-length area must be large enough to cater for the worst case. Dynamic allocation of storage means that physical areas of store are not all pre-assigned to particular processes or data types, but areas are allocated to store programs or data during the running of the live system, as and when they are needed, being afterwards freed and available for re-assigning for other use. The methods of allocating store dynamically are discussed further in Chapter 5. Dynamic allocation postpones the assignment of temporary data areas until running time when the space is actually needed to run a task. The control programs then assign blocks of store from the areas which are free at that time, and these are returned to the free status after use by the task. Besides these overheads of storage management, there can arise dynamic problems if under some traffic conditions there is inadequate free core or if there are insufficient contiguous free blocks. It is harder to detect when buffers have become unduly long, and the whole situation can fluctuate widely under external real-time events. To cater for worst traffic combinations may require as much store as in a fully dedicated system. Dynamic allocation is only likely to help where worst cases can arise in very different ways in the same systems but where it does not have to cater for all of them at once, and there are few systems like that. However, where large workspaces are required and there is control over the sequence of processes, an area could be assigned for use as general workspace by processes in turn, the data in it only being valid while a given task runs. The authors prefer to see a firm grip kept on the situation and not allow the traffic to decide how store is used. To defend a dynamic allocation system as being powerful, flexible, and catering in an optimum way for varying traffic and new processes has too often been found an inadequate substitute for honest analysis, producing no demonstrable hardware saving but an additional overhead and an unnecessary dimension of uncertainty. In simpler systems these supervisory costs are saved.

However the store is divided up, permanently or dynamically, estimates of the size of program, files, and other data areas are required as a stage in the engineering development. They are necessary for planning and to monitor programming progress, in order to ensure that the storage limits are not being approached. News of projects whose computer hardware has had to be unexpectedly increased in storage late in the project development is disappointingly common. In other cases projects are delayed while the software is squeezed down. Such situations bring the industry into disrepute. Some arise through estimates not being made and adhered to, some owing to specification changes, and others are simply due to software engineers failing to convince their managers of the store required. All are cases where the remedy lies in clear management rather than increased computer magic or sophistication. Where there just cannot be enough store, a responsible approach to revising the specification may be needed to see if the aims of the system can be met more frugally, for one sometimes finds a specification contains unwanted features which only crept in through a designer's over-enthusiasm.

If negotiations fail, the software designer could take the same attitude as an architect when a bridge contractor stipulates to him the limit on concrete content, and withdraw from the project before it damages him and the industry!

4.4.2. Multi-level Store

When a system is sufficiently large and does not have tight response times to meet, it may be more economic to keep some of the system stored on a cheaper storage medium until it is needed, rather than to keep it all in directly addressable store. Alternatively one could consider a cheaper, slower, one-level store, or some combination of these.

Devices on which data and programs are merely stored until needed, but on which they cannot be operated *in situ*, are called *backing stores*. Common examples are magnetic drums, disks, cards, and tapes. Ferromagnetic films are easy to deposit and information can be closely packed without interference. This is also true of photosensitive coatings, and either type has the advantage of easy conversion of stored data back into electronic signals, but magnetic films have the further benefit of being reusable. At present, therefore, most backing stores are magnetic in nature, but there are current developments in laser memories and other technologies striving for closed packing of information, faster access, or just cheaper storage. Some do not retain information if the power is switched off.

The devices which store the most information are not only compact but also happen to be the cheapest. Unfortunately they are also the slowest. As a happy result of the nature of things, the most bulky information, the largest files, are generally the least often or least urgently required. Therefore it is usually possible to find an economic balance point — the least-expensive storage arrangement which meets the demands of the real-time system. It is basically cost which dictates the use of backing store, though sometimes the vast quantity of information would be physically impossible to store in direct-access mode.

In this book we do not go into a detailed analysis of the ways of arranging storage at different levels on various devices, and indeed such analysis in a generalized case would be of little use and even confusing. The same goes for the various ways of indexing and accessing these stores. All we can do here is to stress the need for formal written analysis in any particular case, and to discuss some of the ingredients for this analysis which arise in real-time systems, referring the reader to the bibliography and specialized literature for backing-store techniques and indexed file structures. The same rules apply in real-time systems as in any other efficient computer applications.

The constraints of real-time systems pose similar and additional problems for the system designer when using backing store as compared with, say, an off-line multi-programming bureau computer system. Reducing running time in order to get a job finished on a batch system is with the aim of freeing other resources including main store so as to start another job and attain a high throughput, whereas for a real-time system there are the considerations of response time to meet as well as the need to provide throughput at lowest cost.

The general rule is to design the system so as to minimize the number of backing-store accesses, since each may take 10,000 to 100,000 times as long as a direct-store access. For maximum throughput one clearly wants the most frequently run processes to reside in and refer to data held in primary store. Where backing-store accesses are necessary, it helps if associated data can be accessed at one time. Appropriate indexing can reduce the amount of searching through backing store. If the physical storage address is related to the record number, data can be retrieved in "*direct-access*" mode, using a fixed formula to retrieve records on a given file. These points are amplified in the next section.

The other running-time consideration, that of meeting response times, may mean processes other than just the most frequent must be similarly treated. This whole area of design can be considered as an extension of the choice of algorithm in the way discussed earlier in this section; still, the algorithm including storage accesses and transfers has to meet the running-time limit for each process. The designer selects the algorithm and storage which meets the time constraints with the least use of dedicated main store.

Backing-store accesses may be needed not only for file accession, but also for calling parts of actual programs into primary store. Routines which are not frequently run and which are not involved in fast-response processes can be kept in backing store until required, transferred into main store just like data, and then executed. They need not be written back if, in accordance with the suggestions in § 4.2, programs are never modified during running. Either the application programs in main store can decide to call a section of program down from backing store, manage the transfer, and provide some of their own main storage, or they can call on facilities in the control programs to perform the operation. It depends how the index to the backing store is set up. Control programs must be told which section is required, and then perform the operation in a fixed way; the application programs, if they have the index, might do a more optimized transfer. Generally, the standard way is preferred as it can use a well-proven software mechanism in the control programs which is the same for all accesses. So here is a useful facility of the operating system, but we are advocating that transfers even of program should be consciously initiated by the applications programs.

Some computers offer *virtual memory* or *virtual storage*. This is an automatic facility supplied with the computer hardware or with the manufacturer's operating system — the supervisory software described in Chapter 5 — which allocates areas of storage on a multi-level system, so that the programmer need not be concerned with the physical limits or particular level of storage used for programs or data. However, this does not allow estimates of running time to be made, and for efficient, dedicated real-time systems this, we have seen, is an essential part of the analysis and software design. The subject is considered further in § 5.2.6.

4.4.3. Data

When backing store is accessed for data, it is important that the overheads of the transfer management are minimized because accesses of data may be frequent. The indexing needs to be a very simple transformation from file-record name to physical backing-store location, and this index may need to be kept entirely in main store. For these two reasons so-called *"direct-access"* indexing is preferred, where the file-record number has a simple fixed logical relationship to the backing-store location. Then no cross-index has to be maintained, only the base address of the file. For example, to access the nth record in a 4-byte-per-record file, add $4n$ to the base address for the file. It does mean records in a file must be of fixed length, consecutively numbered, and conveniently blocked on the backing store. This method may not make the most efficient use of space on the backing store, but often this is not too important. The direct-access method of backing-store file indexing is much favored in real-time systems.

Where several references to the same file or record are made by a given task, one access can bring an appropriate part of the file into main store so as to minimize the number of backing-store accesses. This needs the file to be conveniently organized. Again, elbow room in main store helps to speed the process by allowing a larger block to be transferred.

The general rule, stated earlier, is that data files should be organized to benefit the most time-critical and the most frequent procedures.

4.4.4. Overlay Patterns

In dedicated systems the job mix is known and the program sizes are estimated. Where not all programs can reside in main store at once, the designer must first decide which programs and files have to be permanently in immediate access store to meet the required response and calculate which they and their task data need. The remainder of the store is then available for data and programs called down from backing store. This area will contain different data and programs from time to time, the new contents overwriting the previous ones. The new contents form an *overlay* or *page*.

The designer can plan which overlays will fit into core at the same time so as to save unnecessary overlaying, and can draw store maps showing the spatial occupancies in various situations. These patterns can be optimized to allow the most urgent and the most frequently used overlays to be overwritten by others as rarely as possible. Each pattern needs to be known to ensure that the response and throughput can be met in the worst cases. As a simple example, if overlay program A needs to call a disk-resident subroutine B, it would be best if overlay B is placed in a different store area so that A is still available to complete the task. Similarly one might need to avoid overlaying a suspended task with an overlay for a different process. This means that the mechanism in dedicated systems for allocating areas of core to overlays should be pre-planned, cater for all worst cases, and be optimized to alleviate these cases for time-critical processes. So the rules for locating in main store the blocks or pages accessed as overlays from backing store need to be tailored for each application.

The choice of backing-storage medium for given data or program depends on the range of device available and the permissible access time. For economy one would usually choose the slowest which meets the requirement, but from time to time advances in technology produce a new medium that is both faster and cheaper than another. Where the computer configuration has not been fixed, this consideration is one of the most important for the real-time software designer and is second only to the primary consideration of meeting response and running time.

Before core store was available, programs were executed directly off magnetic drums. This was slow of course and nowadays does not make efficient use of processor time, so drum-resident programs are now overlaid into core and executed from there. In the case of *extended core store*, however, the main core is augmented by usually large sections of less expensive core store which are only a few times slower, typically a few microseconds access time. Where the processor allows, the designer has the choice of executing the program which is resident on extended core either *in situ* or by first overlaying it into main core. To execute *in situ* not only saves transfer time but also saves overwriting anything in main core. It may be efficient for random, rare, short routines, but most configurations in practice only execute programs in main store.

Accesses to slower backing-store devices such as disks and drums take between 15 and 150 ms. This is mainly the time to seek the right track and search it for the start of the data rather than the subsequent time for the actual transfer. Such devices are more efficient when a large block of data is required. For accessing small blocks such as random file records, a faster response medium such as extended core is more efficient and can be an economic place to keep medium-sized random-access files which are frequently referenced. The saving over main-store costs can be significant with little reduction in response for it is only the file access which is slow (yet fast enough for the CPU to wait), other instructions being at full rate. The rest of main store is free to run other programs faster with fewer program overlays since it is not cluttered with a large permanent file.

Such considerations give the real-time software designer the whole dimension of choice of storage medium for each process program, file, task data, and control program. This can become confusing to the point where inefficient designs result if the paramount considerations of response and running time are not borne uppermost in mind. To meet these requirements for each process individually may not be too hard to plan. Where choices for one process affect another, the solution can quickly become complex, but is simplified if the following general approach is taken. First remove urgency from all processes wherever possible and design the file structure to suit the ones which remain most time constrained. Then select for each process the least-store algorithm and cheapest storage medium which still meet their individual timing constraints. If there is then an overall running-time problem for the combined processes, optimize overlay patterns and use faster algorithms before resorting to faster storage of additional processors.

This general approach can yield an efficient solution, but often there are other constraints such as a large step-function in the cost of an extra hardware facility or a limited range of storage device available on a prescribed processor, or the computer configuration already having been selected, or worse still the hardware budget having been fixed independently of the software cost estimates.

Besides the hardware purchases and maintenance costs, there are also penalties in development and commissioning on a large, diverse-hardware system, as well as the software overheads in programming, running, and storing the necessary control software. There can be justifiable bias towards a simple configuration with the fewest different types of peripheral.

4.5. Languages

4.5.1. High-level versus Assembler Language

For individual problem-solving projects a program might only be run a few times. The computer time taken is of little importance. For many commercial and other batch-programming tasks, greater emphasis is placed on the size of data storage required than on running time, because the prime question of cost is the size of computer required rather than how long the machine must be run each day to process all the jobs. Only in those cases where a machine starts to become overloaded does time become important, and even then multi-programming may ease the problem if it is a slow resource such as disk or printer which dominates the running time. For such types of computing, the choice of language does not have a fundamental effect on the success of a job, so the choice is often made for the language that is easiest to program. The tendency has been to use *high-level languages* that are nearer to common language than the individual machine operations are. Programs written in FORTRAN, ALGOL, COBOL, and so on are compiled into machine instructions and stored in binary code before the program is executed. Compilers can be designed to check programs to some degree or to create a program to occupy least store or least running time, depending on the requirement. Some large machines even have an instruction set matching a certain high-level language, and this is a trend that may be expected to continue with the decreasing costs of hardware logic.

In real-time systems, however, the paramount question is usually one of running time. In dedicated systems there is a strong desire to keep down the computer hardware cost and use a small machine, so storage is also at a premium. In the past, real-time computing has tended to be part of a technical system and so, as discussed in Chapter 1, a different approach was adopted than if a project was seen as a computing task. Real-time projects have always been pushing at the bounds of hardware technology, starting with small machines and finding tasks that need larger and faster ones, so there has been pressure on having the programs very efficient. The tendency here has been to use *assembler level languages* where each instruction corresponds to a machine operation. There are as many such languages as there are types of machine.

As a generalization, a programmer is found to design, produce, and test programs at a steady number of lines per day, irrespective of language. A statement in a high-level language might compile into say five machine instructions. The equivalent steps might be written in assembler language in say three instructions. That is to say the assembler code takes less store and running time but in this case three times as long to program. For a single system, the cost of storage is very much smaller than the cost of writing the program instructions to be stored in it. With adequate room and running time it is therefore advantageous to use a high-level language even if it means buying a computer with larger store.

In those cases where one is up against the maximum processor loading or more often the maximum storage available, then there may be no choice but to use assembler language. Real-time computers have been of small storage capacity in the past, but there has been a tendency for maximum core storage available to double every two years. Minicomputers now have up to 100 Mbytes plus large-capacity disks. With falling storage costs and rising programming costs the benefit of high-level languages is increased.

There are applications where it is not storage that is the limiting factor but running time. Sometimes the task can be split between processors, but this increases the cost of equipment and of installation. It also increases complexity and often one prefers to use one processor if possible. The running-time calculations suggested earlier in this chapter could be estimated for programs in a suitable high-level language. To obtain accurate figures it may be necessary to code roughly a few routines found to have a strong influence on the percentage load.

To obtain a feel for the relative efficiency of languages for a certain type of operation such as a formula calculation, data manipulation, searching, and so on, an appropriate short *benchmark* program can be programmed in each language and the relative lengths and theoretical execution times compared. With this kind of knowledge a more informed choice of language may be made. Because high-level languages are designed to be easy to use rather than to suit a particular computer, less programmer experience or expertise is demanded. Moreover, programs (and programmers) are more readily moved from one kind of machine to another, keeping the same high-level language. Such software is said to be *portable*. The language for which a certain computer has compilers and libraries of software should be a consideration in the choice of computer for a project.

4.5.2. Mixed Languages

The running-time calculations may indicate that a few processes have a much greater effect on overall processor loading than the rest, and that these processes need to be very efficiently programmed. One alternative is to consider the use of special hardware for these functions, whether it be in handling many transmission lines, a special mathematical function, or data manipulation. Another possibility is to program just these processes in assembler language while the rest of the software is written in a high-level language. This mixing of languages requires that the compiler can handle the combination. This is a demand on the particular compiler rather than on the language or the computer. One should ensure that this facility is available before planning on this assumption.

There are two other snags in using mixed languages. The first is that once assembler-level routines are allowed, there may be enthusiasm for coding more processes this way than necessary, because the programmers see opportunities for more efficient assembler programs until they see the speed of producing programs in high-level language. Secondly, where the high- and low-level programs interface or share file data, the assembler-level programs may need to know more exactly how the data is stored than is evident from the high-level programs, the very essence of which is to take care of many such things for the programmer by making them *transparent*. The programmer of the assembler routines may need to see the compiled version of the high-level routines and files before he can write his own programs. If, however, assembler level coding does not creep in except where essential, the greatest advantage of the high-level language can be realized in producing software quickly.

Debugging techniques are quite different in the different types of language. Assembler programs, being much nearer to the hardware, induce a low-level approach to logic checking, and frequently one needs to examine hardware register values. For high-level programs testing tends to be done by running test data and examining results. Many of the types of errors made in assembler coding just do not occur. Moreover, checking results on printout or a CRT screen is easier in a high-level language and requires less time on the computer enabling programmers to share it better. In real-time systems there will still be time-dependent errors that are only apparent during real running. These may be harder to pin down if the programs were in a high-level language unless a low-level compiled version is provided by the compiler. However, if the majority of the software is buffered from real time as suggested earlier in this chapter, most such time-dependent effects are eliminated.

If it is necessary to write large amounts of assembler-level software, the task can be reduced by the use of subroutines and macros. If a certain logical operation occurs at several points in the programs, a subroutine not only saves store but also enables the same logic, once proven, to be confidently used by reference from other programs.

A *macro* is a group of assembler-level instructions on a parameter set which is given a name recognizable to the compiler. Wherever the name occurs, the compiler substitutes the group of instructions to operate on the parameter set declared for this occurrence. Therefore a macro has one same advantage as a subroutine in that reprogramming of a frequently used logical function can be avoided by using a proven routine, but store is not saved, the full group of instructions being stored each time the macro appears in the program. Macros have the advantage of less overhead in parameter setting and avoid the jumps to and from subroutines, so they are useful for short functions. Nested macros can be used to build up a function library for ease of programming, effectively raising the level of the language. Care must be taken to see the storage estimate is not exceeded.

4.5.3. Language and Data Organization

Some languages provide easy means of defining complex data structures and of accessing the data stored in them. These tend to be more oriented to organizational processes than to either mathematical or input-output functions. Where an application is largely one of manipulating data, forming and using various associations of the data, examining, sorting and so on, such *list-processing* languages can have great relevance, not only in reducing programming time by automatically providing features for accessing and associating data but also in enabling fast processing. However, manufacturers of small computers which tend to be used for real-time applications do not usually provide list-processing software and users have developed their own systems.

A general feature of list-processing data structures is that data are often not stored by item as in a file of records where the fields of an entry or item are kept together, but by parameter, topological attributes, or other association, the fields which are related in various ways being linked together in the structure. This makes for simple programs both to add data for further items and to carry out functions which require these relationships. Examples arise in statistical data analysis, information retrieval, and layout-design work. Generally the overheads of such languages are high by real-time standards and are geared to large systems. Much of the list-processing work is in getting the data organized, in accepting data changes, and building relationships, and this is the kind of work normally done on receiving data. This means that the data is then held in exceptionally convenient form for accessing to produce an output result with little further work, so giving a short response time to later enquiries. The structure is usually oriented to fast access rather than to fast handling or storing of received data. Whether a full list-processing approach is made or not, such considerations are important when designing the file structure for any real-time system, whether the system must respond quickly to absorb and store data which can then be worked upon when necessary to yield results steadily, or whether the data will be offered up more gradually to the system which can then work on them and organize them so that when a call for action is made results can be very promptly output. That is, it depends on whether the most urgent real-time work is to be done before or after data storage, so the software designer is guided as to whether the data structure should be most directly indexed by enquiry parameter or by data as received.

Contrasting examples illustrate this. In an information-retrieval system data is stored with relatively little change for long periods, but an enquiry must be promptly answered, so the data when it has been received must be well organized in advance for quick access. In a statistical-analysis application, however, dynamic data may be constantly pouring in and from time to time an analysis of the data is required. In this case the data structure does not have to be oriented to the analysis but to rapidly absorbing the data continually received. A management information system lies somewhere between these two examples; both data handling and output of information make comparable real-time demands.

4.5.4. Interpreters

An *interpreter* performs a similar function to a compiler, but acts at execution time each time the program is run. The program is stored not in a binary or machine code but in the language in which it was programmed, instructions being stored as ASCII character strings for example. When the program is run, the string for each instruction is interpreted into the machine language for execution. This occupies a great deal of CPU time and is only suitable to undemanding projects. The advantage of programming speed in a high-level language applies, but interpretive programs are inefficient in both storage and running time. In dedicated systems, where the software, once commissioned, is only rarely changed, interpreters seem inappropriate.

Interpretive languages would be more attractive for a computer with fast ASCII conversion and string-handling hardware, or if some of the programs could be compiled if desired. This latter feature would allow the advantage of programs which were easy to change during development with the option of then compiling those which had become firm in order to improve efficiency. Such a mixed-language arrangement, a run-time mixture of high-level source and compiled code, looks attractive.

Another possibility is to have efficient assembler or compiled programs but to keep data tables stored in a higher level. Although not efficient in storage, running time might not be too long yet one still has the ability to change the table contents rapidly. This compromise approach requires compiler or assembler options but does not need any special language; just the table data is stored uncompiled.

4.5.5. Language Choice for Real-time Systems

Before selecting the computer configuration and before plunging into assembler coding, we have suggested that the possibility of using a high-level language be quantitatively examined. If it looks feasible, one has to make a choice of language. With assembler level one has no choice once the computer is decided.

A large number of high-level languages are available but most are not of general application. Those which may be appropriate to a given project should be considered, otherwise there are only a few general ones. Even some of these do not have real-time facilities, do not allow mixed languages, or depend on a large, possibly slow-operating system. Some minicomputer manufacturers do, however, provide versions of FOR-TRAN, ALGOL, BASIC, and so on suited to their machines and having real-time features to allow interrupt handling and mixed code. The choice in practice, however, is small. One should consider languages designed for the appropriate type of application such as time sharing, process control, computer-aided design, or communications. A powerful language developed in the US for real-time use is JOVIAL, of which CORAL is a subset. In the UK efforts were made to find a concise version of this without too many redundant features and CORAL 66 was settled upon (3). These languages have found favor in air-traffic-control, military, and automation applications.

Despite standard definitions, manufacturers of minicomputers find it hard to agree on standards to fit different machines and special versions appear. For a given project this does not matter; one still has the advantage of faster programming although less *portability* of the software to other machines. The fact remains that owing to the historically small storage, the absence of standards on minicomputers, and the carry-over of the hardware logic approach in assembler coding, the adoption of high-level languages for real-time projects has been lagging. Now, with larger projects, such languages may be essential for achieving the task in a finite time. In projects of many sizes there are potential benefits in reducing programming time and producing software that is easier for others to maintain. Where running time has to be minimal or where there are many identical systems, assembler-level programming may be essential.

4.6. Nature of a Program

We summarize in this section what a program would look like, given the considerations so far encountered in this chapter, and then discuss how such a program might best be developed.

4.6.1. Program Aspects

First a separable function is identified and called a process. Its interfaces with outside hardware, with other programs, and with files can be described. For a subroutine, for example, these interactions are with calling programs and with called routines, devices, and files. For an interrupt routine they are with external hardware and with software buffers. The designer has determined the running time to meet the response and throughput required of the system.

For a general process such as we have been discussing, within the software design that shelters it from real time, several aspects of the program are progressively laid down by the designer and these are now listed.

The identified function
Boundaries with other processes and devices
Running time
Structure of files accessed
Algorithm
Language
Storage medium and size estimates
A place in the scheduling system
Interface formats
Organizational operations before and after the function
Workspace

All these aspects of each identified program are documented at the program-specification stage. A programmer can go ahead on definite information. Detailed description of the way the program is then written should fall under the same divisions as the specification and not erode function boundaries by spanning several processes.

4.6.2. The Shape of a Program

Consider the stages in carrying out a task. When the control programs have decided to schedule the task and made sure the process is loaded in main store, control is passed to the process.

First the organizational part of the process is carried on. It picks up any data for the task from its input area which may be the top of a buffer or the output area of another program. This data is then checked for feasibility and error routines are entered if necessary. The data contains active values and information enabling the process to collect any other data it needs from files, using lockouts when necessary. All this data is gathered into the "workspace" for the process (or for the task, see § 4.2). The workspace may be one area of store or distributed among buffers and files with just pointer values held in the process area; the notion is the same, that the workspace holds the variable data for task.

Then the actual algorithm part of the process, the useful separable function for which the process was originally identified, is allowed to proceed. It operates as far as possible just on data in the workspace and permanent data, but may need to refer to other files and may want to use subroutines. Where the files and subroutines are held in main store they are executed immediately and the process continues. When the files and subroutines are held on slow backing store the process calls the elementary (disk) handler to index the physical file and exchange control signals with the device. The process elects to suspend and returns control to the control program leaving its resumption positions with either the handler or the control programs. Other processes may be scheduled. When the transfer is complete the control programs detect this and reschedule the process from its resumption point. This is illustrated in Fig. 4.6.

As the algorithm progresses it may need to make other voluntary periodic suspensions just in case urgent tasks are waiting. When the algorithm has completed its transformation on the workspace data, the results are still in the workspace. The final organizational part of the process puts away in files any results yet to be stored and sets up the task output area. This either forms the input area for another process which this program tells the control programs to schedule or it contains results ready to be picked up by output routines when required, on interrupt for example.

4.6.3. Program Development

At this stage one can say the program has been specified and designed. Now the actual program has to be written. The programmer will be thinking at a detailed level and relies on this design specification. To obtain a clean program, without rework, the programmer needs to encompass the whole task in hand with his understanding in order to "see" the process. Therefore there is an upper limit to desirable program size. Programs that are too small are a nuisance, so there is an optimum size. Above this, efficiency in obtaining and maintaining a correct program will drop, for the programmer can no longer keep a grasp of all aspects of it all the time. A program that is too large becomes a collection of code which is difficult to test and which no one dare touch. A programmer presented with a large process may wish to make his own division — perhaps into the organization and the algorithm parts just discussed, or to define stages in the algorithm — so as to cope at one time with the detail of each part and the more quickly to write and test the program. With this approach

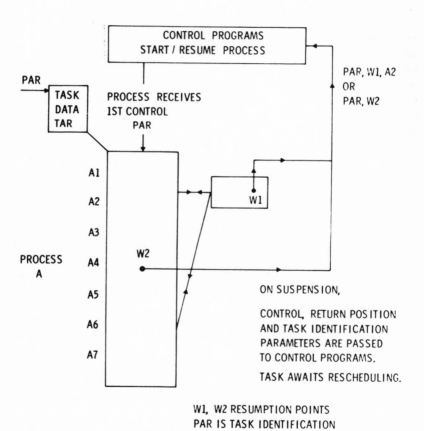

Fig. 4.6. Suspending a program.

the optimum size depends on the programmer and a software manager allocating work should recognize this. Typically we have found the most efficient size to be 100-150 written lines, whatever the language. Concentration is narrowed to the application immediately in hand rather than being diluted by spanning the whole process or system.

The program specification defines structures of external files used and interfaces with other programs. This not only allows programs to be developed independently but also allows changes to be made to one program later without affecting others. This independence of programs allows them to be regarded as modules in the same way as hardware units are made up of separately developed replaceable modules, with all the same benefits of organized design for step-by-step development and easy understanding and maintenance which stem from good engineering practice. The alternative is a mass of interlocking interdependent programs where a fault is hard to find and in which a program cannot be altered without risk of affecting others. The documentation of each coded section will naturally fall under the specification for that process. This should include description of the decisions made on how to organize and code the program. If a process is a *naturally separable function* of the overall system, this division into manageable modules gives the greatest benefit in understanding and ease of testing. It is also more likely to coincide with areas of future changes.

As programs are produced they can be tested. Each can be thoroughly checked by someone else against the specification. The logic can be tested using all sorts of input data and checking the output. The fewer interfaces a module has and the fewer files it accesses the easier it is to test. With processes of the nature discussed in this chapter such testing does not require external system hardware or real-time operation, yet the testing can be adequate to ensure that the programs will work just as well when built into the real-time system. Furthermore, tested processes can be incorporated under the control programs in phases as they become available, allowing the system to be built up gradually. A basic system can be quickly provided and then added to, the additional processes having been envisaged and allowed for at design stage. These steps in implementation are discussed more fully in Chapter 6.

Many programmers like to express individual style in programming. Some of the suggestions above have placed many of the decisions such as language and choice of algorithm on the designer. While this seems right, there is a danger that no one will want to program to a restrictive specification — except of course the designer himself! Difficulties may arise if programming is seen as a menial task. No one wants to be regarded as a mere coder and many analysts think programming is beneath them. One should not copy the engineering equivalent where designs are passed to the drawing office, for we know it is better for the draftsman to be part of the team. Two solutions amount to more or less the same thing: to seek programmers' advice in design, or for the designer to code his own programs. The latter helps cut out relearning and reduces staff numbers — a frequent formula for success.

4.7. Ruggedness

The term rugged software means software that can withstand a battering or attempted misuse and still function with little maintenance over a wide range of conditions in just the same sort of way as a piece of hardware. Consider the horrible tortures which certain hardware must withstand and imagine the equivalent software punishment. Similar standards of robust design, sound engineering, good materials, and product test are required. Higher development costs may be justifiable to achieve the required quality. In the foregoing sections of this chapter some design aims have been stated towards achieving reliable software. Reliability is one attribute; others are correctness, availability, security, and maintainability.

To be reliable, software must always function in the same way. Its function should not depend on data being correct in value, timing, quantity, source context, or consistency. The function must be impervious to data; therefore data which the function uses for making decisions, for constructing addresses for accessing, for counting, and so on must be checked to lie within bounds required by the function. Similarly certain data must stay reliable and needs protecting so as to be incorruptible by programs or other data.

To be correct software must be tested or proved. Thorough testing in all situations would pre-empt the usefulness of the system, and one usually settles for testing in all types of imaginable situations using representative data and checking results. Proving that a program is correct is attractive but not yet supported by most programming techniques. Well-structured programs, arrived at by working progressively downwards from the specification, are more likely to be amenable to logical proof of correctness and are certainly easier to hand-examine.

To remain correct, software must not only be reliable in itself but must also check for hardware or external effects. Periodic self-examination or rerunning of test data helps to show when software becomes incorrect. At extra cost a program can perform self-consistency checks on data and results. If a program becomes faulty one may want the rest of the system to continue, but the fault must be detected.

Continued availability even in fault conditions is a subject discussed at system level in Chapter 5.6. A correct version of the software may need to be kept loaded or ready for reloading in known good hardware within a time constraint imposed by continued real-time operation. As we shall see, this constraint has vital bearing on system design and must be explicitly and realistically specified.

To be secure, software must be protected from unauthorized access by user or other programs by means of code-checking, capability checking, or other designed constraint. The protected areas cannot rely on the observance of disciplines by those unauthorized to access them, and hardware store protection is required.

To be maintainable, software has to be well documented and easily understood to allow short time to repair, and well designed to allow changes and replacement parts. It is essential to be able to see how the program is laid out.

There are many ways in which software can fail. Some arise internally and can be protected against; some may arise externally and cannot all be allowed for. One can always ask the question "What happens if . . .?" of even the most unlikely situations, and arrange wherever possible and economic that the software would not be unacceptably damaged but could continue.

When the software does detect a fault, either the system can stop itself and await maintenance or it can attempt to continue some level of service. To carry on, the software must resume from a known point; it should not just press on or leave a task half finished. Generally it is best to go back to a point in the logic which was last known to be correct, for instance to the start of a task. One then has the option of repeating it, known as *retry*, or omitting it. If repetition gives the same error, another means of carrying on is reverted to. The software might, however, realize that programs or files had been corrupted and want to go back to the last known correct version. This action of going back to a known situation is called *roll-back*.

As an example, suppose a system has been in operation a long while, yet during a process a self-consistency check suddenly fails on a task —

it finds the results should not have been obtained from the data given. One can restart the task in case there was a transient fault, but if the first attempt had updated files, the second attempt would then leave a false value. The process would be more "*robust*" in that such roll-back and retry would not have an ill effect if files were updated only after the checking. As another example, it is surer to carry out initializing at the start of a task rather than rely on the state which should have been left by previously completed task for that process. Considerations of this sort, each of benefit in rare fault situations, combine in large systems to increase significantly the probability of the software being impervious to stray effects and able to continue its real-time work.

Alternative ways of handling tasks in the presence of hardware faults may be provided either by parallel processing in two processors with frequent cross-checking or by simply aborting the task in a controlled and reported fashion. A calculated error rate and economic assessment will indicate the degree of sophistication needed to meet the required reliability. Generally it is more important when faults occur to preserve the system than to save every bit of transient data. These aspects are discussed in Chapter 5.6.

To summarize, the high importance generally attached in real-time systems to maintain continuous service in varying conditions requires more rugged programs than, say, batch programs which can be rerun on a job if necessary. Programs can be sheltered from wide-ranging real-time effects by buffering and controlled scheduling rather than being interrupt driven, and can protect themselves from data and from each other. There are various ways of improving robustness against outside effects and of achieving adequate levels of roll-back or even restart to meet a specified real-time requirement. As far as individual programs go, they need to be thoroughly tested before they can be regarded as tough bricks for building into a real-time system. The system can then regard these robust programs as resources which can be relied on faithfully to process their tasks.

References

1. Dijkstra, E.W. The structure of *THE* multi-programming system. *Comm. ACM 11* (5) 341-6, May 1968.
2. Wilkes, M.V. *Time-Sharing Computer Systems*, pp. 56-9. Macdonald, London, 1968.

3. *Official Definition of CORAL 66*. Her Majesty's Stationery Office, London, 1970.

Control of
System Operation

5.1. The Role of Control Programs

5.1.1. Introduction

We discussed computer hardware in Chapter 3 and some techniques for application programs in the previous chapter. The present chapter is concerned with the area in between, with software which is not necessarily special to an application but which enhances the computer system as viewed by the application program designer by providing such facilities as enable him to concentrate more fully on the application itself. These are fairly general software facilities of two types. They help organize applications to work together in the same system on the one hand (e.g. a dynamic allocation routine), or provide a useful library of commonly needed routines on the other, (e.g. a disk handler).

This area of application-independent software is called by several names, reflecting points of view. Some call it "software", others "systems programs", "system software", or "operating systems". Whatever its name, the purpose is to present the computer as a more convenient tool to the application program designer, reducing his need to consider computer reliability, other applications present, or details of storage and peripherals, and helping produce an economic system.

The range and nature of this general software can be expected to

147

vary not only with the computer configuration, but also with the type of application. That required in a batch bureau system is very different from that required in a power-station control system; so different that most of the bureau "software" will be useless in the control system. In the bureau case the computer system is expected to handle a wide and unpredictable range of applications, to run jobs as best it can on average. In a dedicated real-time system the current applications are known and must achieve a specific performance. Typically, programs will be much shorter, and run more frequently and with tighter time constraints. Because it is dedicated and cannot share costs with other odd jobs, the computer system will generally be smaller and highly-optimized to the specific tasks. Each kind of system has to be economic in its own way, and clearly an optimized system cannot contain as high a proportion of general overhead software Nevertheless, in any system there will be some general principles and some general facilities which will ease the program designer's task and still lead to economic software. In the following sections of this chapter we discuss some of those which are applicable at least to many real-time systems.

In small companies the experts are both managers and doing the specialist tasks or applications. This is very efficient. In larger companies managers are appointed to co-ordinate the system and enable the various experts to remain efficient, and to supply supporting services. Similarly, in a computer system, application programs have to perform efficiently a certain range of activities, working within a co-ordinating framework and with assistance in areas where special application knowledge is not required. In a dedicated system the range of functions is known and steady and probably of a narrow range. Therefore they are less likely to need as much co-ordination as if widespread, but are still likely to benefit from certain services.

This chapter, then, is concerned with management software and service software for dedicated real-time systems, to control and organize on the one hand, and to provide good working conditions and services on the other. We look first at the management side.

5.1.2. The Management Software

A company buying a factory building in which to operate does not expect the construction company to provide a management. Rather, the company sets up its own. If the builder included a management "kit" it would be unlikely to be suitable for the particular company. So we should not expect computer manufacturers to supply management software for dedicated systems. Some do supply useful executives, but care is needed to see that these ready-made ones do suit the application. If not, they should be rejected in deference to tailor-made management. Recently some good executives have appeared for real-time minicomputer systems. The designer should first decide what, if anything, is needed as a management framework and then see if available software is suitable. We now consider what management aids might be needed.

The organizational software is responsible for two main areas: (i) to maintain the computer system; (ii) to supervise the sharing of resources among application processes.

Maintaining the system means ensuring that the availability is kept both to the outside world by providing a sufficiently reliable system and to the application programs by helping them to meet the required performance of continuous operation. As an illustration of maintaining reliable service, a system program may output a confidence pulse periodically to show some monitoring equipment that the computer is still functioning or that a spare machine is really available. Software may need to take action when it is advised that an equipment failure has occurred somewhere in the computer system, to restart, recover, or reconfigure the system. Systems programs can also help for instance in allowing continued running while a log tape is changed. In a system like a reservation system such software has little to do with the application, but it may be quite different for other applications such as in a message-switching system. This "maintenance" software forms the foundation on which the application programs are built. It has to be decided upon early in the design. It needs to be carefully matched to the required system availability which must be explicitly set out before internal technical design can proceed with confidence. So many real-time system designs leave this important consideration until it is far too late for an economic or successful solution, and a major catastrophe results.

The supervisory or management software shares out the available space, CPU time, and other resources to each of the application programs in such a way that each can still meet its required individual performance. This kind of software may be called an executive, supervisor, or operating system, where these terms are generally associated with systems of increasingly general facilities — and size. They reflect the extent to which organizational management is required, being skeletal in small, simple configurations and comprehensive in more complex systems. While the latter can simplify and reduce the size of application programs, the system designer needs to watch that they do not occupy a disproportionately large amount of space and running time. The decision is similar as to whether to use a higher-level language. Can one afford the inefficiency? Does the saving in programming time justify further equipment costs? In fact, are the overheads economic and well balanced? A dedicated system makes less use of generality, but how much flexibility is wise in order to accommodate future changes more easily?

To answer these questions, some quantitative work is necessary. The size and main store occupancy of each overhead facility and the typical percentage running time which will be spent in the purely organizational parts must be estimated. Simple application tasks might be run immediately in less time than required to put them on and off a queuing system. On the other hand, there might be an existing convenient way of allowing several processes to share, say, a store area such that application programmers need not re-invent it. A quantitative analysis is required before either deciding to use possibly heavy general overheads or re-inventing a possibly basic system facility. Good system design can sometimes save the need for certain overhead features entirely.

5.1.3. The Service Software

This is a more straightforward concept. Service software consists of useful routines which the application programmer can use to save programming time or repetition among programs. Examples are library routines such as code conversion or mathematical routines, input and output control procedures including peripheral handling routines, disk drivers, timing facilities, and so on. These are above the level of microprogrammed instructions and range from simple macros up to, say, complete transmission-line handling routines for communication systems. Obviously it is convenient to be able to select just those routines which are exactly right for the application, saving programming time and store space. One still has to guard against incorporating needlessly long or accurate routines. Because they may be frequently executed in the system, estimates of their running time are important. The overhead penalty is usually low and one can benefit through using a well-tested set of utility routines. These service routines tend to be of a general nature, being the same for widely different applications even if the whole set is not required for any one system. This means that computer manufacturers can supply useful utility software, and some do.

Because they can be supplied as standard options, these utility routines could be available as hardware logic modules. These would no longer be restricted to simple multiplication, but would handle standard byte manipulations, input, output, and disk-transfer operations, and so on, replacing common macros and short subroutines. Manufacturers could supply standard sets of such microprogrammed operations suited to each category of application: communications, time-sharing, process control, etc. They can be stored as *middleware* or *firmware* in read-only memory as discussed in Chapter 3. Such basic functions need to be matched to the compiler or assembler. They are fast in execution, leaving more time and more storage for the programs that are specific to the particular application.

One danger is to be too ambitious and over-optimize service routines. For example, a general disk-access routine which presents a whole block may be more robust and faster overall than one which can extract just a desired record if it is given additional parameters which need to be set up and passed over by the calling program. This is a tendency in "home-brewed" utilities. Another temptation is to "pyramid" general utilities by nesting them to make special utilities. The slight saving is usually not worth the confusion engendered; it is often better to stick with just one level.

A way of looking at utility routines is as a functional dictionary which the application programmer can use to construct programs quite quickly by stringing together these basic units from the dictionary. These utility units may be available from the manufacturer, from a library, or from other projects. They include not only the service routines discussed above, but also useful elements for management and application programs.

5.1.4. Summary of "System" Software

The "systems" software has two sides: the organizational or management side and the service side. The organizational side looks after maintaining the computer configuration and allocates shared resources among applications. The service side provides useful routines to save work for the application programmer. Both sides enhance the computer as a framework or tool for the applications programmer. They tend to be lumped together as "control programs" or "systems software", but this software has both the supervisory and the service aspects. These can be separated out to reduce confusion when thinking about either area.

We now further break down these software aids and consider especially those most likely to be useful in real-time systems.

5.2. System Performance

If it is decided that some sort of organizational software *is* going to give an economic enhancement to the computer for an application, then its design must be checked for compatibility with the real-time constraint of the application. The main constraints referred to in Chapter 4 were: response time, data acquisition, throughput, maintaining service, and recovery from failure.

5.2.1. Consideration of Response Time

Supervisory software can achieve two useful things for the application programmer in the area of sharing processor time: it can decide which task to start or resume next and when to do so. This part of the software is called the *scheduler*. When called upon, the scheduler decides which program or task shall run next and passes control of the processor to that chosen routine. There are many ways of deciding which to run next — many scheduling algorithms. Simple examples are (a) to take each process in turn, or (b) to schedule tasks in the order they became ready. However, if a task must be executed within, say, 1 second of being ready in order to meet the required response, then it is no good having a scheduler that gets round every few seconds. Some more urgent tasks may need to jump the queue. In Chapter 4 we suggested ways of reducing this need, but it cannot always be avoided and a priority scheme may be necessary to satisfy the response times. When called upon, the scheduler will look for high-priority tasks first.

It may be that one task takes so long that, if run uninterrupted, some urgent tasks could not meet their response time. Therefore ways of breaking off from long tasks must be used in order to call the scheduler. In some cases a short urgent task generated by an interrupt can be carried out directly in interrupt mode, but we advocate the minimal use of interrupt routines for the reasons given in Chapter 4. Instead, any of three main ways can be used to call the scheduler and handle the urgent task in a more controlled way. First, the processes for long tasks can be programmed to make sufficiently frequent *suspensions* or breaks to allow the scheduler to decide if they should continue yet or if more urgent tasks should be executed first. This is a simple and very controllable method, but relies on all application program designers and coders observing a discipline. The second method is to make regular interrupts. This, like the first method, may result in unnecessary interrupts, especially if there is one urgent but rarely used process, but it is useful for calling regular processes. Each process is given a fixed maximum time-slot.

The third method is to allow the data, when ready, to give rise to an *interrupt* that calls the scheduler. The latter then decides whether to go back and finish the current task first or to start the new task at once. This is a software equivalent to a hardware system of priority interrupt levels. It has the problems of multi-level software discussed in Chapter 4, but can be very time efficient in cases of occasional urgent tasks.

This diversity of scheduling methods is one reason that it is hard to find a ready-made operating system that is suitable for a wide range of applications. However, the first method given above requires few facilities, and the last two — regular or random calls on interrupt — can appear the same to the scheduler. Their main common requirements on the scheduling mechanism are to flag waiting tasks in the ranked order, to scan these flags efficiently, and to start the selected task. Therefore, so long as the scheduler mechanism provides for flag setting from interrupt and from other software levels, then it can be quite general, because the calling frequency and priority order can be separately set up outside the scheduler and tuned to each application once the traffic mix is known. Although this leaves the scheduler as a rather skeletal function, it still gives the benefit to application programmers of a common, defined way of changing task that is also efficient.

The scheduler should be decided upon as soon as the "shape" of the processes and the rough traffic mix is known, before starting detailed design of application programs, because an area of uncertainty in real-time systems is then removed from them. A simple scheduler can be understood by all and minimize overheads.

5.2.2. Consideration for Data Acquisition

Chapter 3 (§ 3.3.) considered the possible ways of transferring data in or out of the computer, by programmed transfer, by hardware interrupting the processor, or by direct access to the computer memory. An operating system can include useful utility routines for handling interrupts and performing programmed input or output transfers of data. In addition, special hardware is required for direct memory access (DMA) channels. A scheduler driven by a real-time clock can provide a polling facility to check regularly whether a peripheral device or channel requires data transfer. However, the choice of facility, level of interrupt, polling frequency, and so on must be determined for each interface by the applications program designer. Incoming data must be stored away within the *survival time* — before it is overwritten by other data — and this is commonly the most critical consideration for input handling.

The choice of input-output facility depends on the number, types, and mix of data channels and on the speed and main processing purpose of the computer. A minicomputer as a front-end to another machine can happily spend all its CPU time servicing data lines; it may be efficient to poll all the lines regularly rather than jump to every interrupt. On the other hand, an on-line control computer may need to get on with a task, relying on interrupt servicing to buffer any data that arrives meanwhile. Still again, a high-speed input or output channel may deserve a DMA facility to leave the CPU free for its main work.

One facility which systems programs can provide to application programs is the easy ability to switch channels or type of peripheral device and to buffer up any input or output if the process or device is not currently available to deal with it. For example, if a magnetic tape is being used as a log, the systems program could buffer the data on disk while a tape was changed, and subsequently log it on the new tape without the applications programs being concerned. Similarly, output data can also be buffered for a printer or for a VDU screen. An input handler can buffer received data and then call (or flag for scheduling) the appropriate task, for instance one which had suspended awaiting a disk access.

These are all service routines, often available from the computer manufacturer and of wide application. They should not be confused with the management software.

5.2.3. Considerations for Throughput

Most dedicated systems do not have a wide traffic mix, but tend to handle large numbers of similar messages. The greatest throughput is achieved using fast algorithms for the processes and least overhead, just pressing on with one message after another, maybe overlapping if they have to suspend. In these cases, there is little that systems programs can do to help because the more that individual tasks are assisted, the sooner they reach the bottleneck which limits throughput, whether it be to make a disk access or wait for core space, CPU time, or an output line. Indeed, if the bottleneck is main store space or CPU time, one prefers to *reduce* system overheads. If, however, the traffic mix or the internal processing stages are sufficiently diverse and other resources are limiting factors, then systems programs can sometimes help to increase throughput by providing suitable suspension facilities and a scheduling system optimized like a batch multi-programming system to schedule jobs in the most efficient manner. For instance, if a task suspends for a disk access, a task waiting for a lot of CPU time can be run. Usually, in a dedicated system the optimized mix in worst traffic conditions can be precalculated so that the systems programs can then be rather simple — they do not have to analyse the resources required for each job in the same way as in a batch-operating system, but can make a quick decision. This low overhead is essential if advantage is to be gained by running useful work during the brief period of, say, a disk access.

If the operating system assigns programs and data to disk at build time, bringing them into main store when required during execution, the software designer may wish to override this facility; the required throughput may demand that very frequently used routines or data which are often accessed have to be kept in main storage all the time.

5.2.4. Availability

The *availability* is a measure of the continued functioning of the system from the point of view of the user. It specifies the probability of the functions performed by the system being always available. In telephone exchange systems, it is called the *grade of service;* if a call fails, a second attempt will have a certain high-percentage chance of connection. To maintain the required availability in a system which will occasionally fail, there must be a speedy enough means of *recovery*, that is, a return to system working soon enough and without unacceptable loss of data.

In many real-time systems the mean time to repair individual faults would be an unacceptably long down-time, and replacement equipment is needed at some level. The level of spare units, whether boards or whole configurations, needs only to meet the realistic and predefined availability requirement. The faulty units may be repaired off-line, but still spare parts are needed. Further, the nature and maximum amount of data which can be lost needs to be consciously decided. There is often a subjective requirement for perfection — the cost of that and of alternative less-perfect solutions needs to be considered at system-design time and a conscious choice made and recorded. The criterion for acceptable loss of data is expressed in different ways in various applications. A message switch must not "lose" a message, but could be "down" for a period occasionally. A control system must recover with sufficiently current data to regain stable control before the controlled process goes out of limits. A reservation system must not lose its data base. For each particular system the availability requirement must be specified and be included in the feasibility study, discussed in Chapter 2, well before any choice of computer configuration is made.

Thus the maximum down-time and data loss when types of fault occur are decided. To ensure that these levels are never exceeded, the control programs or operating system have certain roles to play. Fault detection logic in hardware and software may advise the operating system which then gives an orderly switch over or closedown whenever possible, recording the cause and the restart values. Equipment substitutions may be necessary, carried out manually or automatically, and the system is *restarted* from the most recent point of adequate confidence. This might be the start of the current program, the current transaction, or even the start of that day's transactions. Going back to a confident point was called *roll-back* in Chapter 4. The system has to receive traffic again by the end of the allowed down-time. This period and the data loss have to meet criteria defined in agreement with the user. The definition of the most recent point of adequate confidence or *roll-back* point is different for each kind of system. In some systems where no semi-permanent data is stored it may be that the system can be restarted from scratch. This might apply to, say, a small road-traffic-control system. In cases with a large dynamic database, such as airline reservations or banking, one could roll-back to the last dump state and reprocess transactions since then, perhaps using a magnetic-tape log. In other systems, such as power-station control, certain parts of the data base must carry on with little or no roll-back so it may be necessary to keep an up-to-date duplicate of this data on a standby store. Yet further systems require duplication of the processing itself as discussed in Chapter 3. The important decision is to define explicitly what the roll-back point is; how far back to go in order to have correct data yet retaining as much of the accumulated files as possible and resuming adequate service promptly.

The operating system can provide several different useful facilities in this chain of actions to maintain the availability. It may include regular checks and fault-detection routines, fault-handling and close down logic, equipment interrogation to ascertain the present configuration, and possibly reconfiguration rules and recovery programs. Ideally the operating system ensures that the application programs have a reliable computer to run in, by apparently smoothing out faults in the configuration. The application programs still have to handle faults in application hardware. Thus the operating system might be thought general purpose, but the criteria of recovery time, data loss, and the implied roll-back allowed are different for different applications and the operating system needs to be tailored to ensure this availability.

Some computer systems not only indicate faulty parts, but also isolate them and recover the running system automatically either in a reduced form or by switching standby equipment into use. This is called automatic reconfiguration. Such features are the responsibility of the hardware and the operating system, to provide continued processing and storage to the application software. The detection and location mechanism must itself be immune to the fault, and the recovery mechanism must know how much of the system to change. After repair, the system must be able to accept the repaired unit. Such self-reconfiguring systems exist and are of proven field reliability, but one should always check whether the availability criteria can be met more economically in simpler ways.

In § 5.6 methods of ensuring availability according to several different criteria are described, with examples from major real-time systems using multi-processors.

5.2.5. Multi-processing

To achieve throughput capacity or to maintain availability, or both, more than one processor may need to be simultaneously active. Such multi-processing systems have already been discussed in § 3.6.3 and an example of such a system is described in § 5.6.3. This section discusses some of the implications this has on the operating system.

Multi-processing systems are like multi-level systems inasmuch as the problems of shared data arise, and these can be dealt with by flags and carefully preplanned scheduling as already discussed in Chapter 4. The parallel processors of a multi-processing system, however, might not by synchronized, so the scheduling algorithm in the control programs has to cater for this. In some configurations there are two overall approaches to scheduling to choose from: either to schedule the load of each processor independently as if each were a single processor with its own scheduler, or to regard the processors as resources which can be allocated to carry out a certain task by one scheduler spanning the whole system. That is to say, a given process might not always run in the same processor: the scheduler would decide dynamically which to use, and where code is re-entrant could even allocate the same process to carry out different tasks in different processors contemporaneously.

Where this flexibility in dynamic traffic sharing is not required, there are worthwhile overhead savings and advantages in simplicity if it is *not* provided but rather the job mix of each processor is pre-allocated. Where, as often, the worst case has to be positively catered for, there is little or no advantage in dynamic allocation of parallel resources. If things go wrong, the situation is more easily defined and diagnosed when there is no dynamic scheduling.

If there is one scheduler per processor, the considerations of response time and capacity are similar to single-processor systems. If, however, there is one scheduler considering the processors as an array of resources to allocate dynamically, whether to tasks or to processes, then it is immediately like a multi-level system, whether re-entrant or not, and the considerations of response time, capacity, and interaction have to be considered across the whole system. An advantage held out for this approach is that additional processors can be added more smoothly if the traffic system increases and processors can be taken out of service or brought back on line fairly easily. In practice, however, large changes in traffic patterns are often accompanied by the need for changes in processing data files that require a revised software system altogether, and anyway if a processor in a pre-allocated job-mix system goes down, a spare could be assigned the appropriate same mix. For dedicated systems pre-allocation can usually give as good a performance with less complexity than the nevertheless nice notion of processors as allocatable resources; one would want to see quantitative analysis to be convinced otherwise for any particular project.

There are two distinct reasons for using more than a single processor in a system: to provide enough capacity in processing power for the heaviest specified traffic, or to provide a short time to repair the system where high availability is required. These two reasons are separable, but sometimes there is muddled thinking when systems are designed. In many systems only one of these considerations requires additional processors. Always the reasoning for the configuration needs to be examined against the specification for both capacity and availability to ensure that both can be continuously and simultaneously met. For instance, it may not be adequate to rely on a spare to handle peak traffic.

5.2.6. Virtual Storage

In computer systems which have backing store it is necessary to decide which programs and data are to be stored in main store and which are held on the backing store ready to be called into main store when required. Some operating systems take care of this, allowing one to write programs as if the computer had a very large main store. This is called *virtual storage*. That is to say the storage medium is "transparent" to the programmer, who merely writes a reference to a file or a program call without having to consider the type of storage device on which it is stored, or remembering to make appropriate disk accesses or to provide space in main store. A machine, system-builder program, or operating system with a virtual storage facility can do this automatically at system-build time.

However, it fundamentally assists running time, and hence both the response time and the throughput, if the number of backing-store accesses is kept to a minimum. In particular, frequently and urgently needed programs and data should be in main store. Except in sophisticated adaptive systems, the operating system cannot know in advance the frequency or urgency of application programs and their file reference, so it is not in a good position to arrange the files and program storage in the best way. For dedicated systems the designer *is*, however, in a very good position to organize the storage in such a way that the backing-store accesses are minimized since he does know what the programs are and what data files they use. Moreover, the programmer needs to know this organization so he can ensure that running time limits are not exceeded.

The real-time software designer needs not only to ensure that the overall mapping is adequate, but may also want to set up his own indexing or arrange disk layouts to reduce seek time and so on. If this is automatic, the expected performance is hard to calculate.

So, for efficient dedicated real-time systems, we do not want a virtual machine but we need to be aware of the real one. Virtual memory may help reduce the costs of program development, but it is likely either to decrease the efficiency and hence the response and throughput of the system, or to need a more expensive machine to handle the full traffic because it is less efficient than if purpose-built store mapping is used.

5.2.7. Mini-computer operating systems

This book is concerned with real-time computer systems that are dedicated to one particular application. It is generally true that their function does not change much during their lifetime. When this book was conceived, computers were usually only a small part of the total system, large machines were not good at real-time operation, and minicomputers were limited in size, for instance to 32K words of core. Therefore real-time computers and their programs were small. In recent years, better communications facilities and real-time operating systems have been incorporated into large machines, and the scope of minicomputers has risen to support larger systems. As the cost of direct access store has fallen and as disc storage capacities have improved in value for size, it has been appropriate for the cost-effective mini-computer approach to extend into larger systems, to undertake more functions in a system, and so the stored program element has moved further away from its hard-wired origins.

These developments have brought the need for operating systems on mini-computers and now several manufacturers offer a variety of these to suit types of application such as time-sharing, process control, multitasking and, more rarely, multi-processing. This "system software" saves re-inventing the wheel each time. There is a ready-made framework to do common tasks. Sometimes the mini-computer operating system is needed to overcome hardware limitations, such as a poor addressing range, which it would be onerous for application programmers to deal with. It is this kind of software which is valuable and which has enabled mini-computers to grow: another gap with the larger machines has closed. When selecting a mini-computer, the existence of good system software is a major consideration, generally more important than the languages available. It should support the configuration and type of application being considered, not only during the continuous operational running, but also during program development.

There are pitfalls, however, beyond those already mentioned in this chapter. Some minicomputer operating systems may require a larger computer. They may give rise to an overhead in learning time, merely for the programmer to read and understand the documentation. There may be restrictions on programming or, worse still, bugs, that are outside the control of the applications programmer. The system designer or analyst must therefore be sure that the manufacturers system software is going to be more of a help than a hindrance.

We have suggested that helpful facilities are usually those which take care of the hardware, schedule tasks, help with the handling and general utilities, and manage input and output to peripherals such as printers, disk drives and communication lines. These may be extended to print spool routines, disk file handling, and terminal servicing routines. The system software can look after the hardware-related aspects of protection, fault handling, memory mapping, etc., and can also provide a degree of device independence. It should schedule tasks efficiently and may include swapping on and off disks and a priority scheme. The latter should be simple in real-time systems and operating suit the application; some operating systems can take almost as long to stop one task, decide on the next and swap over, as it would take to complete most tasks naturally. File handling routines are a real help if they are suited to the application, and similarly general utility subroutines can save programming time and cost.

The ideal mini-computer operating system therefore would save the application programmer worrying about the same hardware-related functions that occur in most systems, would provide an appropriate scheduler, and would perform common input/output, file-handling and utility routines. It would not require a pile of manuals and a training course nor call for a significantly more expensive configuration. In particular it should be a low real-time overhead. One should look for the least that one requires and for the greatest help, not a priori for the maximum of facilities.

If one can find system software that is well-suited to the application and the configuration of equipment and peripherals, the possible savings can be a significant factor in the choice of manufacturer, even in dedicated systems that require only basic system software.

5.3. Computer Characteristics

5.3.1. Processing Power

In most minicomputers the processing speed is primarily determined by the speed of main store — of the order of 0.5-1 μs cycle time for core store, with semiconductor store currently of similar speed but heading towards 100 ns ore less. Ingenious overlapping, use of alternate stores, and so on can increase the power by a small factor. A longer word length can allow a more powerful instruction set or wider direct addressing which decreases the number of store accesses. With cheaper processor logic now available, separate sets of registers, special function logic, or even separate processors can be used for scheduled purposes and then, as discussed in Chapter 3, multiple operations can occur simultaneously on different stores. Main-store speed remains the dominant factor, and word length next. All the available combinations of ingenious hardware might make a difference of up to about one order of magnitude. It needs a radically different approach such as special-purpose processors or associative or other techniques to affect the processing power dramatically. Therefore only in cases where the calculations show computer power to be marginally adequate need one be too critical of the exact instruction set or look for fancy hardware functions. Rather, one should watch out for missing facilities that would make a machine cumbersome for the application. Basic features such as some sort of index register or modifier, a reasonable direct address range, single access instructions, a real-time clock, and a simple interrupt mechanism, perhaps a hardware multiply/divide and direct store access, are in general more beneficial than more sophisticated multiple registers, overlapping access, stacks, multi-level interrupts, and fancy instructions.

5.3.2. Available Storage

Again, the chief parameter is the main store. Capacity depends on word length and the maximum number of words. A good base for comparison between machines is the maximum byte capacity. In certain applications particular word lengths are favorable, for instance multiples of 8 bits or 6 bits for character handling, a 12-bit word for graphic displays and other digital-to-analog work, and 18 or 36 bits for decimal working. As basic considerations one should check how much store typical program instructions will each occupy — it may be one or two words of store — and whether the available byte or word lengths which can be stored and manipulated are well matched to the field lengths of the main data for the particular application.

Real-time computers have traditionally had small main stores, largely for cost reasons. Changing technology and wider fields of application have been and are continuing to raise the maximum size of main stores.

Fast-access stores command a higher price than slower media, and therein lies the reason for continuing with slower mass stores and the need to map programs and data onto the available media in the most cost-effective way. This mapping has a profound effect on performance since access times of typical media such as disks are several orders of magnitude longer than core, plated-wire, or semiconductor stores.

Some machines use paging or segmentation in the main store to overcome a narrow direct addressing range of the instructions by setting base registers, so even in main store there are efficiency advantages to be gained in manually optimizing the store layout. Such procedures are tedious, however, and lead to less flexible software. Machines which do not require them are preferred. This again favors a longer word length, enabling a wide addressing range.

5.3.3. Input and Output Methods

These have been discussed in Chapter 3. Direct memory access channels which allow devices to store or access data do allow very-high-speed input or output. For some applications their cost may be acceptable and this facility may be essential. An interrupt mechanism is often necessary if only so that the real-time clock can cause regular scheduling and polling. Multi-level interrupt mechanisms lead to data complications mentioned in Chapter 4, and, if the design can be simplified in the ways mentioned there, the need for these facilities can often be removed. All machines allow for programmed input and output transfer, and in some applications where there is a heavy data flow and complex processing, advantage might be found in a machine using separate processors for the transfers and for the data manipulations.

Sometimes operating systems include an *input-output handler*. This usually consists of driver routines and buffering, to acknowledge and send the transfer signaling to peripheral devices and to save data as transmitted. Such programs are useful utilities for handling standard devices provided that the interrupt or other mechanisms used fit in with the rest of the software design. The same comments apply to disk-driver routines and other backing-store access routines supplied within the operating system. Their usefulness is in saving reprogramming of standard signaling protocol and buffering. In real-time systems one may want to keep them short, performing other functions such as data checking in the inner software away from real time, as mentioned in Chapter 4.

5.3.4. Further Performance Aids

Some applications benefit from special-purpose processing features in hardware such as multiply/divide floating-point arithmetic, parity checking, Fourier transform units, and so on. As mentioned in Chapter 3, some of the smaller functions can be performed by specially tailored microprogram instructions. Some frequent operations can be greatly speeded up by extending the order code in this way. Computers with this facility can therefore be attractive. This flexibility, however, is no excuse for postponing performance estimates; such devices are hard to incorporate later in the day. Moreover, there are snags associated with microprogrammed extracode functions, as described in § 4.3.7. The usefulness of special hardware is limited to special applications when a general-purpose instruction set is shown to be inadequate.

Stacking is another feature offered on some machines which can improve performance, essentially by keeping probably-needed values in a quick access store in a push-down-pop-up or last-in-first-out method. Useful in nested situations, advantage is, however, lost if software has to be arranged to suit the stacking. Moreover, the situation in the case of a fault may be less retrievable because all data in the stack are dynamic. One aid in the simplistic approach is to minimize the amount of data and control information which is dynamic at any instant. It is not a sin to be pedestrian.

5.3.5. Maintenance

Other computer characteristics affect a machine's real-time usefulness. Basic ruggedness mechanically, electrically, and environmentally may be required for reasons quite beyond reducing mean time between failures. It is no use having the duplicate machine overheat on the same afternoon. Beware of under-engineered systems that may prove too delicate in the field. On the other hand, one should guard against the subjective tendency to insist on a rugged machine just because the application is considered important — the same money might be better spent on more spares.

For a system destined for a prolonged service life, the durability of the machine (and its supplier) is a significant factor. In the competitive world of minicomputers, the emphasis is usually given in the technical specification to the side of performance and processing features. The traditional engineering qualities of suitable materials, tolerant components and power supplies, sound electrical jointing, durable hinges, motors, cabling, and so on are just as important as in less electrically sophisticated equipment and can have a considerable effect on the actual MTBF when the machine is in a practical environment.

The availability of a machine is clearly affected by the mean time to repair it when it does go wrong. Ease of maintenance and quick unit replacement might well save the cost of an extra spare machine, and also make for greater satisfaction as well as lower running costs. Fault-location aids can indicate the faulty module which is to be removed. Off-line repair facilities are needed to identify the fault within the module and to check it out after repair, so that the repaired part can be kept as a confident spare without taking the system down again just to prove the part is now correct.

5.3.6. Monitoring and Logging

An operating system can keep a record of the usage in store, time, or disk accesses which certain procedures make, possibly for accounting purposes, but more often to ensure that the system is comfortably handling the current traffic patterns and to give useful diagnostic information. Periodic reports may be produced giving performance and utilization figures. If a fault occurs it helps to know the program and store patterns that were current. A *log* can show the pattern of events over a period not only for statistical use, but also to trace the lead-up to a fault similarly to an aircraft "black-box" flight recorder. This system logging is distinct from whatever transaction logging of application data may be necessary for use in the recovery from a fault stoppage.

Features which enable specifiable parts of the system to be monitored during normal or test running are highly desirable for checking and debugging.

5.3.7. External Control

The system has to provide a means of loading the software and starting or restarting it. Whatever flexibility has been specified for on-line changes must be provided. The computer operator or controller may need to set, reset, or adjust certain variable parameters in the control programs while the system is running, or to indicate configuration changes, priority changes, request a report, change a monitor point, or to input other information relevant to the management software. These data may be distinguished from information or adjustments made to parameters for the application programs, for instance to adjust a transmission error threshold, a temperature level for a process control value, bring in a certain function, and so on.

The means usually favored for communication between the computer controller and the configuration's operating system is a control typewriter or special keyboard with a display. Very small systems rely on the settings of the switch register on the computer control panel as an economic control method. A typewriter has the advantage of moderate cost and standard across many makes of computer, often being supplied as part of a standard configuration. It is operated in a standard way and has print-out facilities which are usually fast enough for the monitored data. While normal indicator lamps are used to show the state of hardware units, a useful overall and up-to-date picture of the software interpretation of the configuration and of software and traffic states can be shown on a standard visual-display unit (CRT). This is useful for larger systems where a fast device is needed. Standard devices like these should be examined before going to the cost of special-purpose keyboards and displays for the computer controller, even if special devices are needed for the *users* of the system in its particular application.

5.4. A Simple Executive

As an example of the simple approach to management software, consider the scheduler for a medium-sized single-processor configuration which is dedicated to performing a certain number of functions, some related and some unrelated. This might be an installation for a commercial company, handling a number of telex lines and also providing some management information input and retrieval services via display units.

An array is set up in main store as shown in Fig. 5.1. Each element of the array indicates whether a particular process is required to be run. The elements are in a priority order. Each time the scheduler program is entered it scans the array, starting at the highest-priority element until an element is found set. Control is passed to that process to carry out any task that may be needing that process. At the end of the task the process clears the element in the array if there are no further tasks queued ready for that process, and in any case returns control to the scheduler. A long process might be programmed to return control to the scheduler at regular intervals or when it has to suspend awaiting a disk access in case more urgent jobs are waiting; in this case the array element remains set until the final exit.

The array elements can be set in two ways: by program or by interrupt. They can be set by software tasks which, having processed some data, require other processes to be run on the results. This means processes can be very independent in the software structure; instead of passing control directly, it is done via the priority array, keeping the processes as structurally separable modules. The second way in which array elements are set is by interrupt programs. Newly arrived data is collected and buffered, and the appropriate element is set for processing when scheduled.

One important source of interrupts for this purpose is the computer's own real-time clock. Each clock interrupt increments a counter. Processes which need to be run at regular intervals, for instance to poll the display-unit keyboards, are indicated in a table. The real-time clock-interrupt program sets the array elements for those processes indicated in the table

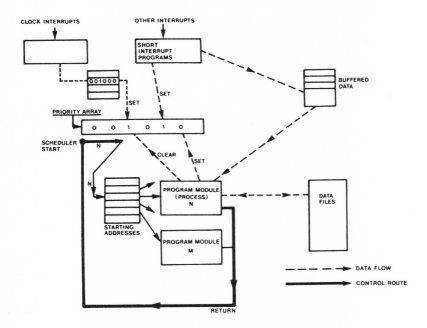

Fig. 5.1. Simple executive — module structure for real time.

entry appropriate to the counter value. In this way certain array elements can be set, say, every fourth clock interrupt, while others are set every second or every minute.

So programs and interrupts can call further modules indirectly, the communicating data being stored meanwhile. The restriction is that no module runs continuously for longer than the shortest response time; the scheduler must be re-entered often enough to activate any urgent tasks. In a dedicated system this time is predictable, and process modules can self-suspend at convenient points to ensure this. Care must be taken in setting the relative element order so that data being used by suspended processes cannot be changed by higher-priority tasks.

The array and clocked table readily allow insertion of new modules. The modules, whether related or not, are nicely separated structurally, and the scheduling program is extremely short, helping maximize through-put capacity. In some computers the array can be provided in a very efficient way, as simple bits in one word of store. The bits are in priority order. The processor scans the word, using a "normalize" instruction if available or else consecutive shifts until, say, the Nth bit is found set. An indirect jump is then made via the Nth entry in a table of process-starting addresses. Figure 5.1 illustrates this structure. If the processor also has a merge facility (an OR instruction), then the elements corresponding to the bits in the clock table can be efficiently set.

Such a scheduler occupies only a few instructions plus the array, clock table, and starting addresses. It can return to the useful application programs within a few microseconds. This may be contrasted with the complex management software encountered in large multi-programming systems where each job is assessed every time, a good job mix calculated, resources allocated, and tasks run according to possibly sophisticated, even dynamic, priority order. Such software with associated queueing areas can occupy many thousands of bytes of store and uses valuable processor time in calculating which task to continue next. In many real-time systems tasks tend to be shorter, so such overhead time would be disproportionately high. In dedicated systems much of the calculation can be predetermined and a simple scheduling algorithm such as that mentioned above can be used with the advantages of low programming cost and easy understanding, leaving maximum store and power for the useful work and getting high performance from an economic computer.

5.5. Software Facilities

This section summarizes the management and service facilities discussed in this chapter which control software can usefully provide in typical re: '-time systems.

5.5.1. Control Features

An executive primarily enhances the facilities of the computer toward application programs by providing a control over these programs. It decides when to start which programs and if necessary when to stop them. It allocates resources to programs. Basic components are a scheduler to decide on some priority basis which program to run next or to reactivate suspended tasks, a timer facility to start regular procedures or detect overlong ones, and in varying degrees of sophistication the power to call necessary actions in fault conditions.

Some of the problems of multi-level systems and some of the considerations within schedulers were discussed in § 4.3.5, while multiprocessing was discussed in § 5.2.5.

5.5.2. Input-Output Handling

The utility side or service software may include routines to handle control signals to and from devices attached to the computer and to handle the data received or sent over these lines, whether by programmed transfer or on interrupt. The data-handling routines may just buffer the data and signal the device or the scheduler, or call application routines directly. Kept short they are efficient and general purpose. Kept general they can enable easy reconfiguring if devices need to be changed or extended.

5.5.3. Memory Management

The management software can sometimes take care of the storage allocated to processes, at load time, or to tasks, at run time, simplifying programming and allowing processes to share the available store. In dedicated systems, in order to meet the predictable worst traffic mix effectively, the software designer can be more deterministic and carry out the store allocation himself to optimize store use. Dynamic storage allocation can be a heavy overhead in both occupancy and running time of the allocation routines themselves (see § 5.2.6).

5.5.4. Resource Management

In sophisticated operating systems the management software may be considered as organizing and providing all the requirements of the application programs and ensuring their continued availability even in fault conditions. Besides the basic features the operating system provides, in a way of which the application programmer need not be aware, other co-called "transparent" features such as full management of storage including backing stores, virtual storage, indexing of data and file structuring to the point of database management, program and data protection, all aspects of configuration checking, enabling devices to be changed, repaired, substituted or added, buffering over "long" periods for certain processes or devices, for instance allowing several different report programs to be run while the line printer is engaged or the paper is being changed, printing the output later, and so on.

Some of the problems of resource allocation in multi-level or re-entrant systems were discussed in § 4.3.4.

5.5.5. System Facilities

Besides the software facilities to assist the application programs, the management software needs to interact with the world outside the machine because the computer system is not entirely automatic but is part of a wider system including the operator. It needs to indicate that it is indeed running, how well, which parts need attention, and so on. It can also accept information to direct its running, allowing some degree of external control. This requires a computer operator's console such as a typewriter or display unit. Its purpose is quite different from that of the consoles for the application controllers.

5.5.6. Summary

Although a whole operating system may be complex, it can be broken down into separate parts each of which is usually straightforward. If only designers of operating systems were not so secretive and wrote down in simple terms descriptions of the methods and algorithms used for each of the component parts and showed clearly the relationships of these parts! Such published documentation would give many an application program designer the confidence through understanding to go ahead and either *use* the operating system instead of possibly needless redesign, or *reject* it wisely. Some references given in the bibliography may be useful, but the designer should assess the efficiency an existing operating system would have in his particular application and also ensure it had been actually proven. Even manufacturers sometimes publish the facilities of such software before it actually exists.

The designer for a particular application system must assess which parts of the software should be of "management" nature and which parts of available software he can use, retaining an understanding of how the whole real-time system will behave under such management. It is too early, at this design stage, to relinquish this understanding and rely on the operating system to take care of things. The application software designer is responsible for response, throughput, data checking, and so on, as well as for the application algorithms themselves. The management software can present a more reliable flexible computer configuration with facilities presented in a way that is easy to use, reducing programming effort, but the application designer needs to understand the capabilities of each of the management tools he is going to work with.

We have tried to identify separable parts of management and service software, showing which are basic and which are sophisticated, and emphasizing that their purpose is to provide an environment for application software which is an enhancement of the bare computer hardware. Those features which do help through giving a clear or reliable organization for programs or which save re-writing standard utilities can simplify the application task. Those features which are a heavy overhead or not fully understood should be discarded. In dedicated systems the argument of providing an indefinitely flexible operating system to allow for undefined changes beyond those envisaged does not apply and a simple executive may be adequate and efficient.

5.6. Control of High-Availability Systems

5.6.1. Self-Reconfiguring Computer Complexes

The systems software as discussed so far has two tasks: managing the operation of the system and providing common utilities. There are, however, systems in which the systems software has to perform a third task.

Several ways of achieving high-availability systems have been described in Chapter 3. Some of these methods require computers which are redundant in the sense that they are not needed to share the work load; they are either stand-bys or else are repeating work done by other computers to allow comparison or majority voting. The amount of redundancy can be reduced by providing just redundant modules, such as central processors, special processors, or store modules, instead of complete computers. A module which develops a fault is switched out of the system and replaced by a redundant one. To achieve very high availability in such module-redundant complexes the identification of the faulty module and its replacement have to be executed so rapidly that these operations must be performed automatically rather than by manual intervention. One then has a *self-reconfiguring computer complex*. The self-reconfiguration capability is achieved by special systems software which usually comprises fault detection, fault location to within a module, reconfiguration of the computer complex, recovery of the database, and restart of operation. Reconfiguration can only be carried out under software control if the interconnections between modules are capable of being switched between operative and non-operative states by appropriate software commands. This means that self-reconfiguring computer complexes also need specially designed or modified hardware.

A number of high-availability systems based on various variants of module-redundant self-reconfiguring computer complexes exist and have been in operation for a number of years, one with hundreds of installations. They are briefly surveyed in the following subsections outlining the operation of the reconfiguration software.

5.6.2. Automatic Digital Relay Center

One system uses hardware which is standard except for the feature of software control of inter-module interfaces. This system is a military message-switching center known as Automatic Digital Relay Center, or ADRC, at an underground combat center in Colorado. It uses D825 hardware for its computer complex. It contains two central processors, ten store modules, and three drums. The latter are used as working storage. Out of this hardware one central processor, eight store modules, and the three drums make up an operational subsystem. The remaining modules make up a monitoring subsystem. This latter subsystem is not a stand-by computer in that it is not large enough to take over the operational task. It is engaged in monitoring the operational subsystem and in self-checking, and also serves as a pool of redundant modules to replace modules in the operational system when a fault develops in the latter. The operational subsystem similarly checks itself and the monitoring system in addition to performing the operational task. Note that little redundant hardware is used.

Fault detection is performed by software. On the detection of a fault productive processing stops. Diagnostic programs are loaded and take control of all the hardware. The diagnostics locate the fault to within one module. If the diagnostic programs do not show up any fault the central processor which reported a fault is itself assumed to be faulty. At least one module is thus declared faulty and switched out of the system. A message reporting this is produced on the high-speed printer.

Then the diagnostic programs are overwritten by the data-recovery program. The data-recovery program recovers all the variable data which were in the machine when interrogated, where necessary relocating the data that were in a faulty store module into other ones. The data-recovery program is in turn overlaid by the operational programs and normal operations resumed.

ADRC keeps track of all the messages received and requests retransmission of any message which is lost or not received properly. All messages sent out are similarly monitored. All messages received and transmitted have to be stored for a certain period for retrieval purposes. The database must be preserved come what may. That this has indeed been achieved is demonstrated by the fact that the system has never lost a message since it came into operation in 1967.

The system has subsequently been enhanced by the addition of two fixed-head disks. This reduced the recovery time. A method of overcoming malfunctions caused by residual software-design faults has also been added. For this purpose validity checking of results was introduced and the executive has been extended to include validity checks on the data submitted with calls for the executive. If an inconsistency is discovered the message which has caused it is identified and removed from the system to be handled manually.

The system has been supplied on a monthly rental basis, rental for any one month becoming due only if a specified level of availability is reached or exceeded during that month. A certain number of recovery periods not exceeding 5 min are allowed. Occurrences in excess of this number or non-availability periods exceeding 5 min are counted as non-available time. On this basis the availability increased from 0.9965 initially to 0.9981 by 1970, and to 0.999977 in 1971, while in 1973 an availability of 1 has been achieved. There is on-site maintenance by a highly experienced team.

5.6.3. NAS Air-Traffic-Control System

In the ADRC described in the preceding section the operational load is carried by a single central processor. The NAS (for National Airspace System) air-traffic-control system, however, uses a multi-processor system (2-4). It also differs in using hardware with built-in fault-detection circuitry. The computer complexes used in this system are known as 9020A, 9020D and 9020E. The main modules are central processors, input-output processors, and core-store modules. In the 9020A the major modules are derived from the system 360 model 50. The built-in fault-detection circuits are part of system/360 design philosophy. Several fundamental modifications were, however, needed for multi-processing. One of these was to provide multiple ports on the store modules so that they could be shared by a number of processors. Another one was to provide *system addressing* by means of so-called address translators. With this system the address of a location in store is independent of the central processor addressing it and of the physical store module where it is located, so the address remains unchanged if a store module is switched out of the system and replaced by another one. Also the input-output operations were separated from the central processor, so that a 9020A central processor has no input-output capability. The 9020 input-output processors are also based on the model 50 central processor and can communicate with any central processor and any store module. The 9020D is a more powerful variant with its central processors and core-store modules derived from the model 65. The same goes for the 9020E, a multi-processor complex which will process input messages from up to 96 air-traffic controllers, afford them access to the central database, and compose and refresh their graphic and data displays. It contains two additional, specially developed module types, namely display buffers and display drives, providing space diversity so that no display position is lost even with the failure of a display buffer and a display drive.

The system/360 design had to be modified to bring the interface under software control, in order to enable the executive to isolate a faulty module from the system and replace it by another one. Indeed, to increase the security of operation, the control of the interfaces between modules has been developed to a highly sophisticated level. All modules have system-configuration registers and special privileged instructions have been added to the order code for setting up these registers. The contents of the configuration register determines with which other modules in the system the module may communicate and from which other modules it may accept the special configuration register-setting instructions. Two bits in the configuration register determine whether the programmer's manual controls and the maintenance controls are operative, and also in the case of a central processor whether the processor may issue the configuration register-setting instructions and thus control the system interconnections.

A 9020 computer complex typically contains three central processors, two to three input-output processors, and 8 to 12 store modules. Of the three central processors two usually share the load and are termed "on-line" processors, while the third one is available for carrying out off-line tasks. Of the two on-line processors only one will be in the highest operational state, enabling it to control the system interconnections. Should a fault-indication signal be generated by this processor the other on-line processor will automatically have its state changed to the highest one. An off-line processor can run diagnostic programs to locate the fault in, say, a store module. Such a processor does, however, remain connected to and under the control of the system (unless a special switch on it is turned on for maintenance work on the processor itself). So a maintenance engineer may suddenly find that his processor has dropped the diagnostic program to take over an operational task and that it will no longer respond to his commands even on the manual control panel. This lack of response to manual controls is due to the fact that in the higher operational states in which the on-line central processors operate the manual controls are disabled.

Error signals from the built-in fault-detection circuits call in microprograms to preserve data which could help analyse the fault. These microprograms also send out fault-indication signals to the other central processors. A special program known as Operational Error Analysis Program, or OEAP, is then called in (5). The central processor which discovered the fault enters the actual error-analysis segment of this program. This has two tasks: firstly to determine in which module the fault has occurred, as this is not always clear even with the built-in fault-detection circuitry, and secondly to determine whether the fault is a transient or solid one. The fault-indication signals sent out to other processors generate calls to the executive which in turn cause these processors to enter the monitoring segment of OEAP. Productive processing thus stops on the detection of a fault; one processor diagnoses the fault while the others time the first one. If this processor does not report within 350 ms that it has succeeded in recovering from the fault it is isolated from the system. The period allowed for recovery is lengthened to 7 seconds in the case of a fault in the store module containing OEAP itself to allow for recovery of this program from magnetic tape. The executive also refers to OEAP for analysis of interrupts caused by violations, both those trapped in system/360, such as store-protection violations, and also unauthorized attempts to reconfigure the system. Input-output malfunctions are analysed by the executive and appropriate action is taken by it. The executive reports all such occurrences and actions taken to OEAP which maintains records of all malfunctions. The results of the error analysis are passed on to the error-control segment of OEAP. This segment decides what actions should be taken according to the type of fault, i.e. whether solid or transient, and in the case of transient faults, depending on the fault record of the particular module. If the decision is to remove the faulty module OEAP will do so and inform the executive. The executive will then indicate to OEAP which module should be used to replace the faulty one. Then OEAP will execute this task, setting the configuration registers as required and in the case of store modules also the address-translator registers. Having recovered the configuration it then becomes necessary to recover operation. The preservation of the database relies on periodic dumping. Every 30 seconds all tables containing variable data are locked out and dumped on to magnetic tape. The variable data dumped include both operational data and system-control data, e.g. the contents of the address-translator registers. The dump is carried out in the order of frequency of usage of these tables, and as tables are dumped they are released for operational use. Some 56,000 words are dumped and the complete dump takes 3 seconds. A segment of the executive called *restart* is responsible for system reconfiguration and also for recovery of the database when necessary. Restart is performed by one central processor with the others in a special wait state. The executive and OEAP each contain some 10,000 instructions. The modest size of the executive is due to the fact that it has been specially tailored to the particular application. The overall NAS system comprises 20 centers covering between them the whole of the continental United States. About half the centers have 9020A complexes and the rest have 9020D complexes. Some of the latter ones also have 9020E complexes. These 20 centers communicate with each other, transferring data as flights pass from one area to another. Each center also supplies flight-plan data to the terminal area systems within its area. (The terminal area systems control the areas around major air fields.)

5.6.4. The No. 1 ESS and T200 Complexes

The No. 1 ESS (for electronic switching system) is a high-availability complex specially designed for stored program control of telephone exchanges. It is intended for exchanges of between 20,000 and 50,000 lines. The complex contains two identical computers. It is nevertheless not a duplicated computer system of the type described in Chapter 3. The duplication is used as the means of fault detection and as a source of redundant modules. Reconfiguration in the case of a fault is achieved not by switching over from one computer to another, but by detection of the faulty modules and exclusion of such modules from the system (6).

The computer modules are central processors, program stores, data stores, and the buses interconnecting them. The program stores are semi-permanent, using a technique known as *twistor* in which zeros or ones are differentiated by the presence or absence of small bar magnets in aluminum sheets. The program store modules contain 13 k words of 44 bits. An exchange will have three to six such modules. The data store modules have 8 k words each of 24 bits and there may be between 2 and 40 such modules in an exchange, depending on the size. At any one time, one of the central processors is designed as the active one and the other as the standby. The standby processor normally carries out precisely the same operations as the active one. Both processors are, in fact, clock synchronized. In each processor 48 comparison circuits continually compare the signal levels at up to 48 circuit points in the other processor. In each processor 288 circuit points can be connected to the comparison circuits. These connections vary with the machine instructions so that those circuits affected by the execution of a specific instruction are compared in the course of that instruction. A number of other special circuits monitor the operation of critical parts such as the clock and power supplies. The store modules have their own built-in monitoring circuitry to monitor their operation. The program stores also employ error correction. Seven out of the 44 bits are error-correcting bits based on a Hamming error-correcting code which enables single-bit faults to be corrected. This enables operation to continue in the case of single-bit faults, thus increasing the availability of the system. A record of all fault corrections is maintained by special hardware.

When a fault is detected productive processing ceases and the system switches over to fault analysis using the data available on the fault. If the fault is found to be a transient one it may not be necessary to switch out the affected module, depending on its fault record. If the fault is a solid one the location of the fault to a single module can be postponed until productive processing has been resumed, since it is possible to switch out a number of modules and still have a working system. If necessary, test programs check out the store modules to find enough good modules to make up a working system. The fault might be in the program store module containing the fault-location program, so part of this program is also kept in a data-store module. Reconfiguration is performed by the active central processor which determines which of the duplicate buses will be connected to each of the two central processors and which store modules will be connected to each of the buses.

The No. 1 ESS has been designed for unattended operation with no maintenance personnel on site. For this reason the design includes a special hardware module, known as *emergency action*, which times the reconfiguration program. If this module is not reset within 640 μs it takes over control of the hardware, setting up successive minimum configurations and checking them. Messages on all fault-detection occurrences and the actions taken to overcome them are printed out and also transmitted to a remote service center. Service men would expect to find a reconfigured working system with a print-out identifying the faulty module which has been removed from the system, and a further print-out produced after reconfigurations identifying the replaceable plug-in submodule within the faulty module.

The first No. 1 ESS controlled exchange went into commercial operation in 1965. By the time of writing over 700 such exchanges have been installed. This growth provides hard evidence that the design has met the requirements put on it. These were that total system down-time should not exceed 2 hours in 40 years; also the percentage of mis-dialled calls should not exceed 0.05. This figure, incidentally, is some 20 times higher than that achieved with electromechanical exchanges.

There were at first a number of instances in which the computer complex failed to configure. None were due to simultaneous faults in corresponding modules, but two of the failures were traced to servicing errors. Maintenance operators removed by mistake the sound module rather than the one indicated as being faulty (7). Some configurations put together by the emergency action module described earlier, which were apparently sound and should have functioned properly, failed to do so owing to corrupted memory contents. Even in such highly protected stores transient faults could still corrupt the memory contents. However, only about 10% of the memory corruptions were due to this source, the remainder being caused by servicing errors or software bugs. A special technique of program audits was developed to discover and rectify store corruptions (8,9).

A great deal was learned in the course of this vast and highly successful project, and most of this is applicable to other high-availability complexes. Much of what has been learned has been published and is extremely useful to anyone interested in high-availability computing (10,11).The No. 1 ESS design approach was successfully adapted to other telephone applications (e.g., 12).

Compared with the No. 1 ESS, the T200 telex exchange is very much a newcomer. The latter is a much simpler and less ambitious design with no built-in circuitry for hardware fault detection. The computer complex of the T200 exchange has triplicated central processors with majority voting, duplicated data stores, and duplicated input-output processors (13). The program store is read only and is not duplicated. The triplicated central processors are clock synchronized and the duplicated stores are accessed in parallel. Parity checking is relied on to determine which are the correct data in the case of a fault in one of the stores. The data stores also store the reconfiguration programs. In the case of a failure of the program store the programs are loaded from a backing store into one of the data stores. The usual means for the detection of software faults such as trapping attempts to write into the program stores are provided. There is also a watch-dog timer.

The first T200 exchange was in Hong Kong. In its first 17 months total down-time due to faults was 683 minutes giving an availability of 0.999075. (In addition 123 minutes were lost because of power failures.) Of the 683 minutes about one-third were in the first four months, during which three generations of software were loaded to correct software bugs. There were 50 system crashes of which 14 were found to be attributable to the hardware and 25 to the software, while the cause of the remaining 11 was not identified. The fact that the program store was not duplicated turned out to be a design weakness as transient faults in this store were a major source of system down-time. The overall ratio of transient faults to solid faults was in fact somewhere between 1-10 and 1-100. (This accords with experience on other systems.) The triplication of the central processor was found to be most effective in overcoming both transient and solid faults.

5.6.5. *System Availability and Integrity*

The self-reconfigurating computer complexes described in this section all rely on specially designed hardware and software. The special hardware designs are primarily processors and stores, since faults in peripherals can be overcome by the use of redundant peripherals provided the processors and main stores remain operational. The design of special hardware and software for high-availability self-reconfiguring computer complexes demands protracted and thoroughly painstaking "walking-through" in the sense defined in § 6.2.2. to foresee and allow for all the possible circumstances. In the case of the 9020, for instance, special methods had to be developed to gain access for fault diagnosis to a central processor which failed in an operational state in which its manual controls are disabled. Software modifications continue long after the systems first went into operation. The design of a high-availability self-reconfiguring computer complex is therefore a major and protracted task not to be lightly undertaken. The systems described in this section have all been large enough projects to justify such an undertaking.

Most hardware faults are transient, and these are more easily detected by fault-detection circuits than by software and more quickly rectified by error-correcting or retry hardware than if a full recovery operation were required. When reconfiguration becomes necessary it may be manual, as in the BOADICEA system described in Chapter 1, or automatic, as in the multi-computer complexes in Chapter 3 or in the multi-processor complexes described in this section. Automatic reconfiguration is faster and may allow unattended operation but presently requires specially designed hardware and software. Redundant-module self-reconfiguring computer complexes may require less equipment than redundant computer complexes, but this possible economic advantage is not achieved because such systems are not commercially available. None of the computer complexes described in this chapter can be bought simply as a computer complex. Nor would they necessarily provide a full solution to the problem because the systems software, which as has been seen is essential to complement the special features of the hardware, is tailor made to particular applications. One self-reconfiguring computer complex which is commercially available is system 250 (14-16). Its system software (other than the high-level language compiler) is intended for communications applications.

In most cases the main cause of malfunctions are software bugs.

This is still true even of a system like the No. 1 ESS after six years and several hundred systems in the field. Research has been done on formal methods of proving the correctness of software using propositional calculus. This appears to have come up against the problem of ensuring that the task to be performed by the software has been correctly specified in the first place. At any rate this approach does not appear to have matured into practical usefulness. So far, the methods of designing and engineering software to give a simple and straightforward structure and full and meticulous documentation as discussed in Chapter 4 provide the most potent weapon available against design errors. Nevertheless, such errors will still be there when the system is in operation and for high availability so-called *defensive programming* techniques are essential. These techniques consist of a variety of audits or validity checks followed by suitable corrective action which may in the limit be the removal of a transaction from the system for manual processing.

Whatever the source of the malfunction in a high-availability system, the first objective must be to stop the system from crashing. As long as the system remains operational and provided it contains the required software, it can then meet the integrity requirements. Correctness of results can be achieved by such well known methods as validity checks and computation of the results by different methods. The preservation of a database is usually required both for availability or integrity. The database may be damaged or lost owing to a malfunction. Once the equipment is reconfigured, the previous data state may be recovered by some kind of roll-back to a confident checkpoint. In some cases at least a duplicate is maintained of all variable data, as in the ARDC and No. 1 ESS. In other systems, such as the NAS system, all variable data are frequently dumped to allow recovery to the most recent checkpoint. This can be supplemented by a transaction log, on magnetic tape for instance, to recover from the checkpoint up to a state just before the fault. For even more accurate recovery it may be necessary to have facilities to request repeat inputs of data lost since the last dump or the last transaction successfully logged, and the system would therefore need to be aware of what data could have been lost in the fault. These techniques of ensuring integrity of data must guard against the same faulty data being faithfully recorded on the back-up store. This is hard to achieve in the face of software bugs. Various kinds of store protection can localize the effect of software bugs.

In general, appropriate software methods can be found which give satisfactory data integrity for each particular application without special hardware, though base and limit registers, capability limitation, and parallel processing by identical or alternative logic can give additional means of data protection.

The choice of the optimum approach for achieving the needed availability and integrity depends very much on the requirements of the specific application. A message-switching system where occasional non-availability for 5 minutes is acceptable but which must never lose a message may need a very different approach altogether from a telephone exchange where a 5-minute break in operation is a major disaster but a mis-dialled call is not. The availability and integrity requirements will subsequently continue to permeate the whole of the design. The amount and nature of the hardware, the operating system, and the manner of writing the application software are all highly dependent on the overall system configuration chosen and on the methods for validating results and preserving the database.

It can be seen that the two criteria of system availability and data integrity both need to be very carefully assessed for each particular application. To over-specify the standards required may make the system unobtainable in a realistic time scale or budget. Under-specification of the criteria will result in an inadequate system. The user has to consider his application carefully because the designer is not the best person to decide the degree of perfection required, so the user must give a conscious and realistic specification of the system availability and data integrity; he must state the acceptable down-time in duration, frequency and level of degradation, and state for each type of data what occasional loss is permissible consciously or unconsciously by the system. The decision will have a great effect on the cost of the system, yet a well-considered design can often achieve satisfactorily high standards without great expense or sophistication. It is one of the most fundamental ingredients of the specification.

References

1. Armstrong, R., Conrad, H., Ferraiolo, P., and Webb, P. Systems recovery from main frame errors. *Fall Joint Computer Conference*, 1967.

2. Blakeney, G.R., Cudney, L.F., and Eickhorn, C.R. An application ori-

ented multi-processing system. II. Design characteristics of the 9020 system. *IBM Syst. J. 6* (2), 80, 1967.

3. *National Airspace Systems (N.A.S.) Fact Book (NS-5)*. FAA, NAFEC Facility, Atlantic City, NJ, 1968.

4. *System Description National Airspace System En Route Stage A (SPO-MD-109)*. FAA, NAFEC Facility, Atlantic City, NJ, 1968.

5. Lancto, D.C., and Rockefeller, R.L. The operational error analysis program. *IBM Syst. J. 6* (2), 103, 1967.

6. Downing, R.W., Nowak, J.S., and Tuomenoksa, L.S. No. 1 ESS. Maintenance plan. *Bell Syst. Tech. J. 43* (5), 1961, 1964. Part 2, 1964, p. 1961.

7. Staehler, R.E. No. 1 ESS. service experience—hardware. *Proc. Conf. on Switching Techniques for Telecommunications Networks, IEE Conf. Publ. No. 2,* p. 88. Institution of Electrical Engineers, London, 1969.

8. Nowak, J.S. Tuomenoksa, L.S. *Memory Mutilation in Stored Program Controlled Telephone Systems*, Bell Telephone Labs., Naperville, Ill.

9. Nowak, J.W. Emergency action for No. 1 ESS. *Bell Lab. Rec. 49* (6), 176, 1971.

10. Higgins, W.H.C. Survey of recent advances in Bell System switching. *Proc. Conf. on Switching Techniques for Telecommunications Networks,* IEE Conf. Publ. No. 2, p. 447. Institution of Electrical Engineers, London, 1969.

11. Johannesen, J.D. No. 1 ESS Service Experience — Software. *Conf. on Switching Techniques for Telecommunications Networks, IEE Conf. Publ. No. 2,* p. 459. Institution of Electrical Engineers, London, 1969.

12. Delatore, J.P., LeRoy Hinck, L., and Petschenik, N.H. Solving software problems in TSPS No. 1, *Bell Lab. Rec. 49* (10), 316, 1971.

13. Kreis, W. Computer systems design for real time telecommunication control. *Proc. IEE Conf. on Software Engineering for Telecommunication Switching Systems, IEE Conf. Publ. No. 93,* pp. 196-205. Institution of Electrical Engineers, London, 1973.

14. Cosserat, D.C. A capability oriented multi-processor system for real time application. *Proc. Int. Conf. on Computer Communications, Washington, D.C. 1972.*

15. Hamar-Hodges, K.J. Fault resistance and recovery within system 250. *Proc. Int. Conf. on Computer Communications, Washington, DC, 1972.*

16. Repton, C.S. Reliability assurance for system 250 — a reliable real time control system. *Proc. Int. Conf. on Computer Communications, Washington, DC, 1972.*

System Design and Development

6.1. Approach to Projects

6.1.1. Introduction

The three previous chapters have discussed the various tools available to the real-time systems designer in the computer part of the system: the computer hardware, the application programming, and the control software. We now return to the overall system design at the point where it was left in Chapter 2, namely that the requirement has been stated, a feasible solution within time scale and cost has been found, and the decision has been made to go ahead. This chapter goes from this decisive point through the stages of design and implementation in the order they need to be tackled, referring to the tools discussed in the earlier chapters. Real life will prevent an ideal approach, but the system designer and development team still have to strive to complete each stage as well as may be possible. Often one has to iterate and find the best compromise, but at least one can keep the organized approach in mind, knowing the sequential stages that have to be reached before starting the next. One has to *plan* ahead. There are many instances where prematurely plunging into detail on unestablished assumptions has led to chaos and an ultimate need for rework in any case. One cannot say there is not time to complete a stage. If there is not time to obtain a specification or complete the design

185

or document the decisions, yet implementation goes ahead, then it is likely that much rework will be needed later. This will not only escalate cost but also lengthen an already tight time scale. Short cuts are almost always expensive. So we suggest in this chapter some of the sequential stages in system design and ways of controlling the progress of design and implementation.

The principles of this section (§ 6.1) apply not only to computer systems or to the computer part of systems, but to a wide range of projects. For the rest of the chapter we are particularly concerned with computer systems. Where a total system involves other areas, including the user environment and possibly other major equipment areas, an all-embracing specification is needed first and then for each area its own "functional specification" is required. Moreover, when each area has been developed it needs co-ordinating and integrating into the total operational system. These aspects are discussed in Chapter 7; for now we concentrate on the real-time computer system. The major phases of the task, with the relevant sections, are shown in Table 6.1.

Table 6.1.   Major design and implementation phase

Design and implementation plan	§ 6.1.2
Checking the functional specification	§ 6.2.2
Working out the design specification	§ 6.3
Software design and implementation	§ 6.4
System documentation	§ 6.5

6.1.2. Outline Plan

Before embarking on the design stage, the project manager responsible for the system needs to list the major stages for design, implementation, and bringing the system into use. He needs to estimate the time required for each stage and the resources in terms of staff, space, equipment, and cash which will be required. Typical stages for a project may include the following:

Project definition
Outline plan
Design
Procurement of subsystems

Development and manufacture of other subsystems
Unit test
Subsystem test
Integration or system build
System test
Shipment
Installation
Acceptance tests
Field trials
Training
Post-acceptance support
Maintenance
Enhancement

We assume the procedure discussed in Chapter 2 has been completed. A project manager is appointed. He has to assess the project by reviewing and defining the task of implementing the system. This is the project-definition stage. The *outline plan* is just a diagram showing the consecutive and parallel stages of implementation. Completion of each stage is shown as an event or milestone on the outline plan. It does not have to be in detail or dependent on the exact equipment involved. It is just a *scaling* exercise, and a plan for one project may be very similar to another. An example of an outline plan is given in Fig. 6.1.

The purpose of the outline plan is to show and remind the project staff and the user that not all the time available can be spent on design and

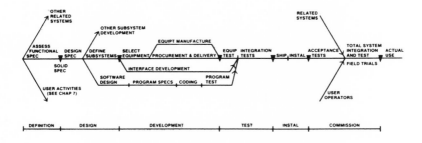

Fig. 6.1. Project outline plan for scaling, planning, and monitoring.

development. There are the shipment, installation, commissioning, and test stages as well. From the user's point of view there is also staff training and perhaps some parallel running before the system is fully operational. All these considerations affect the "ready-for-service" date. At the outset of a project, one is often too enthusiastically preoccupied with system design to remember that significant time is required for these later stages. So if an outline plan is produced at the start, one is reminded to think in terms of an earlier date for completion of development, typically the completion of system test in the factory or development environment. The outline plan should be made public to all involved.

As the project develops and system design proceeds, a more detailed version of the plan can be produced. If appropriate, a full critical path analysis or PERT chart might be produced, showing interdependent events, resources of labor and cash required, etc. Very often, however, the value of such a plan is in the drawing of it, not in the slavish updating of it. There is another danger of a detailed plan; it is usually heavily detailed in the design and development area, these stages covering most of the paper, squeezing the time out of the essential and unavoidable later stages of the project. Let the development plan be recognized as such, observing the completion date for development which is required by the outline plan.

Sometimes plans are drawn up without a date scale, just to show an event network. We believe they should be at least drawn to scale, so that longer activities are clearly seen, and preferably against a calendar baseline, not so as to fit into the desired time scale but so as to highlight at the outset any problems in meeting the ready-for-service date. If it is impossible to meet the date, the biggest crime is for the project manager to ignore the problem, burying his head in the sand, and pretend that, for instance, his design team can prove a subsystem the day the underlying equipment is received from a supplier. A solution must be found at the start, whether it be a revised plan, revised system, or a revised and agreed commissioning date.

Having got the whole job into perspective, one can now turn to the particular stages of design and development.

6.2. Preview of Design and Implementation

The functional specification has to be translated into a description of what is involved internally to provide those externally apparent functions. This is the *design specification stage*. As an example from the process-control field, if the functional specification asks for the control of flow of ingredients in, say, paper-making to maintain a selected quality of output, the design specification will indicate the measurement of the output, comparison against the quality required, and relevant adjustments of valves to control the flow. Already the major internal functions and external equipment interfaces are identified.

The next stage is to identify appropriate subsystems, some of which may later take the form of hardware, a computer configuration, software or transducers, and then to define the characteristics of each subsystem so that working together they will meet the overall functional specification. These characteristics are then used to define the internal nature of the subsystems. The important difference between the function and the design specifications at any level is that the former define the requirement while the latter express the outcome of systems analysis, deciding what is logically involved in meeting the requirement. That is to say, a translation of what it must do into how it could do it. The outline plan just shows this progressive breakdown as the *design stage*. The end result of the design is a list of subsystem design specifications against which hardware, software, and so one can be evaluated, selected, or built. As an example of a non-technical case such as setting up a company organization, the end result of the design stage is a list of job specifications against which candidates can be selected, with starting dates.

It would be a mistake to draw the design of the subsystems as separate events on the first draft of the outline plan as one should not skip the progressive analysis of the requirement and jump to preconceived ideas, but work out the requirement critically, lest alternative new techniques be overlooked or needless traditions propagated.

As the design specification progresses in increasing detail, the functional specification is found to be a simplistic definition. More internal detail has to be defined, first in terms of related subsystems, then within each subsystem, and so on. This detail must be agreed with the user to whom constant reference is therefore absolutely necessary. The method is one of increasing detail, breaking each area down progressively, defining smaller and smaller elements. At each level the definitions are checked for completeness of each element, relationships of elements are set out, and together they must meet the requirement described in the level above. Such an approach is called "*top-down*" design and can be applied to many types of systems. Both the functional and the design specifications can be developed in this way.

When it comes to implementing such a design, sometimes the elementary bricks are first created and tested. These are used to build the next larger units which are tested in turn until the whole structure is complete. This is called "*bottom-up*" implementation. One snag is that sometimes success or failure is not indicated until a late stage. Another approach is to build a framework first, then build a section of the system completely and prove it before starting further sections. This gives good feedback and less risk but can lead to non-optimal or even "Topsy-like" growth and vague completion. Whatever approach is taken on phases of implementation, it needs to have been consciously envisaged at the design stage. In this chapter we assume a top-down design approach and an independent "*bottom-up*" implementation of sections, modules, or packages which can be incorporated when ripe into a framework which is the first thing to be built. We rely on the framework being sufficiently robust to take ultimately all the envisaged sections. This requires a plan before detail is commenced. Then it is safe to go ahead on the framework and sections.

6.2.1. The Functional Specification

The nature and purpose of a functional specification are discussed in Chapter 2. Because of its importance to the success of a system, the considerations are summarized again.

The first stage is to identify the requirement, to state the overall objective. This is stated by the intending user, possibly with help from consultants and maybe as a result of a study in operational analysis. In any event the user is the prime force and is unlikely to be happy with any system foisted on him or which misses his basic need.

In meeting the requirement the system will provide a benefit to the user. This benefit should be quantized in economic terms to decide the maximum appropriate budget. A more expensive system would be inappropriate. A lower figure should be set as a target so that the benefit will exceed the cost. A user who omits this fundamental step will find it hard to select from alternative systems proposed; a well-engineered car may be attractive and better value for money than a cheaper one, but either type is too expensive if the real requirement is for somewhere to shelter from rain.

A functional specification is drawn up to describe what the system will do and the intending user should check this against the requirement. The contents of a specification and the method of arriving at it were described in Chapter 2. An endeavor is made to be definitive and complete. The user may need advice as to what is possible. The designer needs to put the user's wishes, as stated in the requirement, above his own ideas of useful functions. Discussion and comparison of alternatives will yield a preferred specification. Before adopting it the cost is compared with the acceptable budget. If too high, adjustments and alternatives are considered. Ultimately an economic specification acceptable to the user may be found. Only then should real technical design proceed, having defined and agreed what must be achieved. This discussion is the design, evaluation, and optimization procedure depicted in Fig. 2.2 (Chapter 2).

The specification includes another important element, the time scale. Without a date set for completion no-one can say a system does not work, only that development continues, with no goal and no way of stopping it. Likewise there is no incentive for the user to agree the work is complete or be happy to use a stable, tested system. Acceptance dates must therefore be agreed, deciding in advance when the design and implementation people are to show the user that the system meets its specification, so that it is available by the time the user expects to use it.

The three fundamental elements of the functional specification are thus agreed: functions; cost; time scale. For the rest of this chapter these fundamentals are assumed to exist.

6.2.2. Checking the Specification

So we think we have a functional specification. Whatever the system, it is certain that the specification will not be perfect, even if the method described in Chapter 2 for producing it has been earnestly followed. There will be errors, things taken for granted, omissions. The functional specification will also leave many questions of detail to be answered before definitive implementation can be completed.

The first task, therefore, is to check the functional specification for understanding, completeness, and consistency. To check for consistency is first to determine whether the system is possible, whether the outputs can in fact be derived from the inputs, and then to check for minor inconsistencies or conflicts between requirements. The next step is to check for completeness, to determine whether inputs and interfaces are fully defined, and then to examine the specification of the functions to be performed and outputs required for exactness or loopholes. A useful way is to "walk-through" the possible data paths. Here, one is continually asking the question "What is to happen if . . .?" until the imagination is exhausted and until answers have been obtained. A method sometimes used is "rule-writing" in order to say exactly what is to be the result of each possible situation. This has the benefit of focusing attention on the useful application function for discussion with the user and for going into more detail than the functional specification, without the discussion becoming confused with considerations of the equipment or software structure that may be needed to execute the functions. So now we really do have a functional specification.

The design task is to translate this description into a method of meeting the requirement, indeed the most cost-effective one. This does not necessarily mean a computer-based solution; a broad view is needed when searching for ways of meeting the specification. In this book, however, we are concerned with those systems where a computer-based solution is the most cost-effective one; as seen in Chapter 1 this is becoming true for more and more systems.

6.3 Methodology for Overall System Design

This section sets out a general method for determining the overall architecture of a real time system. The problem here is not unlike that presented by the Gordian Knot, for the design of any one part depends on the design of many other ones, so where does one start?

6.3.1. Design of the Input and Output Functions

The natural starting point for the design of a real time system is with the input and output functions. By this is meant the equipment which interfaces with the outside world so that it can seize the required input data and offer it up to the data processing functions and which introduces the results of the data processing into the outside world in the required manner. This portion of a real time system is mostly hard wired but there is now an increasing use of micro-processors with programs in read only memory. The input and output functions are the starting point for the design because, being the interface to the outside world, their capabilities are determined by the operatonal requirement and they are also less dependent than other parts on the rest of the system.

The transducers, which are the actual interface with the outside world, must enable the system to meet the operational requirements, including all the specified constraints. A fragile terminal or one needing subdued lighting is unsuitable for an industrial environment. An alphanumeric keyboard may impose too high a load on the operator; an audio output device may allow the operator to carry out other tasks whereas the visual display terminal will not. The choice of operator input or output devices and the way in which they will be used determine the final shape of the man/machine interface.

These aspects, therefore, have to be thought out rather carefully at this stage. One needs to consider the type of operators who will use the devices and to envisage the instructions that would appear in the user manuals. These decisions will have considerable bearing on the usefulness and workability of the system.

As with any other design one has to find the most cost-effective devices which will meet the requirements. A visual display unit may be superfluous if a hard-copy record is necessary in any case. Having determined the minimum array of transducers necessary one moves on to the choice of individual devices where such a choice exists. Obviously, one is after the most cost-effective devices but one has to consider more than just the initial purchase cost. The reliability of a transducer may be a determining factor, since even if it is possible to replace faulty transducers by spare ones the cost of doing this and the cost of the ensuing temporary loss of system facilities may well outweigh the difference in initial costs. Also, the cost of the interface equipment, which may vary for different transducers, has to be included. Transducers also vary in the extent to which they will load the computer; for example, one transducer may need processing to linearize its output while another one may not. This factor may be disregarded at this stage on the provisional assumption that the extra processing load will not be a factor in the design of the processing function. The validity of this assumption and the possible consequent revision of transducer choice is examined in § 6.3.3. For the design of the interfaces assumptions have to be made as to which inputs and outputs will be by programmed transfer, polling, interrupts, or direct memory access. In most cases this is determined by the data rate, the interrupt frequency of the device, and the extent to which different devices all require a similar treatment. The choice between direct memory access and one of the other methods is a trade-off between computer loading and more extensive interface equipment. Where the balance of this trade-off is not obvious the preferred choice at this stage is again to put the load on the computer, as a provisional assumption prior to the final decision as described in § 6.3.3.

The methods of seizing input data and presenting data for output having been determined, the design process has reached the stage indicated in Fig. 6.2. The next step is to determine the internal (software) interfaces between these input and output functions and the main data-processing functions. These interfaces are typically buffers of data held in store to contain messages of known types delivered at specified maximum rates for each type.

Buffers should be long enough to accept these rates for periods approaching the appropriate response times; longer buffers would allow messages to lose their essential "freshness". The processing capacity for the main data-processing functions should be adequate to handle these peak rates averaged over the response-time periods. Only if these two conditions are met can one be sure that all the input data seized will be captured and processed and will not be overwritten or become stale.

Similarly the interface between the main data-processing functions and the output functions is determined. The response times referred to are somewhat shorter than those specified in the operational requirement because of the times spent in the actual input and output functions.

To complete the specification of the interfaces between the input and output functions and the main data-processing functions, as shown in Fig.

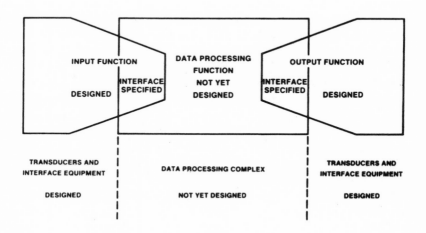

Fig. 6.2. Input and output functions provisionally designed.

6.2, it is necessary to decide what processing if any is included in the input and output functions so as to define the format of messages in the buffers. In Chapter 4 it was suggested that this be minimal. It may be restricted to little more than the functions performed by the input or output hardware, such as parity checking, checking or adding message envelope, and other "message-conditioning" operations. Definition of these interfaces now allows the design of the main data-processing functions to proceed.

6.3.2. Marshaling the Design Data

We come now to the design of the main data-processing functions. System analysts who grew up on software for batch processing may tend to see the main data-processing function as the whole of the system, but as has been seen there is more to a real-time system than just data processing. However, following the procedure of isolating the main functions from the real-time world, the task of designing for these functions is simplified again and becomes similar to multi-programming in batch systems.

For the design of the main data-processing functions the following information is necessary: (a) the data processing capacity to be provided; (b) the availability requirements; (c) the number of systems to be built.

Estimating the required data-processing capacity is known as sizing. The sizing task provides an example of the problems caused by the interdependence of the various parts of the design process, for the required capacity does in turn depend on how the data-processing functions are designed; use of a backing store or splitting the work between several computers will give rise to additional processing overhead load. This conflict is resolved by making the initial assumption that the processing will all be carried out in a single computer using only main store. This gives estimates of the essential processing power and storage required. This capacity is then adjusted to allow for increases or decreases caused by particular trial designs. One can examine whether it is appropriate to carry out certain functions in special hardware, to use more sophisticated input and output functions, to use backing store for various programs and data files, or to split the processing load in various ways between processors. The effect of each factor can then be clearly seen against the initial estimates of the essential capacity required if one simple computer was used. When the possibilities have been explored in this way, the most cost-effective solution meeting the requirement can be decided upon. We now examine this procedure in more detail.

The term processing capacity includes both storage and throughput. The latter is expressed by three separate parameters: direct memory access load, total of overheads due to interrupts, and the actual processing load. These have to be separated because the performance of any one computer in these three respects is not necessarily correlated. It is not necessarily the faster machines which offer cycle stealing as defined in § 3.4, while the interrupt overhead depends on the design of the computer and not just on processing speed. The amount of storage needed for data is not computer dependent, and has to be determined separately from the program storage which varies with the instruction set.

The loads due to direct memory access and interrupt overheads are determined directly from the specifications of the interfaces between the data-processing function and the input and output functions. The direct memory access load is expressed as so many words or bytes per second in or out (items shorter than a byte being counted as bytes). The load due to interrupt overheads is expressed simply as the number of interrupts per second; the load resulting from the actual processing of the interrupts is included in the processing load as is the load due to polling and programmed transfers. This gives the total processor load of the input and output functions.

The processing load for the main data processing is now estimated. A complete list is required of all the processes to be carried out. This includes not only all the actual functions of the application, the algorithms, but also any programs needed to process the buffered input data ready for the actual functions and to prepare the results for the output buffers — this chain of processes is shown schematically in Fig. 6.3.

The chain can be broken down into more detail showing each of the listed processes and the relationships between them as in the block diagram of Fig. 6.4. The main data files required for each process are determined and an integrated list made. Various ways exist for showing diagrammatically how each process or block on the diagram accesses the files or database in the system (1,2). The loading estimates for each process are derived as described in Chapter 4, choosing algorithms to enable the response times to be met. These loads are calculated for the worst traffic case and added to give the total processing power required by the main data processing.

Besides these processes there is the processing load due to the systems software which controls and assists the running of the other programs as discussed in Chapter 5. At this initial stage the minimum essential system software may be assumed and its processing load estimated. The load due to the control program overhead can be significant and is often underestimated. To these figures are added the input and output function loads to give the total essential processing power required in the initial case of one simple computer. This may be expressed as the number of instructions that have to be performed in a given time.

It is usually a somewhat easier job to estimate the storage capacity required for program and data. The buffers and file sizes are calculated, and the size of input, output main and system programs estimated. Program estimates will depend on the envisaged instruction set and on the programming language. Since these factors determine the number of words of store which will need to be accessed to execute each process, they affect both the processing power and the store required. A machine instruction set and programming language have therefore to be assumed.

In some cases it may also be worthwhile to prepare a histogram of the data items on which individual machine operations will have to be performed. From this, one can then deduce the most efficient word length.

When the procedure just set out is implemented thoroughly, the es-

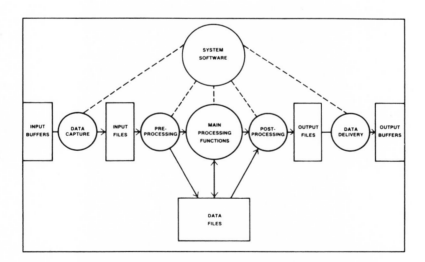

Fig. 6.3.   Input-output and supervisory tasks separated from the actual main functions.

timates of storage and actual processing load should be accurate to within 20% and this should be allowed for in the subsequent design. If the work is rushed a higher contingency has to be allowed. The estimates of the direct memory access and interrupt overhead loads follow more directly from the functional specification and may be expected to be more accurate. In some applications the input-output load turns out to be negligible compared with the actual processing load. In other applications the input-output load may be paramount.

The data-processing capacity as determined so far needs to be augmented to provide reserves for errors in the specification and design, for inefficiencies of implementation, for modifications, and for enhancements. The magnitude of such reserves depends very much on the particular circumstances, e.g. on how well the system has been specified, on how good the design and implementation team is, or on what enhancements might be expected, all of which are not easily evaluated. As a rough guide reserves of 100% increase on the actual processing load, 50% on the input-output load, and 100% increase on store needed would be appropriate when the functional specification has been thoroughly prepared and where the design

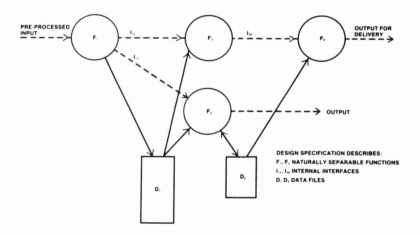

Fig. 6.4.   Separable processes and data files.

and implementation team is well experienced in the particular type of system. Higher reserves are needed if there are doubts in any area.

Thus the processing capacity which must be provided in the design is now determined. Of the five figures which quantify it three are largely independent of the instruction set assumed: data storage, DMA load, and total of interrupt overheads. The actual processing speed and program storage do depend on the computer assumed since the number of instructions and the speed at which they are executed can only be estimated for a particular machine. A method of transferring these estimates to other machines is discussed in § 6.3.4.

Some real-time systems have to be designed to cover a range of task sizes. Furthermore, the individual configurations catering for the various sizes may also have to be capable of expansion on site. The classic example here is a telephone exchange, where sizes vary greatly, depending on the number of subscribers, and which have to be capable of on-site expansion. It is necessary to size the two extremes of task sizes where the maximum task size is the limit for expansion for which the design is to cater. Further sizings, of intermediate task sizes, may be required in the course of design. Where it is known in advance that the system will be implemented as a computer network, like the BOADICEA system described in Chapter 1, sizing has to be carried out separately for each component.

Having estimated the processing capacity required for the functions and traffic in the application, a decision is needed on the best method of achieving the required availability. As explained in Chapter 3 there is a watershed in the choice of possible configurations depending on whether the availability can be satisfied by a single computer within the limits of the maintenance facilities specified. These parameters in the specification need therefore to be analyzed to determine whether this is the case. Should it be found that the availability requirements of some functions can be met with a single computer but those of others cannot be so met, it may be necessary to size these two groups of functions separately.

The design of real-time systems is affected by the number of systems to be produced in the same way as the design of any other product, the cost of the software constituting part of the development cost. Even in the case of an order for a single system, one should consider whether further systems to the same design are likely to be produced. Design for multiple systems will, as always, swing the cost balance in favor of specially designed components, whether hardware or software, and may also affect the balance between hardware and software. Design for similar systems encourages the use of parametrization and of modular techniques.

One more task remains to be done before starting out on the actual design. In choosing the transducers and in the course of sizing a great many provisional assumptions are made. A complete written record of these assumptions must be prepared for reference in the subsequent design stages.

6.3.3. Determining the Overall System Configuration

The first step is to asses whether the processing capacity, as determined in the sizing, can be satisfied with a single minicomputer. The reason for limiting this assessment, in the first instance to minicomputers, is that someone designing a real-time system himself, as opposed to buying a ready-made system, is unlikely to be justified in buying a big computer. If the load cannot be met by a single minicomputer, or is close to that point, the composition of the load is to be analyzed. The starting point for this is the list of assumptions made during sizing, mentioned in the previous section. The guideline during sizing was to throw the load onto the computer. However, in many cases quite substantial processing loads may be transferred from the computer to more elaborate input-output equipment and, indeed, it may prove more cost effective to do so, as will be discussed shortly. If the load divides neatly into a number of tasks with little interaction between them, a multi-computer configuration may be a cost-effective solution. If a large part of the processing consists of many repetitions of comparatively short programs, these may be speeded up by using a minicomputer with an extracode facility, Alternatively, processing may be transferred to another, possibly specialized processor. In this case it may be desirable to introduce some dual access storage common to the two processors. If direct memory accesses constitute a large component of the load, consideration may be given to a multi-bus configuration which will enable these accesses to take place simultaneously with processing. These last two possibilities belong to the spectrum of configurations between the multi-computer and fully fledged multi-processor configurations mentioned in Chapter 3. Here one is considering multiple processing units for reasons of meeting the processing capacity required.

A whole new set of problems arises if the availability requirements cannot be met with a single computer. Special hardware for high-availability systems is much more expensive than minicomputers produced in large quantity. Software for special high-availability configurations such as multi-processor complexes is also much more complex. Hence one tries first of all to achieve the demanded availability using standard minicomputers. Without the addition of special hardware this is possible only in two cases: if the nature of the system allows distributed processing in the manner described in § 3.5, by far the best solution if possible, or if the availability requirements can be met with a duplex computer system with manual switch-over. Even if a solution with standard computer is possible, it is necessary at this stage to decide on the right solutions to all the problems of recovery and integrity discussed in § 5.6.7. If neither of the two standard computer approaches is feasible, a dual computer system with automatic switch-over, or a triplicate or partly triplicate system may be considered; both of these use standard computers with the addition of special hardware. A multi-processor configuration is another alternative, and one using hardware with special availability facilities built into it may be required to meet very stringent availability requirements. This may in fact be the right solution for a very-high-availability system which has to cover a range of task sizes and where the quantities involved justify the design of such hardware together with the software needed for it. One needs to keep separate the requirements of a multi-processor for capacity reasons from those for availability reasons. These different requirements often become confused. It must be clear how the availability will be met in terms of equipment, recovery method and degree of automatic action.

When the overall system configuration has been arrived at, stand well back — not because it may blow up, but because there is almost certainly a simpler overall solution. To discover it a detached, new approach is needed. This may be brought about by asking oneself just what it is that one wants to achieve and what is logically necessary to achieve it. (Recollect that in Chapter 2 a case was described where operators were required to put in data which was already there.) It may help to call in someone, who has not been involved hitherto, who can probe the validity of assumptions which may have led to the proposed design. The savings achieved by a simpler solution may well go far beyond anything that can be achieved even by the most thorough optimization of the first solution arrived at. The main opportunity for cost-effective system design lies in being able to select a fundamentally cheaper method or type of configuration, not just cheaper equipment to do the same thing. However, the search for a simpler solution cannot go on indefinitely, so the time comes when the overall configuration *is* decided on. One then goes on to optimize it.

In doing this it should be borne in mind that there are trade-offs between development cost and cost of the final product, as well as between various ways of designing it. Costs can be reduced by easing the squeeze on store to allow the use of more relaxed programming, less experienced coders, and maybe the use of a high-level language for all or part of the system. This is one reason for avoiding a configuration which comes close to the limits of the processing capacity available with a given computer range. Another good reason for avoiding such a configuration is the lack of reserves to overcome unforeseen difficulties or enhancements. One of the areas to be looked at during optimization has already been mentioned earlier in this section, and this is the division of tasks between the computer and the input-output equipment. The optimum boundary will depend on the number of systems to be designed, the types of expertise and resources available within the design team during the relevant periods, and on the state of technology. Until now the design of special input-output equipment may have meant a considerable amount of design work; this has been greatly reduced with the advent of the very fast simple microprocessors mentioned in § 1.4. Another area to be looked at is the possible use of two-level storage. Here, feasibility as well as cost effectiveness have to be checked. This is done by re-estimating the processing capacity which will be required, assuming that the appropriate programs and files are held on the backing store under consideration — mostly disks. This re-estimate is complicated by the need to allow for the worst case of queuing for transfers to and from the device. It is sometimes found that the higher processing load resulting from two-level storage cannot be accommodated. This is why real-time systems like, for instance, the air-traffic-control system in § 5.6.3, need millions of bytes of main store. If two-level storage is feasible, will it be more cost effective? The gain will be the saving in main store shown by the re-estimate and possibly a relaxation in the use of store which will reduce the cost of programming. Against this have to be set not only the total cost of all the additional equipment and software, but also the cost of the extra complexity which will manifest itself in, for instance, a greater commissioning period, space requirement, and spares holding.

Throughout all the stages of the work the chief designer will seek advice and information from experts in the various specialized design areas. This is not to advocate design by committee but simply acknowledges the fact that the chief designer cannot possibly match the specialized knowledge of the experts in a rapidly growing field like computers. This exploitation of specialized expertise becomes essential at the configuration optimization stage. Specialized hardware and software engineers, some of whom may subsequently assume responsibility for the design and implementation of the major system components, should be brought in to participate in the preparation of functional specifications for these components. These experts will then work out design specifications to meet their functional specifications as illustrated in Fig. 6.5, together with provisional implementation plans and estimates. Given such data, the various major components are juggled around with the aim of optimizing the overall configuration.

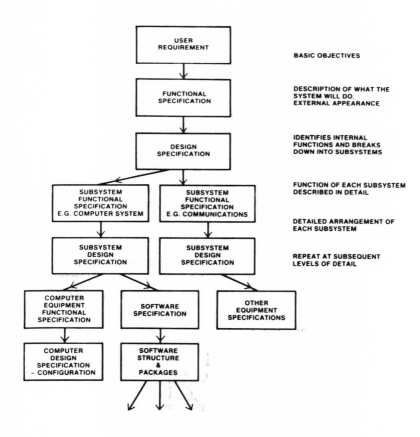

Fig. 6.5.   Documentation reflects stages in design.

Two more tasks have to be carried out before the optimization can be regarded as complete. One is to check the functional specifications of the main components to ensure completeness, consistency, and irreducibility. At this stage this boils down to the following three checks: (i) that the sum of all the functional specifications meets the overall functional specification; (ii) that every component does in fact do whatever it is that the other components assume it does; (iii) that no component performs tasks already done by another one.

The final task is to list all the design decisions with the reasons for them, and all the components affected by each decision. In the course of implementation, problems will arise requiring modifications to the design. By that time the reasons for the decisions may no longer be remembered, and some of the implications of the modifications may not be realized until it is too late to do anything but patch it up somehow. If there is a full list of design decisions and it is consulted every time a modification is considered such occurrences should be eliminated.

6.3.4. Choice of Computer

Two conflicting factors underly the problems of selecting the most cost-effective computer for a given system. One of these, sometimes referred to as "lock-in", arises from the fact that the use of a given computer in a real-time system inevitably leads to an investment which is specific to the particular machine. In addition to know-how and experience, the investment may also include a program-development facility and software or interfaces for special input-output equipment not supplied by the manufacturer. On the other hand, the rate of obsolescence is such that a given model is unlikely to remain competitive for longer than two or three years. To keep their existing customers, many computer manufacturers now make their new models at least upwards compatible in software and interfaces. The circumstances on any one project may, therefore, range from a situation where the best solution is obviously to continue with the same computer even if it is wholly obsolete to situations where a wide-ranging assessment of all possible computers is required. Within this range there are situations where the choice is limited or even determined by non-technical factors such as customers' preferences or national policies. Where a comparative assessment has to be made, a list is first drawn up of the manufacturers who may have suitable products and who also meet the other conditions which may have been imposed. The invitation to tender which is sent to the selected suppliers must give full information on what is required, in the form of a configuration-design specification. The computer configuration decided on (e.g. single computer or dual computer with or without common store, etc.) should be described, with a block diagram if appropriate.This is then followed by all the relevant performance parameters for all items of the configuration, from the processing capacity of processors and main stores to full specifications of any interface units to which special input-output equipment is to be connected. This also applies to any items of software, such as operating systems, which are to be included in the operational configuration. Also, if appropriate, the supplier should be instructed to increase the specified processing capacity, e.g. program or backing storage, by the amounts required for his software items. The optimum configuration for a given task is sometimes computer dependent. The basic design data, i.e. the processing capacity and the availability requirements, should therefore also be stated in the invitation to tender. This should enable the suppliers to judge whether with their computer a better configuration than that decided on by the designers is feasible, and if so to offer it as an alternative. Any special requirements, whether parity checking on stores, environmental requirements, or special features of operating systems must also be stated.

In addition to the functional aspects the invitation to quote has to state all the other requirements, i.e. numbers of and times at which units are to be supplied, warranties to be given, back-up and spares requirements, training and maintenance facilities, when and where these are to be provided, and anything else that will be needed to produce the system or systems and to keep them going when in operation. Lastly the invitation has to specify the combinations for which prices are to be quoted. These are determined by several factors. There are the reserves of processing capacity which have been added — there is no need, for instance, to purchase the reserve main store at the outset. A mixed-origin configuration may be considered with various items from different suppliers. Also, separate prices for some items may be required in order to determine whether it would be better to procure them from outside or to produce them internally.

The operational system may not be a suitable configuration for developing the programs. A quotation may be required for the purchase or rent of such a program development facility. This should match available support programs such as editors and compilers and take advantage of other aids like multiple-programmer use.

Two of the processing capacity parameters, the actual processing load and the program storage, appear in the invitation to tender in a computer-dependent form. The supplier needs to know the instruction set with timings of the computer assumed in the sizing, the type of processing involved, e.g. bit manipulation or fixed-point arithmetic, and how much multiplication and division is involved. This should enable the supplier to assess which model in his range will provide the required processing capacity. He should be asked to attach to his quotation an instruction set with timings of the model he proposes so that his assessment can be checked.

It is sometimes suggested, particularly by people who are more concerned with the justification of the choice than with actually in making it, that the decision on the offers submitted by suppliers should be made in two stages: all proposals are first screened to see whether they meet the requirements; then the cheapest one of those that do is selected. Unfortunately, this is not a practical proposition. In the first place determining with certainty whether a computer will or will not meet the requirements may involve a lot of work; secondly, the real point at issue is which computer will result in the most cost-effective system or systems, which is not necessarily the same thing as the cheapest machine which meets the specification. Furthermore, from the information in the quotation varying degrees of mixed-origin procurement may be found appropriate for different machines; similarly, there may be different choices as to what items should be bought in or produced internally. The configurations which would be bought in from different suppliers may therefore not be comparable.

The correct procedure is to carry out an initial assessment of each offer to determine whether it is likely to meet the requirements and, if so, the approximate total cost of the system or systems. In the case of machines which do not provide adequate processing capacity but which are particularly cheap, and when it is also known that there is a model with greater processing capacity, it may be worth inviting the supplier concerned to make a further offer in terms of the more powerful model. Similarly, when a manufacturer appears to be offering too powerful a model he may be invited to offer a cheaper one.

Computers which are clearly unsuitable technically or appear to be far more costly than the cheapest one are eliminated and one goes on to a more thorough assessment of the remaining machines. For this a more precise measure of the actual processing capacity will probably be necessary. To do this appropriate *benchmark* programs will have to be used. Benchmarks have been criticized as inaccurate. However, this largely arises through attempts to cover a wide area of applicability, e.g. all process-control applications, and through attempting to include input-output operations. As has been seen, the latter is quite unnecessary, since input-output operations can be quantified in a computer-independent manner anyway. Benchmark programs specific to the type of actual processing in the particular application have to be prepared. Since speed differences between computers greatly exceed variations in the efficiency with which they pack instructions into store, the benchmarks should be representative of the tasks taking up the bulk of the processing time. This is normally not too difficult to achieve, since by the nature of automatic computing most of the time is spent on the innermost loops of the repetitive routines. Several short programs representative of the types of processing involved are thus selected. These benchmark programs are coded and timed on the computer assumed for sizing.

The actual processing load is now analyzed to see what proportions of the total time are taken up by the several types of processing. The results may need correcting for any special features of the machine used for sizing. For instance, if it is considered that multiply and divide take an unusually long time compared with other instructions, the percentage of time spent on tasks which use these instructions heavily should be reduced accordingly. Weighting factors for each of the benchmark programs are then determined such that, within the total of the weighted execution times of all the benchmark programs, the percentages taken up by the various types of processing match those in the actual processing load. This total of weighted execution times provides a measure of the actual processing capacity of the computer assumed for sizing, for that type of application. Similarly, a mix of the instruction types weighted in proportions appropriate to the application give store-occupancy benchmarks. This provides a measure of the program-storage efficiency of the computer assumed for sizing. Some machines may run a program faster, but occupy more words of store for the program than another machine.

The tasks performed by the benchmark programs then have to be specified in a machine-independent, complete, and unambiguous manner. These specifications are sent to the remaining potential suppliers to have them coded by experienced programmers and to return the listings with timings and store occupancies. The listings are checked for conformity to the specification, for errors in the timing and occupancy computations, and also to see whether the manner and quality of coding are those which one would expect to find in normal use of the particular computer. Any coding which does not comply with this should be returned to the supplier for re-coding. The logical way to use the benchmarks would have been to ask the suppliers to propose a machine for which the total of weighted times to execute the benchmarks does not exceed a given limit. This, however, is a dangerous procedure as it may lead the suppliers to optimize their coding to a degree far exceeding that which would be achieved in normal use. When the benchmarks are used in the manner just described, one would expect an accuracy of some 20% in the results.

The results of the benchmarks, coupled with a more thorough evalua-tion of the other features of the machine, allow greater certainty in deter-mining whether a machine meets the requirements. Those which do not are eliminated. A more accurate assessment of the total cost of using each of the machines is now made. The more promising machines are subjected to in-depth evaluations. The various experts on specific aspects of system design will have to be involved in these evaluations until they are all satis-fied that the machine really does meet their specialist requirements. All too often these specialized checks are not done thoroughly enough. It is seen that the selection process consists of a pyramid of assessments of increas-ing depth of progressively smaller numbers of computers. Two further considerations often complicate the selection process. One is the possi-bility of reducing the total cost of bought-out items by purchasing various items from their individually cheapest sources — the so-called mixed-origin approach. It will unavoidably extend and complicate the administrative aspects of the project implementation. The technical risks involved in the mixed-origin approach depend on the extent to which the particular combinations, whether of hardware items or hardware and software, are field proven. Information on this should therefore be sought. The other complicating factor is credibility. With the rapid rate of development of computers, machines may have to be considered off the drawing board from an established manufacturer. This situation is not unique to the com-puter industry and can usually be resolved by assessing the technical status of the new design, coupled with an assessment of the place of the new com-puter in the supplier's product-development policy and with an appraisal of the supplier's track record. Another credibility problem is that of the newly established supplier with no track record. The key question is whether the management and backing of the new company is of a caliber which will ensure that they will succeed in achieving their objectives. The investigation needed to answer this question has to be carried out to a depth commensurate with the risk involved. The offer in question will therefore need to have a big enough competitive advantage to justify starting this investigtion.

6.3.5. The Use of Simulation

Simulating a system means developing a model of the system and then seeing how it responds to inputs, refining the model and drawing conclusions to assist the design of the actual system. The simulation technique can be used at several levels in the development of a real-time system.

To simulate the complete operational policy to check and improve the design.

To simulate the computer system as so far described in § 6.3, to check that it can handle the traffic, and to verify other design aspects.

To simulate the chosen computer equipment on another machine so that programs can be developed before the actual computer chosen is available. This is called emulation.

To simulate the environment for the computer system in order to test this new system, once developed.

Well-known examples of the type of simulation needed to check an operational policy are management and war games or the Club of Rome simulation of the future of our planet (3). The problem with such simulations is that they have to be so simplified as to become unrealistic.

The next level, simulation of the computer system to be designed to see if it is suitable, is quite feasible. One can examine the effects of mapping in multi-level store, of various scheduling methods, and find which processes have the most critical effect on the important parameters in the system. However, this requires very many variables and many of these are highly interdependent. A particular instruction set or interrupt vectoring may only be available on a restricted range of configurations. The effect of scheduling cannot be seen unless processor loads are already estimated for each process. To test in fault conditions or traffic overload would require a highly developed model of the particular application. If estimates are wrong the model will be wrong too and the wrong conclusions will be drawn. When embarking on a project the manager of the design team normally finds he has a definite budget and would need much convincing to spend time and money developing a model rather than the real thing, for adaptable models are not known to exist that can be readily turned to new applications of real-time systems. Moreover, the benefits from such simulation are mainly in the verification of the analysis which was necessary before the model could be built. Models tend not to show up faults which have not already been allowed for; it is just as hard to develop a model which will respond to faulty input as it is to develop the real thing. It is probable that situations not foreseen in model tests are very much the same as those overlooked if one proceeds directly with the project itself. Simulations have been known to prove what the designers wanted proved, even when utterly wrong. It will still be some time before computer architecture and software technology are amenable to simple modeling in a way that will enable specific designs for a variety of applications to be tested economically or rigorously. At present the tools are too expensive and not powerful enough to simulate a whole system.

The third use of simulation, to *emulate* or act like equipment not yet available, has been used by many concerns, mostly engineering organizations who have been developing a new product (4,5,6). Here the economics are better if one is trying to develop or test a design which will go into quantity production. For a single project which uses particular equipment, unless an emulator exists, it may be best to wait for the actual machine, provided the project time scale allows. Otherwise, one could look for a revised plan or the use of equivalent equipment before resorting to the cost of developing an emulator. Simulating the environment to test the real-time computer system when it has been developed is discussed in Chapter 7. The benefits of using simulation as opposed to test gear which is a sample of the real environment will depend on the application.

When considering simulation, the costs in manpower, time, and computer time need to be estimated in advance and justified in clearly reducing the risk of proceeding directly with the real implementation of the design. This should prevent simulations being done just because somebody fancies doing one, greatly exceeding the budgeted effort in the process.

By and large, if analysis and design are well thought out simulation is unnecessary, while if they are not simulation will not help but will merely become an expensive effort sink.

6.3.6. Design to Implementation

The computer-evaluation process may well raise issues concerning the computer configuration. These have to be cleared up and the whole configuration given a final review, after which it is frozen. Complete functional and design specifications for all major components are finalized. Some of the components, whether hardware or software, may be produced internally while others may be subcontracted out. For the former, implementation plans are prepared, while for the latter quotations will be obtained, including delivery dates, against full specifications. The part of the outline plan (see § 6.1) concerned with the implementation of the design can now be detailed and implementation can start.

This book does not go into the methods for producing hardware, as these are well accepted. The next section deals with the design of software, and it will be seen that the methods for the successful production of software are analogous to those which are widely accepted for hardware.

6.4. Software Development

6.4.1. Software Design

Armed with the functional specification, a known equipment configuration, and the system design document, pure software design can proceed. It is still too early to start writing programs. The facilities of the operating system or executive have been listed, and now the design of each facility not already in existence must be undertaken. Similarly the areas of the application functions have been defined and approximate size and time estimates made. Now an exact specification for each process is required and the main data structure must be laid down. Interrupt and other programs to run at higher levels of priority need to be identified along with the method of scheduling or otherwise passing control between programs. Files and programs are mapped onto the various storage devices. Plans are made to gather certain application data for permanent storage and define more exactly system interfaces and user interaction in more detail.

This mixture of activities needs sorting out. The software designer may find it convenient to divide them into broad areas such as software structure, interaction with the outside, and application functions.

The software-structure design defines the functions of the operating system, the level of each program, the data structure, and the store mapping. The relation between application and executive and utility programs is defined, preferably in a simple way that can be shown in a diagram. Programming conventions are laid down, including for instance subroutine calling, labeling, and programming language. This software-structure document may also be suitable for maintaining a list of names of all program packages and files to be in the system with estimates and progress indicators. It will be seen that such a document occupies a central position in the development of the software. It can become an instrument for technical management, as described in § 6.5.

The second broad area, defining interactions with the outside, gives a highly detailed definition of the interfaces of the software part of the system, with surrounding equipment and with operators in the particular application. This part of the design cannot proceed in isolation, but requires discussion with those responsible for the other equipment or for operator functions. For equipment, the signaling, buffering, data content, and error actions are agreed. For operators and users, the input sequences, report formats, and display-screen layouts are defined to the extent that they can be programmed on the one hand and written into users' manuals on the other hand.

The application areas, already roughly enumerated for size estimating, now have to be described in more detail. A good starting point may be found in describing the main files, especially those shared by several processors. The record formats are defined showing exactly what parameters are stored and their units. Next, the input and output buffers for the processes are described, defining pointers, queue lengths, and points of interaction with the executive and utility programs and with those programs beyond the buffers which interface to the outside world. This defines the environment for the application programs, protected as suggested in Chapter 4 from the asynchronous vagaries of real time. Attention can now be paid to the processes themselves, listing their component programs, subroutines, and internal interfaces. If processes are broken down into individual functions, an accurate description can be given for each. At last attention returns again to the useful algorithms which are the main *raison d'être* for the system. The outcome is a list of the application programs with a specification for each.

This software-design phase resulting in the production of these documents is a significant task and may take some time. The broad areas overlap and interact so some iteration is necessary within the design phase. Because of this duration and because the software design should become firm before programming starts, the design stage needs to be a planned activity on the software time scale with an identified completion date. If this date is not achieved in the event, one may find it wise to delay the start of coding.

Without a target date not only is the grip on progress lost, but, more seriously, awkward parts of the design may get shelved. These are just the parts that need attention; if they are neglected the result is usually a dissatisfying reduction in the actual capability of the final system or the need for extra expenditure and delay for additional equipment or further programming.

Typical results of incomplete software design are to find that programs are too large for the main store, that there are more programs to write than expected, that interrupts interfere with shared data, that display or report formats are not as required, that the system recovery programs were omitted, that misunderstandings have arisen between programmers, and that the intended expansion capability has been absorbed either by user requests or by programmer enthusiasm. On the other hand, the reward for completing the software design and producing a written description is to have a means of communication, of checking, of management, and above all a source of confidence and stability. We now have the program specifications.

6.4.2. Software Management

In an engineering system components are produced in a co-ordinated manner, each component being identified, its development or procurement and integration being planned and monitored. Those responsibile for it fit a disciplined reporting structure. In dedicated systems, software is merely a system component, a point made at some length in this book where as much attention is given to the place of software as to its internal nature.

There is no reason at all why software development should not conform to traditional management practices. In the past there may have been an excuse, but now that technology is no longer new. The stages of software design, development, and test mentioned in this chapter and throughout the book are well established. A manager may decide that to follow them need not be a futile striving for an academic ideal. A real worry, however, is how to monitor progress through stages, especially if he is not a software expert fully involved in the programming task. What tools are there? As for other technologies, he can consider staff progress reports, and he can request time scale estimates and agree milestones. These milestones are the equivalent to engineering drawing release, bill of materials, component delivery dates, assembly, unit test, and system-test schedules. To a manager the analogy is encouragingly close.

Given a top-down design, the component list is readily available: a list of programs. The milestones marking the end of each stage for each component can be plotted on a plan. The order of integration of build-up in the bottom-up method of implementation requires considerable thought.

A mass even of perfect programs should not be thrown together at once, but built up through "unit" test, each unit being checked out in progressive stages of build. The phasing of integration needs to match the availability of equipment, information, and other resources. It may be that the supervisory software should appear first, followed by the "housekeeping" utility programs, only incorporating the fundamental application algorithms in the later stages. It seems that the order of build-up is less important than the need to have an explicit plan.

The plan should include stages for testing software with project hardware; because the latter may not be perfect initially, the suggestion was made to build the software from the framework inwards to the algorithms. For instance, the ability to display a CRT picture needs proving before the correctness of data displayed. However, if the suggestion of buffering as much of the software as possible from real time is taken, nearly all the build-up can take place independently of interface testing. A real-time clock can conveniently simulate external events. Such parallel development can reduce project time scales at the usually critical integration stages.

Of course the project manager will have drawn the overall plan before design commenced, but it is at this bottom stage, when programs have all been specified, that much more detail is required. The plan to completion may now look something like Fig. 6.5.

We now have a detailed design and an implementation plan. A further ingredient is required. Programming procedures need to be set: standards defining the language, coding conventions, documentation required, program test, and issue procedures, and so on.

Programs can now be written.

6.4.3. Programming

Designers responsible for particular areas can be encouraged not to look down on the coding task. They may either carry out the task or, for large projects, direct a section of the implementation team, always retaining responsibility for successful implementation. Otherwise the luckless coder has a miserable task to put right any design errors if the disdainful analyst has moved on to other work. A key factor seems to be to have a well-defined team who fully identify for the time being with the project, each member having a responsibility defined in terms of the implementation plan. Indeed names could appear beside events and milestones on the plan. For the designer to carry responsibility through implementation can reap benefits in efficiency in three ways. The first is that of good motivation. The second is through the reduction of relearning. The third is that the tasks tend to fall more naturally into separable areas with this vertical division of the team. For a chief designer to hand over to a programming leader seems a poor approach. In this important respect the analogy with traditional production engineering does not apply — not because of some essential difference but because the engineering tradition is wrong. It is common practice to hand engineering design to the drawing office. Better results through better motivation have been found by assigning draftsmen to the project team for the duration of that activity. No only are attitudes better, but efficiency is improved and there are fewer errors. The advantage of integrated design teams has also been demonstrated by experience in software implementation (7). A career structure in software engineering is also provided in this way.

Coding can proceed very fast indeed, having specifications at the program level, design knowledge in the team, and target milestones. The size of a component program at the bottom level should be such that the programmer can totally encompass it and at all times fully understand that component. Close communication between those responsible for areas of software implementation is needed. As at other levels of design, omissions and inconsistencies tend to occur at the seams between system components designed by different designers. As in other areas of human endeavor, there is the likelihood of one person assuming that his neighbor will look after this or that, or of people making inconsistent assumptions. A programmer often finds it necessary to make assumptions where the specification leaves room for choice. A discipline is for such decisions to be referred, resolved in a consistent way, and documented. One quickly learns what should have been defined in the specification.

Emphasis has been placed on the design stages. The actual task of producing the programs, though they may be numerous, has been minimized. Techniques of coding are not discussed at length in this book because they depend on language and machine, but are essentially the same as in non-real-time applications. The main differences between real-time programs and others is the need to observe the storage and execution-time estimates. Other considerations were discussed in Chapter 4. Minimizing the coding stage makes it more acceptable to analysts, does not require legions of coders, and allows maximum time for the design before programming, where rework is expensive, and for integration tests.

6.4.4. *Program Test and Issue*

As an individually tested program emerges it needs to reach a formal state before being integrated into the next higher level of build-up, otherwise it will, under pressure of time or overconfidence, creep in untested and possibly undocumented. The formal state is the completion of documentation for that program, including test results. It is then said to be "issued". The purpose of subsequent integration stages is to check all the seams, so tests need to be oriented to do this.

The method of bottom-up implementation requires each program module be tested before integration into larger packages. These in turn are tested before incorporating into the growing system. Much of the early testing is off-line, being to test the program logic for correctness and completeness. Test data should include representative sets, extreme cases, and faulty data. If someone other than the programmer writes the test data, unexpected situations may be brought to light. Test data and results may be included in the documentation of programs which are offered for "issue" — a formal state which each program must attain before integration into the next stage of build-up, even where interactive programming is possible.

A quick method of editing and retesting programs is most valuable at this stage. Tested programs integrated into packages can also be tested in this off-line fashion, or in pseudo real-time using, say, a clock interrupt. The real-time framework is separately tested, checking hardware interfaces, interrupt mechanisms, and supervisory or framework software. This minimizes confusion by separating errors in real-time input and output from logic errors in application algorithms.

Because a manager knows which programmers are producing which programs, he can readily judge their efficiency, having regard to the complexity of the algorithms and the completeness of the specifications. It is common to find that some programmers are 10 times more productive than others. Others may be better at checking and documenting. A programmer whose coding runs far ahead of his issued (documented and tested) programs is a liability.

If the designers remain on the implementation team, they are still available for the important stages of system test and commissioning.

The commonest problem in integration is lack of testing time. A finite time is required to check seams and overall functions even if no faults are found. Further time of course is needed to remedy any faults. Check-out time can be estimated. Remedy time can only be guessed at from experience. Some contingency must be allowed, especially if first-time hardware equipment is involved.

6.4.5. Real-Time Test and Diagnostics

The tested packages are incorporated in a phased manner into the framework system for real-time test. At this stage, sources of realistic data are required, real or simulated in some way.

At real-time test a high degree of confidence exists for each program brick and for whole packages. However, unexpected interactive effects are frequently found. Some are hard to trace, being only present in the "real" situation. Therefore one requires diagnostic facilities within the real-time system to monitor dynamic parameters both in the supervisory and the application areas and to permit on-line switching of test points. A very useful debugging aid is to display on a CRT the changing values of selected parameters whether they be queue lengths, application data, or contents of suspect store areas. A further aid is to give periodic hardcopy print-out of selected variables in convenient format. The aids will be needed for unexpected uses and should therefore be flexible rather than sophisticated or too specific. They should allow the option of on-line use and not rely on stopping the system.

Monitoring programs are often needed to record traffic and activity levels, to save certain data faster than can be printed on, say, a console typewriter or seen on a CRT. Therefore a general logging facility is valuable to save selected information in real time for later dumping. A "snapshot" of the software state can be taken in this way for later cool analysis. The period of the "exposure" and the parameters recorded will need to be selected on an *ad hoc* or trial basis. It is unlikely that preplanned views will be those that are required the next day.

A useful utility for the commissioning phase is a subroutine or program which reads in real time a set of switches which can be set and reset by the operator during running. A keyboard can be used, or perhaps more directly the key switches on the computer's own console panel. According to switch setting, temporary real-time actions can be taken in the software, such as a selective trace, measurement of task run times, and so on. Preplanned situations can be prepared and then affected or recorded during running at the instant the tester wishes by setting a switch. Such diagnosis need not perturb the normal real-time running which is under test or examination.

When it comes to field trials or commissioning the system in the real situation with actual operators or user equipment, the performance may need to be checked. The same diagnostics are useful, especially timing measurements and logging facilities. The latter can help to catch that elusive transient fault which only arises in certain rare combinations of instructions or peripheral activity. If a log of the preceding period is maintained, on a cyclic basis, overwriting an area of store, then when the fault does occur the system can be stopped manually or by an automatic trap, allowing subsequent scrutiny of the events which led up to the situation. A repetition of the same events each time the fault occurs can give useful clues to tracking possible causes.

A combined hardware and software investigation may be needed to trace certain faults, especially when both software staff and hardware engineers are each convinced that a fault is not in their area. Simple interface test and input-output logging programs may resolve the simpler cases, proving by undisputed programs just what data was received or sent. For more involved situations staff may need encouragement to co-operate in a combined investigation using hardware test aids and diagnostic software at the same time to look for synchronous events.

If, as is usually the case, commissioning before the acceptance tests has been only partial, perhaps owing to limitations of other equipment or environment available, then frequently there are unexpected faults when a system goes live in earnest. Some bedding-down time or period of parallel running with a previous system may be necessary initially. However, it is generally found that the mean time between failures increases encouragingly as the "last" bugs are removed. Dedicated systems that are not frequently changed quickly become highly reliable in software and are then limited by the hardware.

There remain, however, the occasional "funnies". As traffic increases or patterns change, software timing effects can occur and even logic errors can show up. Selected diagnostic programs should therefore be left in the system. These allow causes of faults to be traced in the same ways as used for testing. Other faults often arise owing to changes in hardware, particularly drift in critical timing circuits. When possible, the periodic routine running of maintenance programs which fully exercise and test the hardware is desirable. The benefits are similar to the required tuning of a car engine and other preventive maintenance. Experience of such obscure or difficult faults in real-time systems is necessarily scattered and so slow to accumulate that a book of collected actual cases would be most valuable to the systems engineer.

6.4.6. Software Acceptance Tests

Very often real-time tests in a user environment, field trials, are not possible until a long time after off-line or simulated real-time tests are complete. This may be due to certain related equipment not being available, or to the user not being ready, or, worse still, to uncertainties arising from possible changes in requirement! However, the software team must have their product checked, to know what may be wrong, to be able to release staff, or possibly to claim payment. From the user's point of view there is then proven software available in a disciplined state and less likely to cause trouble during field trials.

Therefore, it is advocated that there should be acceptance tests specifically for the software or at least for the software and actual computer equipment, even if it is recognized that full commissioning tests, possibly on another site, and field trials may still be necessary. The object is to prove that the technical objectives have been met. If it can coincide with full system tests by the user, so much the better, but if not, as is generally the case, there should be prior acceptance tests for the software. They still need as much as possible of the surrounding hardware. In this chapter we are concerned with these tests in clinical conditions to see if the technical goals have been met. Chapter 7 deals with the user's active involvement and the running of field trials.

The technical goals were set in the functional specification, so this is the source which should be used for deriving the acceptance tests. The tests to be carried out need to be described in detail in an acceptance-test specification. The degree of detail is such that each necessary action, such as loading up the system, is explicit and unambiguous, so that anyone not familiar with the internal system could carry out the tests and so that the tests could be accurately repeated at a later date if necessary. Advantage may be gained by someone not on the design implementation team drawing up the acceptance tests.

Before running the tests they should be agreed with those who are to accept the system as truly proving that it does carry out all the specified functions with the required performance. Acceptance tests should be run in a formal manner with the accepting authority witnessing the results. In this way attention is focused on running the tests rather than on last-minute refinements or discussion of possible changes — these can follow acceptance if they are required — and one knows in a rather definite manner whether the goals have been met or whether certain aspects need further attention. Whatever the result, it is of value to all concerned. A more gradual and implied acceptance is less satisfactory all round: the implementers are uncertain what still needs to be done; the user cannot get sole use of a settled system and may be less inclined to pay for it.

The tests need to show that appropriate output does result from the test inputs for all logical paths, separately and as far as convenient simultaneously with interacting and independent paths. Further, capacity tests should check for adequate storage and power in terms of response and throughput. If full traffic conditions cannot be easily generated, the system should provide data to enable unambiguous extrapolation. It is not necessary to run detailed tests to check the overall performance from outside, at the same level as defined in the functional specification. They may be in a detailed or general form, the point being to agree that they prove the system, so they must not be ambiguous or open to wide interpretation. The time to work out, agree, and eventually run the tests should not be underestimated. Neither should their importance. Without them the software stays amorphous; who can say the job is done or use the system confidently?

6.5. Documentation

Too often development, especially software development, is prematurely claimed to be 90% complete. How can a manager assess the claim and monitor progress to detect and alleviate the tendency for eleventh-hour escalation of software effort putting project time scales and expenditure in jeopardy? This can be done by having two tools: an outline plan of the project with a consistent software plan showing completion dates of each stage with estimates of manpower required, and a list of the documents that have to be produced. If milestones on the plan are identified as documentation completion dates, the manager has a real grip on the situation. This section offers some suggestions for achieving this.

. At various points in this book the need for documentation has been highlighted, to meet technical requirements for having design decisions recorded, programs in readable form, and so on. Documentation is required not only for such communication but also for discipline and control. It can also provide a tangible asset. Here we are just concerned with documentation as a useful management tool.

One can say that the documentation state is the state of the project. If a document is complete, that stage is complete. It does not follow that the contents are appropriate or correct unless the document has some place within it to record that the necessary checks have been carried out. For example, a program's documentation should include the test data and results, the latter being shown as checked for correctness; acceptance tests need a place to indicate when the test has been successfully completed and so on. Approached in this way, the documents can be planned to show when project stages are complete. To complete a whole project every document must be finished, so it follows that a list of these documents is required in order to know when the job is done. If this list is produced at the project-planning stage and if completion dates and effort estimates are given against each entry in the list, then one has a means of measuring progress against the plan and can take corrective action.

Besides the list of documents, it is necessary to state beforehand what shall be in each of the documents, else how can one know if it has been completed? This is equivalent to setting documentation standards. Producing and worse still reading such standards manuals can be boring and time consuming. Given outline standards, being a list of documents and the purpose and nature of each, a more direct approach has been tried with success. This is actually to create all the planned physical documents early in the project, literally meaning a row of empty files and so on, but these files are labeled and have contents lists. Moreover, pages within the files can state what information must be entered on them with an indicated space for signing as checked where appropriate. This means that some forms can be prepared, taking care, however, not to be unnecessarily restrictive. As the project proceeds the files are filled directly. When each document is complete, this is recorded on the list which can be compared against the plan at any time.

Having at the outset a real set of empty documents reduces the need for rewriting notes — one knows what writing is necessary and documents directly. It avoids the tendency to skip retrospective documenting in favor of the next urgent stage. Further, a well-planned set of documents and carefully specified contents headings help ensure that decisions are made and work proceeds in the right order, especially if the "top-down" approach is used for design and phased integration for testing. The set of documents reflects the structure and stages of the plan.

Quite apart from the progress monitoring, the list of documents avoids nasty surprises such as realizing rather late the need for written acceptance tests, user and maintenance manuals, and so on. Of course documents have value for reference, not only during development and test but for maintenance and for future use in similar or related work. To this end they are a real and tangible asset, sometimes even saleable, but always reducing dependence on the memory or the continuity of staff.

Returning to the list of planned documents, this is itself a key standard and may take the same form for many types of project. The list should be included in a *project control document* along with the outline plan and plans for each subsystem, financial estimates, and so on. It acts as an index for other documents at the same time as recording their planned and current status.

Let us consider the entries in this documentation list, created at the project planning stage and kept updated in the project control document. Because the documents reflect the project structure and stages, it is natural that they correspond to the activities cited earlier in this chapter. An example of the list for a software-oriented project is given below.

Project control document
Functional specification
System design specification
Functions of each subsystem
Design specification for each subsystem
Software specification
Software structure
Program specification
Programs
Commissioning plans: installation, build-up, cut-over
User acceptance tests
Training and user manuals
Maintenance and manufacturers' handbooks
Administrative records

We consider each of these in turn.

6.5.1. The Project Control Document

This is a management document containing the following.

Terms of reference for the project
Summary of objectives for the system
Financial budget, current and projected monthly expenditure chart
Outline plan with major milestones
Documentation list
Staff reporting structure diagram
System block diagram

The terms of reference and summary of objectives delineate the responsibility and aims of the project team. The agreed budget can be shown as planned expenditure month by month on a graph so that a further plot of actual expenditure, updated monthly, can be used to assess probable cost to completion. The outline plan and documentation list are described in this chapter. An explicit staff-structure diagram is required and should be no embarrassment — if it is, there are problems to be solved right away, The system block diagram is useful for reference and for explanation to others interested in the nature of the project.

Although the project control document is for the benefit of the project manager, it would be nice if it were available for perusal by his staff, who like to know what goes on, and by his managers who may gain increased confidence or at least awareness. The document should be created at the outset of the project.

6.5.2. The Functional Specification

This has been discussed in Chapter 2 and earlier in this chapter. It is the interface between the designer/developer and the user. Its contents must be agreed before design starts as it sets out what the system has to achieve in terms of function and performance. It forms the basis for the design specification, the acceptance tests, and the user manuals. Everyone concerned needs to read it. It will be a help in formulating future systems.

6.5.3. System Design Specification

As described earlier in this chapter, this states what the system has to do internally to perform the required functions. It identifies subsystems and is the first stage of "top-down" design. Designers with extensive experience in the field of the application have much to contribute to this document.

6.5.4. Functional and Design Specifications for Subsystems

The two sets of descriptions state on the one hand the functions each subsystem has to perform in terms of its inputs and outputs to other subsystems, and on the other hand the method and type of equipment to be used for that subsystem. Notice that the subsystems tend to correspond to separable functions. There may be a number of stages in this progressive breakdown into finer subsystems.

6.5.5. Software Functional Specification

This is that member or members of the set of subsystem specifications that is concerned with the computer functions. Other members are concerned with equipment and related systems. The software specification makes it clear what jobs have to be done within the computer as opposed to those performed by the surrounding equipment. For instance, it will be clear whether in a computer-controlled exchange the computer handles the data or just controls switched connections and whether signaling is analysed by software or decoded by special equipment. The main software functions are indentified and broken down into software packages, each eventually being expressed as a list of programs.

6.5.6. Software Structure

Technically this is the crux of the software design: knowing the computer configuration and the nature and facilities of the operating system or supervisory software as defined. The methods of handling the major data files, of responding to input and output, and of running programs are set out here. This is the software framework into which the useful software packages containing the application algorithms will fit. This document contains the following.

 Description of the configuration
 Outline of supervisory or "systems" software
 Descriptions of structures of main files
 Input–output methods
 Scheduling control to or from application programs
 Recovery techniques
 Computer operator facilities
 Analysis of storage allocation, throughput, and response

Method of using support software in the development

Clearly expressed, the software framework is then understood by programmers and engineers who can then better appreciate the way their part of the work fits in and the way the system responds to traffic and to hardware situations. It similarly gives a better idea of the system capabilities to interested users and to those concerned with similar future systems.

6.5.7. Program Specifications

Two initial things are required. First, there should be a list of all the programs that have to be written, arranged by packages or main functions, including those needed for development, support, testing, diagnostics, maintenance, and any supervisory or "systems" programs not in the existing software supplied with the computer. Secondly, there needs to be a diagram for each package showing clearly the relationships between the identified programs. Each program may be a block on the diagram, the hierarchy of which shows which programs call on which subprograms and routines.

For each program so identified, there needs to be a description of its function, its interfaces with other software, a list of the files and data it accesses, and other details needed for coding the program. Estimates of size and typical or worst running time are required. In this program specification document, the list of programs is the index or contents list. The list and the diagram of program relationships may also appear in the software structure document if the system is sufficiently dedicated so that the application and supervisory software are not separable.

6.5.8. Programs

Each of the identified programs is to be documented. This includes the following:

Name of program
Actual size and running times
Entry/exit conditions
Files accessed
Detailed logic
Program listing
Programmers' comments
Test data, results, and check signature

Some programmers prefer to describe the detailed logic by flow diagrams, others by commented program listing. In either case a paragraph or two of prose can be invaluable to others and little burden on the programmers. As with other documents, completeness is achieved through the demands of the checker. The only way a program can be considered complete and released for inclusion in package build-up is by obtaining his signature. This discipline can save the expense of undue optimism at this stage. Even where programs can be written and tested interactively on an actual or development system, some equivalent form of documentation is required, for checking, future reference, and for progress monitoring. A criterion for documenting programs is a level adequate for others to understand the program and to know when it is complete and correct.

6.5.9. Commissioning Plans

This involves the following.

The build-up of software packages
Integration of hardware and other subsystems
Levels of testing
Installation details
Introduction to operational use

The need here is for a recorded plan, being an amplification of the integration stage on the outline plan, and notes as to the intended method of commissioning. This can include a check-list of points to deal with, resources required, and so on. The content will vary widely with type of project but it helps if the project manager records his plan in advance. The actual commissioning after installation is discussed in Chapter 7.

6.5.10. User Acceptance Tests

This is a document important as one tool in defining whether technical objectives have been met. The need for these tests and the need to write them out beforehand should be agreed with the user at an early stage, often as part of a contract. The purpose and nature of acceptance tests are such that the user will accept their successful completion as proving that the requirements of the functional specification have been met. The document is not just a protection for the developer against changes in the user's requirement, heart, or staff. It is also an aid to the user in helping him realize his own responsibilities as described in Chapter 7. The document and the eventual signatures therein are considered a vital ingredient in the measurement of success of a system.

6.5.11. Training and User Manuals

These are for the user's staff to become acquainted with what are to be their new tasks when they come to work with the system and for reference during their work. In the latter case, for the user manuals, the information may be condensed to a small, handy form. The contents of these books need to be worked out from the functional specification in close liaison with the user, to match the operational procedures as described in Chapter 7. Again the time taken to produce these books is usually significant, but they can contribute enormously to the smooth, willing acceptance of the system by the user staff. They can also help staff get greater benefit out of the system by using it in the way it was intended. These books should be the most heavily used in the life of the system and the only documentation of the system that many user staff will have. They are worth producing well and should be thorough.

6.5.12. Maintenance and Manufacturers' Handbooks

These are standard handbooks as traditionally supplied with units of equipment. In the case of software they are often limited to instructions for running programs that prove hardware. In real-time computer systems one often finds all the equipment passes such tests but still a fault prevents the application programs from running. There will probably be enough faults on a system, besides transient faults and deep software problems, to justify a manual for non-programmers to perform simple tests using the on-line software to help determine the probable area of the faults.

If the software maintenance is to be performed locally other than by the original design staff, documentation is needed to help take advantage of the designer's attempts to allow for easy modification and enhancement. Often such good thoughts go unrecorded, making it difficult for others to make simple changes even to parameter values and tables. In many cases a reference to appropriate sections of the software structure document may be sufficient.

In systems where modularity was intended to be of lasting benefit or where table-driven techniques are used, software maintenance manuals are most valuable and can save time and costs of needing the designers for making simple changes. The presence of such documents determines whether the on-line software does indeed retain its attraction of changeability, being soft, or whether it is a firm knot no one can touch without arduously tracing through much program detail.

There may be opportunity to write software maintenance manuals during the equipment installation period when software staff might be held up. This could be forgotten if the document was not shown on the documentation list.

6.5.13. Administrative Records

These are for the use of project management and are applicable to many types of project. They help in the organization of the non-technical tasks. The following are some of the prepared files that may be useful.

Progress minutes
Contracts and subcontracts
Purchasing and delivery
Accounting records
Shipping and installation
Daily project log
Personnel matters

Of course the list depends on the nature of the project, and many other treatises on project management can deal more extensively with this topic (8). The principle suggested here is to foresee the type of non-technical work and plan to deal with it. One can then follow a plan rather than be driven by events. Because no two projects may be the same, this is only an ideal to which nevertheless one can aspire. The anticipation of the extent of non-technical matters may help the project manager to assess whether he needs administrative assistance before he has become so overloaded with attending to these matters that he cannot keep abreast of fundamental progress and problems. In this respect, an engineering tradition of project management through standard administrative procedures does have an application in computer projects and systems including software. Too often either progress slips because a technical expert has not appreciated the importance of progressing other matters or just as frequently the clerical tasks made inefficient use of his time. In either case, the approach to management through the planned documentation suggested here can and has been found beneficial.

6.5.14. *This Book and Others*

Finally, it is hoped that this book, while not documentation specific to any project, may nevertheless be helpful in organizing the approach to management through documentation.

The authors of the present book would like to see more standard methods established for real-time system design, development, and implementation in order to improve the success rate of such projects by achieving timely, useful, and economic operation. A standard list of the documentation required would help in establishing a reliable method.

References

1. Phillips, C.S.E. Networks for real time programming. *Computer J. 10* (1), 46-52, May 1967.

2. Jackson, K., and Prior, J.R. Debugging and assessment of control programs for an automatic radar. *Computer J. 12* (4), 203-6, Nov. 1969.

3. Forrester, J.W. *World Dynamics*. Wright Allen Press, 1972.

4. MacDougall, M.H., Computer system simulation, an introduction. *Computer Surveys 2*, 191-210, 1970.

5. Huesman, R.L., and Goldberg, R.P. Evaluating computer systems through simulation. *Computer J. 10*, 150-6, 1967.

6. Gordon, G. *System Simulation*. Prentice-Hall, Englewood Cliffs, NJ, 1969.

7. Vaughan, H.E. Development history of No. 1 ESS — software. *Proc. Conf. on Switching Techniques for Telecommunications Networks, IEE Conf. Publ. No. 2*, pp. 475-8. Institution of Electrical Engineers, London.

8. Metzger, P.W. *Managing a Programming Project*. Prentice-Hall, Englewood Cliffs, NJ, 1973.

The User
and the System

7.1. Outline of User Actions

If the procedure described in Chapter 2 led to a decision to adopt a new operational policy, the user is now faced with the task of implementing this new policy. This is to say he has to establish it and bring it into operation. This task, like that of designing the new policy, is one which only the user himself can carry out. Chapters 3, 4, and 5 surveyed the tools and methods for real-time-system design. Chapter 6 described the design and implementation of real-time systems. This chapter resumes where Chapter 2 left off insofar as the work to be done within the user organization is concerned.

The intending user is always responsible for the implementation of the system. It is not enough to agree a specification and, where appropriate, a contract with the suppliers of the computer system and then for the user to sit back and expect to be presented with a panacea to replace his production, communication, or staff problems or be provided with a total smoothly operating system. He needs not just to monitor progress but to prepare for the new system and to bring it into real operation.

The method for implementing the new operational policy has been worked out as part of the design of the policy itself. A full and thorough plan for this task must now be prepared. The various actions to be included in the user's plan are surveyed in this chapter. Because the implementation of the real-time system may require a long time, arranging for its acquisition is often one of the first steps taken. With the functional specification

231

fully defined, the methods for acquiring the system may range all the way from do-it-yourself to the farming out of the complete supply and installation of the real-time system together with the training of the user personnel in its use. This range of possibilities is discussed in § 7.2.1. The user organization may lack skill or experience in any one or more of the various implementation tasks. The possibilities of using consultants to provide the missing skills are discussed in § 7.2.2.

The impact of the new operational policy will range widely within the user organization, often into parts far removed from the computer. A process-control system, for instance, may demand a restructuring of the marketing department to handle the new product mix made available through much closer process control. A road-traffic-control system has been found to affect, among other things, the maintenance of the roadside traffic lights. Such ramifications will have formed part of the design of the operational policy, and preparation for them must now be included in the implementation plan as well, of course, as those parts of the user's total operational system which interact directly with the real-time system. These are referred to as the *environment* in which the real-time system operates (see Fig. 7.1). Section 7.3 is concerned with the preparation of this environment, not just physically, but in preparing new procedures and in staff training. Without adequate preparation the real-time computer system will be rejected — just as a foreign body is rejected by a living organism. It will be rejected as the symbol of and the tool for the new policy, for "new" implies change and change is frightening. The way of overcoming this fear is described in § 7.3.2. Then the requisite organizational and procedural changes can be prepared. This process may highlight points to clarify with those who, usually in a separate team, are implementing the real-time system. This integration to yield workable procedures is discussed in § 7.3.5.

Section 7.4 is devoted to the action following on the actual delivery of the real-time system. The first of these is the conducting of the acceptance tests to determine whether the system as a whole fully meets the agreed functional specification (§ 7.4.1). Once this has been established the actual cut-over to the new operational policy has to be achieved. As can be seen from Fig. 7.2 this is the stage at which the various actions described so far all merge. The several methods for achieving the cut-over are described in § 7.4.2. Inevitably not everything will turn out quite as has been envisaged, nor will it be immediately apparent where precisely the actual fault lies. It will be necessary to compare carefully the actual situation on the ground with the detailed design of the operational policy to determine the precise nature and extent of the fault (§ 7.4.3). Some of the faults identified will be design faults, while other ones will be due to shortcomings in the implementation. Where faults of these two types are interrelated there is the temptation to ask: "Why correct the shortcoming in the implementation to align it with the blueprint when it is already clear that the blueprint will need changing to correct a design fault?" The reasons why this temptation should be resisted are explained in § 7.4.3. Once the new policy is operational as designed, enhancements, either to correct shortcomings in the design or in order to increase benefits, can be evaluated, designed, and implemented in the same way in which this was done for the policy as a whole. The eventual replacement of the system is discussed in § 7.4.6.

So this chapter complements Chapter 6 which was concerned with the technical aspects of real-time systems. Even technically excellent sys-

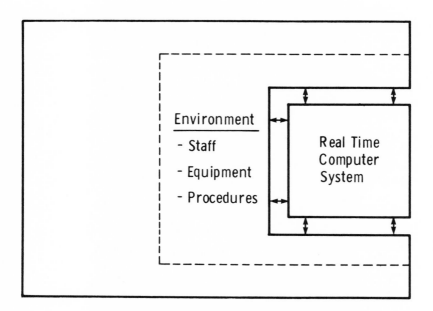

Fig. 7.1. The user's total operational system.

tems have often failed to be useful. This has sometimes been because of the lack of an operational requirement (Chapter 2) or because the user organization has not carried out the actions described in this present chapter.

7.2. Acquisition

7.2.1. Contracting for the Real-Time System

The cost-benefit analysis relied on one or more offers to provide a real-time system to the stated functional specification at a stated cost. Once the decision has been taken to go ahead it becomes necessary to take up one of these offers. The cost-benefit analysis may have been based on an offer from within the user organization. This does not necessarily mean that the user organization will do all the work, or even most of it, itself. Almost certainly the computer will be bought out. Some or all of the software may be subcontracted out, as may be special-purpose hardware. No matter how much of the system implementation is subcontracted, the decisive distinction is where the responsibility lies for ensuring that the resulting system will meet the functional specification. This responsibility cannot satisfactorily be shared between the user organization and an outside subcontractor, not that there has been a lack of attempts to do just this. Such attempts usually follow the situation described in Chapter 2, in which engineers are given the task of specifying the system. Having produced their ideas on the design the engineers then go to outside contractors and ask them to engineer a system to this design which would also provide certain operational facilities — without a full functional specification ever having been produced. There usually follows a period of discussions with one or more of the potential subcontractors to clear up or detail further points in the design. These discussions may even glory in such high-sounding names as project-definition study. The eventual contract is based both on the design, or the part of it, which has been hammered out in these discussions and on an undertaking that the system will meet certain operational requirements. The resulting system will eventually emerge, at best, as the design by committee that it is. The recriminations as to whose fault it was will reverberate for years to come. Sometimes they end up in a court of law, with each party relying on various sections of an essentially contradictory contract.

If the user organization is itself to assume the responsibility that the

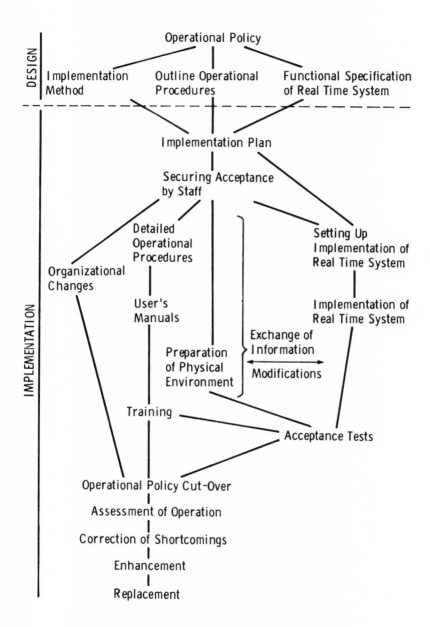

Fig. 7.2. Implementation stages.

system will meet the functional specification, then it must be capable of designing the system in the manner described in Chapter 6 and from this design produce functional specifications for all the subsystems on the same lines as the functional specification for the system as a whole. Any of the subsystems or components can then be acquired from the outside or sub-contracted out on the basis of their specifications.

Alternatively, a contract may be placed with an outside contractor to supply a whole system to meet the functional specification. This is termed a *turnkey contract*. Under such a contract an outside contractor as-sumes the responsibility for meeting the functional specification as such; in this case there is a very clear distinction from other types of contract. In principle, the contractor can supply anything he chooses as long as it will perform in such a way as to meet the functional specification. The acceptance tests are the means of determining whether the system meets the functional specification. These tests are therefore the basis of the con-tract, and the agreement is that the customer will pay the contractor a specified sum if whatever the contractor supplies by the agreed date passes the acceptance tests detailed in the contract. Hence the whole thing hinges on the acceptance tests. The customer must ensure that the acceptance tests are sufficient to prove that the system does meet the functional speci-fication. However, the acceptance tests are not all a one-way affair. The customer has to undertake to provide the means for conducting these tests, for instance if they include tests with real data and traffic conditions or require actual skilled operators.

Before such a turnkey contract can be awarded there may still be a question as to which contractor should be chosen. The cost-benefit analysis in Chapter 2 must have been based on at least one offer which was fully acceptable, and presumably it was the cheapest one of those. There may, however, have been several offers which were close in price. Possibly not all the outside offers considered in the cost-benefit analysis were to the same operational requirement. It may be considered worthwhile to ask all would-be suppliers to requote for offers to meet the operational require-ment finally adopted to see if any of them will provide a cheaper offer. In some cases there may be regulations requiring this to be done. If a number of contractors offer to meet the operational requirement at costs no higher than that assumed in the cost-benefit analysis, differ-ences in cost may have to be considered against other factors. A major factor is the credibility of the supplier. The estimate of this credibility is based largely on past performance. It is necessary to consider to what extent such past performance is a guide to the future. The first point to check when doing this is the continuity of the technical team. If many of these people, possibly the better ones, left to work elsewhere, then doubts must arise about the quality of performance in the future. Another point to be checked is the supplier's financial position, as success in a competitive environment is sometimes achieved at the expense of sound financial management.

Contract terms vary widely, in the nature of the contractor's undertakings, in payment methods, penalties, and contingency arrangements. A contractor's responsibility may vary from just providing software or individual units to purchasing and installing the computer and peripherals, other equipment including tranducers such as control valves, radars, or communication gear, preparing the site, and training user staff. It is important that the user should understand what is not included in the contracts and what remains his own undertaking. He wants a system but may only have bought equipment.

Payment to suppliers is generally on a fixed-price arrangement, with progress payments against clear milestones marking stages of work in progress. Alternatively, regular payments may be made on a "time-and-materials" basis; however, this does not encourage timely completion within a budgeted cost. Arguments for this method often maintain the specification is too fluid for the contractor to make firm estimates. While one can sympathize with a supplier in times of inflation, the user has constraints too, and it is the main thesis of this book that a pre-agreed specification with time and cost estimates is paramount. The user may have to become more specific in order to obtain a realistic quotation.

A third method of payment is to rent rather than buy the system, the rental only becoming due for those periods during which the system meets the specified availability standards. Even this does not protect the user from consequential loss while the system is down, and a supplier is unlikely to agree to such a contract where sources of malfunctions may be hard to identify as design faults, inadequate maintenance, or circumstances not envisaged in the functional specification.

Large contracts can take considerable time to complete. They should therefore allow for changes in operational policy which may occur. This can be expressed as break clauses related to stages in completion of implementation and stage payments. The contractor is paid for completed stages and the customer inherits all work in progress. To invoke such clauses is always unsatisfactory and therefore they should not be arranged to present an easy way out for either the intending user or the supplier. A more positive provision, if changes are thought likely, is to set out in the contract the means of costing modifications. Penalty clauses for delay or poor performance give an incentive but are hard to invoke in practice, especially if a small contractor has defaulted and has small tangible assets.

One should not lose sight of the main thesis that the responsibility for the system meeting the functional specification remains firmly with the contractor, the acceptance tests being the criterion by which success is judged, while the responsibility for the suitability of the functional specification and the adequacy of the acceptance tests is the vital concern of the intending user. Although it may be programmed to order, the purchase of a real-time computer system should still include the precaution and preparations which apply when accepting any new machinery.

From the user's point of view, he has described the system that is required and expects the supplier to provide something which will carry out these particular functions. From the supplier's point of view, he has sold some of his products, perhaps some equipment, and maybe some programs that have to be developed. And that's it. There is a gap.

Consider an airline wanting a seat-reservation system. The system is specified and a contract let to a supplier for the computer, terminals, and programs to be installed and shown to work. Who gets permission to put in the cables and who lays them? Who trains the staff? Who decides when and how training will be done? Which room contains what equipment? Who can judge whether the acceptance tests will prove the system can withstand faulty input? Who will say if the system has passed the tests? Who will be around afterwards to maintain the equipment or discuss changes? How are reservations made or the right passengers checked in when the system does break down? These things are a long way removed from the catalog and price lists of equipment. They need manpower to resolve, arrange, and carry out, and this means more money. How much more is hard to estimate; there is a risk as well as work. The risk is lessened where relevant experience exists, as with any endeavor, for system engineering even in its broadest sense is an identifiable skill.

There are two sources for the necessary experience and effort to fill the gap between a tested machine and its operational use. One is for the user organization to supply or obtain the experience; the other is to let a comprehensive turnkey contract. In the first case there are many decisions only the user can make, so it is essential he be involved. He can add to the experience within his organization by retaining consultants to advise on the other areas. The supplier's role is then straightforward. In the second case, the turnkey contract, the systems engineering experience is bought as part of the package, more responsibility being delegated by the user who nevertheless must still be involved. Because of this overlap and interaction, the dividing line in responsibility needs to be explicitly drawn in turnkey projects. This itself requires knowledgeable assistance in drawing up the turnkey contract. Any contractor will tend to be protectionist and seek a watertight agreement to limit his risk, while a user may try to keep the options open to an unreasonable extent. In any event, the ultimate responsibility for the success of the project in achieving the objectives of the operational policy is that of the user organization and cannot be entirely delegated. There are many decisions only the user can make.

7.2.2. *Assistance from Consultants*

The intending user may need outside advice, whether the systems engineering is to be carried out internally or largely contracted out. In Chapter 2 the use of consultants was discussed for expressing policy, drawing up the operational requirement and functional specification, and evaluating designs for feasibility and cost effectiveness. When it comes to implementation consultants have a further role to play. Because the analysis and implementation skills are somewhat different, the consultants need not be the same ones as those involved in the design of the operational policy and cost-benefit analysis. The selection criteria are similar to those described in Chapter 2 but the relevant main skills should be in project management, installation, and operational experience and complete familiarity with the technology involved. If such a person can be found who also has experience in the user's own application, so much the better. A member of a consultancy organization which has already undertaken similar work may give the user a more stable service on a broader base of support than an individual specialist.

Whatever the source of consultants, they can be of value to the user in the following stages of implementation.

Selection from suppliers proposals.

Assisting to draw up contracts.

Approving the intended acceptance tests.

Monitoring standards and progress.

Assisting the user in the vital task of preparing his organization for the system.

Foreseeing needs for the user's staff to adapt and train.

Supervising the running of acceptance tests.

Helping with the cut-over and integration.

Planning enhancements.

The main contribution is in ensuring that the user makes adequate provision for each subsequent stage in the implementation and that action is taken ideally before problems delay progress. This is not just a technical job but one of improving human communications. The consultant must have the full confidence of the user. This may be easier with a consultant as such unless relations with a turnkey contractor are particularly good.

Whatever assistance is obtained and whatever degree of turnkey responsibility is contracted to a supplier, it has been asserted that the ultimate responsibility for the successful introduction of the system into operational use remains with the user organization. It therefore needs to appoint its own manager whose goal is the achievement of the relevant part of the operational policy. Because the introduction of the new system may affect procedures, staff and methods of reporting, use of space, and other resources, this manager must have adequate authority to resolve any problems with all the departments who may be involved and ensure adequate plans are laid. One expects a major new system to affect a wide cross-section of an organization if maximum benefit is to be gained. The engineering, data-processing, or management-services departments may be very much involved, but on their own might not be able to reach decisions or achieve agreement on operational matters with other departments. The manager should have the authority necessary to see that the operational requirement is implemented.

For the remainder of this chapter it is assumed that whatever the source of experience or degree of delegation of responsibility for implementation, a management structure does exist between the user organization and any contractors, with responsibilities defined. The overall objective is to meet the operational requirement in actual use rather than just accepting the supplier's system. The acceptance tests are considered in § 7.4, but in Chapter 2 it was shown the operational requirement contains not only the functional specification for the real-time system but also the outline of the new operational procedures for the user, so the next section discusses the user's role in preparing the environment for the system.

7.3. The User Prepares the Environment for the System

This section is concerned only with the user organization, and describes the internal activities which are required before the organization can be ready to use the new system. On these depends much of the actual benefit which the user will obtain.

The left-hand side of Fig. 7.2 shows what activities are necessary besides the implementation of the technical system so that both the system and the rest of the organization can act together as in Fig. 7.1 to meet the operational requirement. The following are the main activities.

(1) Preparing for organizational changes.
(2) Preparing the staff environment.
(3) Preparing operational procedures.
(4) Preparing the physical environment.
(5) Preparing to integrate with the real-time system.

7.3.1. Preparing for Organizational Changes

In Chapter 2 consideration was given to the overall operational policy of an organization and the need to state explicit what it was trying to achieve. As a means to achieving the objectives, a change, whether an improvement or addition to operational methods, was found to be not only feasible but cost effective, and a technical system was specified. This specification, though vital before starting to implement a system, could not be drawn up in isolation. It was envisaged *at that stage* how the system would be used and how this would help achieve the operational objectives of the organization. So it was envisaged how the organization would interact with the system. Too often these thoughts are lost or become obscured. One has to remember the improvement or extension to the organization that was intended and then ensure that it comes about. This is the subject of this part of the user's preparation.

When a particular function, say a clerical function, becomes computerized, it may be quite clear what changes are necessary. The organization may change very little; perhaps some staff expansion is saved and reports come out more promptly. This is often the case with batch-processing work, putting another job onto the machine in the data-processing department. In the case of real-time systems, however, this is not usually the case at all. Mainly by virtue of the speed at which information can be returned to answer requests or at which a control response can occur, real-time systems often enable a whole new way of working and call for significant changes in a user organization.

We saw at the start of this book how banking operations had changed, for instance to retrieve a particular statement rather than distribute all of them. In car production the right number of vehicles with certain optional combinations can be produced automatically to reflect the orders received rather than having to predict the finished stock which should be held. In a message switch or telex exchange a torn-tape operation might be replaced, requiring staff to perform quite different roles. The implementation and then running of a public system like a water-traffic-control system for ship-collision avoidance might require a completely new branch of the organization. A real-time foreign-exchange system might need some changes in traditional banking practices if full benefit is to be obtained from the system.

The plan for the new method of working is shown on Fig. 7.2 as the outline of operational procedures. Only when this phase has been completed can the new method be explained to staff and the detailed job scriptions drawn up. The considerations for the new operational procedures will depend of course on the nature of the application and a detailed discussion would not be appropriate in this book. However, there are two general and complementary methods of expressing the results of this work which are usually helpful. One is to show on a diagram the staff reporting structure with job titles so that the chain of command and the composition of departments or operational teams can be clearly seen. The other is again to draw diagrams, but in this case as flow charts of the passage of information or control of the process through the organization. For instance, such flow diagrams can show the stage in operations at which documentation is created or data entered to the system, or the department which deals with certain functions. This flow charting is of course a common practice of many organizations and is not confined to those where computers are installed. It may be the result of operational research or organization and methods study and there are many texts on the subjects, both for clerical office procedures and for production control and so on. The reason for giving this subject particular mention in this book is that the need for such explicit diagrams of the way the operation is to work is that much greater where automated or real-time computer systems are concerned. This is because it is not quite so obvious what roles the machine is entirely covering and where it still needs help or human interaction. Moreover, it has been said that organizational changes are likely to occur, so the need is clear for diagrams explaining the new methods, the new routes of information, and different types of procedures.

Having expressed the outline of the operational procedures in these terms, the user can then turn attention both to the way they will affect existing staff and to the detailed job descriptions or operational procedures for each type of function shown in this new staff structure and flow diagrams.

7.3.2. Preparing the Staff Environment

As discussed at the beginning of this chapter, an important ingredient in the successful introduction of a system is a constructive staff attitude. Whether in a process control environment or in an insurance office, the cooperation of those who will interface with the system is clearly necessary. There are two kinds of obstacles; one a fear of redundancy, the other a fear of changed procedures. Both require education, to remove these fears and to train in new methods. They should be tackled in that order. It is rare for real-time computer system to cause redundancies because the systems are generally brought into expanding, developing or new environments. Total staff numbers scarcely ever fall though they may rise more slowly. It is true however that different skills may be needed, for instance to operate or maintain the computer equipment. Also, retraining in new methods may be necessary. If it was not the case the system would probably be one of limited benefit. How then can the user encourage a positive attitude? Clearly this aspect is not one generally covered in a supplier's terms of reference.

Going back to Chapter 2 and the operational requirement, it can be seen the system was thought necessary in the first place to give an identifiable contribution towards attaining the organization's objectives. The justification might have been expressed as an improvement in, say, the quality from a production line, the capacity of a telex exchange or the convenience or safety of air travel. These objectives are not necessarily aligned with the motivation of the individual staff who will be affected and one needs to explain the benefits in terms of the advantages to those staff. The system might bring greater reward through increased or better production, or simply enable the organization to survive at all in a competitive business. It might be solving a problem in the volume of data to be handled. This might relieve some of the routine, still requiring the interesting special cases to be handled manually. It might relieve some worry or simply help the operator, as in the case of air traffic control. Explained in such terms, staff may find the system acceptable or even start to look forward to its introduction.

If, on the other hand, the system cannot honestly be presented as attractive to certain staff, then there really is a problem. Such a problem needs to be recognized, faced, and solved before the skeptical or obstructive attitude can set in. Some staff may need to be redeployed. If this is to be extensive, one might well question whether the system was indeed of the right nature; it would need to have some clear and dramatic benefit to justify widespread sudden changes in the workforce distribution. As has been said, most real-time systems are merely part of a new or ongoing development in an organization and the benefits usually outweigh this kind of problem. Indeed, since Chapter 2 this book has assumed that a system does have justified benefits. It is up to the user not only to ensure that this justification is correct, but also to ensure that the benefits are realized in practice. There was a horrible example where an advanced information system was installed in a hospital, but the predominantly elderly staff could not read the characters on the cathode-ray tube. The system was taken out again.

It may not only be the direct users, the operational staff in contact with the real-time system, who need to be involved. Many managers may be opposed to change if it is likely to disturb their province or leave them less in control of things they understand. Explanatory and discussion meetings are needed for them also.

The fear of change can only be countered by an exposition of the benefits of the new system. It is no good trying to soothe the fears by the negative approach of claiming that the change will not be all that great. Such a claim will only raise suspicions, for if the change is not going to be all that great and is not going to upset this or that, why introduce it? Fear can only be countered by another emotion, enthusiasm for the brave new world ushered in by the new operational policy. The effective educational approach is for the user to tell his staff the reasons for the new policy and the benefits it will bring. The group of people who have designed the new operational policy now take on the task of explaining to the rest of the user organization the thinking that went on behind the design and what it will achieve. This educational process is not, and indeed should not be, wholly one-sided. Reactions from the future users may be of great value in working out the detailed operational procedures and the subsequent user manuals. Staff currently on the job may be in a position to suggest even slight changes in the facilities offered or the exact manner of use which could prove of great operational benefit.

Explanatory meetings for staff, then, with discussion encouraged should form an early stage in the education process. The staff structure diagrams and flow diagrams described in the previous section will be useful for this. The next section discusses details of the new operational procedures for each kind of operator and the preparation of user manuals.

From these, experimental training courses can be developed. These should be tried first with a mixture of the design staff and enlightened operational staff who will use the system. These latter may become those who train the rest of the operators or users. Such a collaborative effort, even if a desk exercise at first, helps to cement constructive relations between the system, personalized by contact with those designing and developing it, and those who are going to live with it. Additionally the exercise can give valuable feedback to the designers before it is too late! Unless major problems occur to cause a rethink, modifications should, however, be kept to a detail level only. The benefits can still be significant, quite apart from the identification with the system which the operational staff can then feel. It is to be *their* system — they had a say.

This kind of education is quite additional to the formal staff-training courses which will follow and which may be included in the supplier's contract. The user should not think that to order some training courses will take care of the things discussed in this section. It may be fairly true when purchasing individual equipment such as a car or a computer, but not for *systems* which interact more closely with the user's organization at the operational staff level.

When a system and staff are introduced to each other in this way and when the system has passed its formal acceptance tests, as described in § 7.4.1, staff will be ready to participate in trials and then to adopt the system into full operational use. Therefore, training should be at the earliest possible stage so as not to extend the time scale. The system may be "ready for service", but will the operational staff be ready to use it?

7.3.3. *Preparing Detailed Operational Procedures*

The outline of new operational procedures is expressed both as staff structure and as information flow diagrams. These serve to explain responsibilities and the new methods to staff. Now we turn to the detail of these operational procedures, leading to the user manuals and handbooks which will be needed for the formal training courses and for reference in daily use.

It is generally true that the designers and suppliers of the technical system will provide instruction books on *how* to use the facilities which that system provides. For instance, they will say what keyboard functions are available, how to load the paper, the procedure for setting controls, and perhaps what to do if a mistake is made or the system appears to have broken down. These manuals do not necessarily say *when* the user staff are intended to use the facilities, or *who* should use them, or what they are *for*. In, say, defense systems, these things have usually been worked out in a disciplined environment by the user. In other kinds of application, however, the actual translation of these facilities into a particular person's job sometimes is not set out and user staff may tend to use the system in a way that was not planned, with possible confusion and probably reduced benefit. There is, therefore, a need to describe the role which each member of the operational staff has to play.

Only a part of these roles will be concerned with the technical system, for staff will have other functions such as answering telephones, issuing or taking instructions verbally, and so on. Again, these aspects are generally outside the terms of reference of the supplier of the technical system. The user, therefore, has to ensure that this aspect of the preparation is completed.

The result is a set of operational manuals, one for each type of job with different duties. Thus a supervisor will have a different manual from a member of that team, even though many of the functions may be the same. The manuals describe all the duties and operations of the job, not just those concerned with the real-time computer system.

The operational procedures may call for some documents or forms to be used. These have to be designed and printed. This is often a surprisingly long and tedious process involving great detail. By using the approach described above, of an outline and diagram of procedures followed by detailed job descriptions and then the form design, this last task can be done efficiently. One knows the stages, information, signatures, number of copies, and so on required for each document. Care should be taken not to duplicate unnecessarily the processes going on within the real-time computer system, for part of the purpose and benefit may be to automate some of the clerical and record-keeping tasks, reducing the paperwork. However, the *user* needs to check what special stationery may nevertheless be required for use in conjunction with the new technical system.

Armed now with the operational requirement document and the functional specification, the detailed operational or user manuals and forms, the user can perform a highly useful *walk-through* exercise. This is just desk-checking the completeness and consistency of the planned operational procedures. It is not necessary to have the real-time computer system available for this. Given the data which will be input to that system, the expected output in terms of displayed information, reports, or control functions can be assumed to follow the functional specification. One might have forgotten something simple such as the need perhaps for someone to enter the time of day once the computer system is started, or to change the paper at some stage, or to log-in again after breaking off to answer the telephone. This exercise can be the same as the experimental training referred to in the previous section, where it was suggested that imaginative members of the operational staff should be involved. One can guarantee that they will come up with a host of very difficult questions to which answers must be found, and a variety of possible situations which must be provided for and described in the user manuals. This is not the same as the exercise described at the start of Chapter 6 for checking the functional specification. The purpose now is a wider one, to check the completeness of the operational procedures. Staff experienced in actually doing similar functions without a computer system can spot snags at the detailed level.

The result of this walk-through exercise may be to request modifications or clarification of detail in the technical system. This interaction with the designers and implementers of the computer system is shown in Fig. 7.2. This is where the discipline behind the specification needs to be carefully weighed against the benefit of modifications. The user has to decide what action to take on this feedback of information. Once such problems in the operational procedures have been resolved, the formal training courses can go ahead. These can now cover not just how to operate the equipment attached to the computer system, but how to relate those functions to the total role of the specific job for each member of staff. Thus staff are trained not just to use the computer systems, but in the new operational procedures.

7.3.4. Preparing the Physical Environment

The preparation of the computer site, an area, room or building, may be part of a turnkey contract or stay the responsibility of the user. In either case, its timely preparation is required. Real-time systems may, like traditional computer bureaus, contain big computers which generally require their own room with a controlled atmosphere. Where, however, minicomputers are used, the conditions tend to be less critical, requirements being mostly determined by the electromechanical peripherals involved, such as moving-head disks. In other applications, such as airborne guidance systems, the equipment may have been designed specifically for the environment. The manufacturer's recommended operating-temperature range is generally quite wide, and although small variations of temperature within the range can be troublesome, this is less so with more recent technologies. Office accommodation is generally adequate, subject to a good level of cleanliness. Where equipment is on a shop floor, for example, it may need some physical protection from other activities in the area. Once the location and conditions are decided upon, there are several considerations which are common to most equipment installation and so they are merely listed here.

(i)   Floor space is required for computer equipment, plant (compressors, filters, etc.), associated personnel, supplies, stores, spares and records.

(ii)   Construction considerations may include room volume, possibly false floor and ceiling, floor loading, control of access, and physical security.

(iii)   Amenities can involve air conditioning, filtering, and temperature control, power supplies, stability and loading, fire protection, detection, and extinction, lighting and windows, and communication facilities.

(iv)   Installation considerations are physical placing of equipment, route for bringing in equipment, cabling, casework and furniture for equipment, user, and storage, and access for test and maintenance.

While many of these topics clearly fall into a particular area of responsibility and some are less relevant to real-time systems, they should not be overlooked or their cost underestimated. One airline's reservation system required a separate plant building as big as an aircraft hangar and rather more expensive. On the other hand, a small message-switching minicomputer might work happily beside a desk in the general office running off the main power supply. Architects' designs include most of the physical considerations, but the user should ensure that they cover the casework or fittings if not standard from the supplier, and also that the physical disposition or arrangement of the equipment is well suited to the new operational procedures. This means at least outline procedures are needed before the physical layout is finalized.

In real-time systems another aspect is sometimes underestimated. This is the cabling which has to be laid, for most real-time systems have dispersed equipment. Provision must be made in the building for appropriate routing of cables, and responsibility must be assigned for the pulling and testing of them. Some communications will be sensitive to the lengths of cables and so the equipment supplier should be given plans showing the lengths of cable runs.

Very often real-time systems require resident staff to operate, maintain, or enhance the equipment, software, and facilities. As with many technical installations, inadequate space provision is often made for these staff.

Unless the supplier has been assigned a turnkey contract in a very broad sense, including discussion with the architects or facility managers as appropriate, the user should be sure adequate specialist advice is obtained in planning the physical installation for a system of any significant size.

7.3.5. Preparing to Integrate with the Real-Time System

While all these preparations are going on, the real-time system itself will be designed and implemented. There has to be a continuous exchange of progress information between the people carrying out the preparations within the user organization and the team designing the real-time system. Problems arising in the one branch affect the plans in the other one. Problems on the procedure side may reflect on the design of the system and *vice versa*. The interaction here is precisely the same as between teams engaged on the design of parts of any other design project. All the activities indicated in Fig. 7.2 are parts of the design and implementation of the new operational policy, and as in most projects the weak points are at the seams between the various teams. The difficulty is to ensure that the user's development of detailed operational procedures goes ahead in step with the technical development and does not lag. Implementation is clearly more straightforward if the design includes envisaging how it would be implemented. Because human ability to envisage things in advance is limited, a perfect design is never achieved in practice. Problems inevitably arise during implementation, so there must be full communication between the people implementing the technical part and the organizational or procedures part. Problems in one part can sometimes be more easily solved by modifications in other areas.

However, modifications to the design in the course of implementation are extremely dangerous. Many real-time systems have become bogged down in modifications which are really extensions, causing time scales and cost to be greatly exceeded and the benefits reduced to an extent which made nonsense of the cost-benefit analysis. A widespread technique among contractors in competitive situations is to submit offers at unrealistically low prices on the assumption that the customer will ask for modification in the course of work. By that time he will have become a captive customer and have no choice but to accept an effective price increase.

When a problem is discovered which raises doubts as to whether the operational policy with its functional specification for the real-time system will in fact work as originally envisaged, then the cost-benefit analysis immediately becomes suspect. The first question which therefore arises is whether to freeze work until the problem is solved. The decision whether to do this must be based on an intelligent guess as to whether the problem can be solved without reducing the balance of benefits over cost to an unacceptably low level. Whatever the decision on this score, the next step is to work out a modification which will solve the problem which has arisen. Having produced such a modification it becomes necessary to amend the cost-benefit analysis. On this basis one can decide whether to go ahead with the modified operational policy and system. This means a great deal of work for each modification. However, only by faithfully following such a procedure for every modification is it possible to prevent the all too familiar situation of escalating costs and time scales and of vanishing benefits.

7.4. Into Operational Use

7.4.1. Commissioning

After all the preparation by the user and then the physical installation of the equipment of the system, there are still some stages to work through before full use can be made of the system. Staff may have to be trained on the actual equipment and the suppliers may be required to show it all works. In § 6.4 "factory" acceptance tests were recommended, testing that the system performs technically to the functional specification, at least in the development environment. Fuller tests are required once installed at the user's workplace. These may include a repetition of the earlier acceptance tests but in the user's own environment. The object is not to see how the user likes the system, but to prove that it works to specification.

A number of problems can arise in organizing site tests, which if foreseen can be averted and not delay the commissioning. Even before the equipment gets to site, problems can arise. If an international shipment is involved there may be customs problems even if the system is to be used in the defense of that country. Physical loss and damage need to be insured against; systems have dropped into docks, rolled down hills off trucks, or simply stood in the rain or sun at an airport. These are general system problems, but ones to which computers are rather sensitive, and ones which all add to time and cost. Once at the site, quite frequently the equipment cannot easily be placed in position, owing to restricted access routes or risk of interfering with existing machinery.

Anticipating, however, the equipment in place, what will be required in order to run commissioning tests? Real or simulated test data are the main requirement, and plans must be laid to enable connection either to real input equipment, such as sensors, keyboards, data lines, radars, or other parts of the system, or else to lifelike simulated or prerecorded data. These test data are best derived from the actual system, for then it includes realistic error rates, noise, and traffic mix. If it is recorded the tests can be more readily repeated, which may help to track down any faulty responses from the computer system. The costs of obtaining test data by a special simulator of the environment or surrounding system may be justified in the development and early acceptance test phases, but can be a costly and time-consuming waste of effort, because the simulator may only be capable of producing the same types of errors in test data which have been thought of in programming the computer system; other errors arising in the actual system may not have been allowed for. Therefore tests with simulated data are of limited value. To use real data and actual equipment and perhaps actual operators obviously requires a great deal of co-operation between the intending user organization and the supplier. Many of the factors are outside the supplier's control. On the other hand, those who developed the system will be the most efficient at making good any technical defects, clearing software errors, and so on. Because of this overlap and the difficulty in controlling the activity in a predictable way, squabbles often arise over who provides what and who has delayed whom. Except where it can be clearly under the supplier's control, the following solution is suggested as the way most likely to get the system into a ready-for-service state.

The supplier's contract should call for acceptance tests of the kind described in Chapter 6, repeated if appropriate on site, together with inspection and tests of all the units supplied. This tests that the functional specification is met and that all the equipment is installed and serviceable. The contract should then require the supplier to provide support services during the commissioning period at a quality and rate of charge specified. In this way the user is safeguarded against the supplier disappearing or overcharging, yet the user has the incentive to do the advance preparation so as to minimize the commissioning period. To encourage the best support from the supplier, the final payment may be made on completion. The supplier then has a more controllable limit to the fixed-price part of the work and can afford not to charge so much for contingencies. The arrangements would vary to suit the nature of each particular system, but this mixture of fixed and variable costs is recommended for smoothing the commissioning task.

Given the user manuals and trained operators as well as the newly tested equipment, the next stage is an exciting one. It is to try the system as if for real, perhaps even handling some real traffic in a "guinea-pig" mode. This stage is called the *shakedown* or *field trials*. The essence of these trials is that they are carried out by the user, *not* by those who developed the technical system.

Field trials not only test the real-time system for its response, accuracy, throughput, and robustness, but also test whether the operators have had adequate training and whether the new operational procedures hang together in a workable and foolproof way. If the tests are carried out with limited traffic, measurements of system and operator performance will need to be scaled up to check that there is adequate capacity not only in computer throughput and response, but also in the operator load. These exercises will quickly find loopholes in the operational procedures. It is the moment of truth for the designers to see if the system will stand up in the real environment, with site conditions, noisy data, and the actual operators. It is also the moment of truth for the intending user to see if the system really works in his organization, and if his expression of the requirement and his preparation of the environment have been appropriate. At this stage, one *is* going to see whether the user likes the system, so it is a moment of truth for all concerned.

If the user likes the system, a success at least in one sense has been achieved. What to do if the user does not like certain aspects of the system is discussed in § 7.4.4. Once the user is reasonably satisfied, attention is turned to cutting the system over into real use. The ready-for-service date has arrived.

7.4.2. Bringing Into Service

In Chapter 2 it was suggested that the changeover to the new system should be planned before the start of the design phase. It may be necessary or wise to have a period of parallel running or partially divided traffic and run up the new system gradually, or it may be better to switch over completely at a point in time, relying on other back-up procedures for a while. It is not easy to decide, but the method of changeover clearly needs to be well defined so that the physical connection of equipments can be properly carried out and so that there is no confusion as to where and when the new operational procedures apply.

The methods of cut-over are as follows.

(1). To feed real input to the real-time system, via sensors and operators, and just to monitor the output. It does not yet control or feed back into the ongoing operational system but runs in parallel till its output is approved by comparison.

(2). To divide the traffic and process some real data on the new system. Sometimes "guinea-pig" or tame traffic can be found. Often, however, there is a difficulty in maintaining compatible data files between the new and previous systems.

(3). At a stage of sufficient confidence in using test data to switch over completely to the new system, for all real data. There must be a means of reverting to the old system when the new one fails, as it will for a while. The best time to try the changeover is in a slack period, giving time to settle before a busy hour or peak season.

Where the system is a new one or has more facilities than the one it is replacing, there may be an opportunity to bring the facilities into service gradually, establishing the main ones before using further ones. This may help those using the system, to try it out gradually, and may make trouble-shooting easier. However, it should be a planned phasing, not one which occurs by default by lack of preparation or lateness in development.

7.4.3. Performance and Shortcomings

Once the new system is in real operational use, there may be a transient settling-in time when wrinkles in the procedures or in the real-time system have to be straightened out. There comes a time when a reasonably stable situation is reached, with a meaningful traffic. Then one can collect statistical information on the use and on the performance of the system, as well as continuing to check its correct functioning. There are three uses for such figures: to compare performance of the new system with the previous one; to compare against the forecast of use; to measure over time the trends in use of the new system.

To compare the performance of the new system against the old one it is important to have taken measurements of the latter beforehand. Comparison against the forecast is only valid if the new system is actually used in the intended way; changes in the operational use give different benefits from those which justified the decision made in Chapter 2 to go ahead with a cost-effective system. Trends in use of the new system help to predict the actual performance in the future. One can see how response time varies as traffic grows, and how use can rise and then fall as the novelty wears off or changes in demand for an operational facility fluctuate. If the trends are seen correctly and in time, planned expansion or improvement in workload scheduling is possible.

Logging facilities help to gather factual data for analysis of use and save relying on subjective opinions. For instance, the system can monitor the number of calls connected or messages sent in an exchange, can average the transaction time for a reservation system, or can record deviations in a process-control system. Besides giving technical information, such data enables benefits to be calculated from agreed values.

The responsibility of ownership is one of cost-effective use. The manager responsible for the procurement or operation of the installation will want to refer to the original forecast of cost, savings, and benefits in order to check whether the objectives are being met. Costs include original expenditure plus operating costs for staff, supplies, maintenance, and sometimes floorspace occupied. Although these running costs are generally low for real-time minicomputers, some provision must be made. Forecast savings should show the expected return on capital employed. If these have correctly taken account of discounted cash flow and been calculated on inflation-accounting principles, expected savings differ from those required just to cover running costs and simple amortization. Costs and benefits, projected at the stage of Chapter 2, can now be checked in practice.

The benefits may be hard to measure. Most real-time systems do not provide a directly identifiable income in the way that a bureau can for batch or time-sharing work. Benefits may be simply to meet a technical necessity or to increase business through greater service or capacity, or to reduce other costs. If the computer system can be established as a revenue center and realistic charges set for the tasks performed for "users" then the notional benefit can be assessed. Uneconomic tasks become evident if users can reject charges.

From these cost-benefit considerations, the financial viability of the installation can continue to be tested in use. Indicators are available to help decide whether to curtail or expand facilities or capacity. Just as the designer has the technical goal to show that the system performs the specified functions, so the user needs to be sure and to demonstrate that the objectives of the system are achieved in use.

Once a system is installed, however, it is often the case with dedicated real-time applications that the continued appropriate and reliable functioning of the system is more important than the costs already committed. Acceptance tests may have included reliability tests, but faults will occur and the user will be concerned that adequate maintenance is available. If he is wise, he will have trained his own staff or taken a maintenance contract in order to cover more than any limited warranty period. He will have arranged for adequate spares to be available within the allowed repair time.

What happens if the system does not perform in accordance with the forecast or specification? Drastic action may be possible under some contracts or lease arrangements. More usually the user is committed to the system by the time such shortcomings are found and corrective action will be desired. Rarely is it found necessary or economic to reduce the configuration or performance if utilization does not reach expected levels. More commonly an increase in capacity, performance, or function is required to meet the actual situation. The cost-benefit calculations are similar to those in the original design except that there is now a heavy bias towards the existing system. Possibilities are to improve the configuration with more main store, faster backing store or processor, or to improve the software by altering facilities or making critical ones more efficient. Logged or diagnostic information obviously helps to indicate the more beneficial areas to change or optimize. Such changes will need intimate knowledge of the equipment and software. It is one of the claims of software that it can be readily adapted to meet specific situations. However, one should distinguish two types of change: those found necessary to meet the original aim and those arising from changes to the specification. The former may be classed as corrections, whereas the latter are enhancements, discussed in the next section.

The term "*modification*" is used for either type of change: to make good a deficiency, or to change or add a facility. First we consider the making of corrections. It is sometimes difficult to decide if a change is a correction. One has to refer to the operational requirement document and see if that was incorrect or ambiguous. If it is explicit and correct, either the real-time system does not meet the functional specification or the operational procedures have not been correctly expressed and implemented.

The preferred method of correction is, in most cases, quite clear. It may be expensive and any cost needs to be justified before going ahead. One hopes there are not fundamental failings, but, even with small faults in the real-time system, correction at a late stage may be expensive and a supplier may be reluctant to carry them out. This is the case for having thorough acceptance tests which are carefully scrutinized for completeness by the intending user before he agrees to accept the system on the basis of these tests.

Sometimes a correction can be avoided by adjusting the requirement, taking care, however, not to distort the overall operational policy. The user could decide for instance to do without a certain report or monitoring facility if it was seen to be unimportant. He could decide to adjust the operational procedures so as not to require a major system change. However, there may be corrections which do have to be made to the real-time system. Here one may find that software is not quite as readily changed as one had imagined. Frequently it is not the program change itself which is expensive but the process of agreeing it is necessary, deciding whose fault it was, who is to pay and how much, and to keep the documentation up to date. Therefore the user needs to have an agreed method of working with those responsible for this type of maintenance. Once established, there is a common will to fix corrections readily and economically, before confidence in the system is eroded.

Such a method of working needs to honor the difference between corrections and small changes. One hears: "If only it could just . . ." or "but we thought it would obviously have to do that". These reflect gaps in the stated operational requirement, perhaps due to a lack of attention to detail or of forethought. More rarely are they due to an actual change having occurred in the requirement. This is the case for the user's involvement in a thorough specification.

Of course one cannot foresee everything. Moreover, further opportunities for additional benefit from the real-time system may only become apparent at a late date or be suggested by experience in actual use of the system. Incorporation of these attractive changes, as distinct from the corrections considered above, is the subject of the next section. It is important to recognize into which category a particular change falls.

7.4.4. Enhancement and Replacement

Here we are concerned with those cases where the user wants to change the specification as set out in the operational requirement. These are not corrections, as already discussed, but definite changes or additions to the specified facilities. It might be merely to change the format of a display, to handle considerably increased traffic, or to merge with or add substantial further operational functions.

Experience with the system and changed requirements will each call for changes to the specification. While software may be readily altered, program status quickly becomes confused if changes occur too freely. Documentation needs to be maintained and changes controlled so that only those which are approved are implemented. Costs of implementing modifications may be considerable, and therefore proposed changes need to be assessed for their benefit and cost before being approved.

It is here that the user will find a difference between good and mediocre design. A system designed in a modular fashion and with plenty of allowance for various kinds of change will prove very much easier and so cheaper to modify or enhance. Modular design allows particular functions to be changed or added without repercussion throughout the system. A smooth scheduling algorithm will be less sensitive to program changes and alterations. A highly optimized system is more likely to require costly redesign of several parts than if the design allows spare storage and processing capacity. A good designer will have anticipated the type of likely change to the system such as increased number of lines or terminals, altered formats, areas for additional functions, or algorithms likely to need tuning. In many cases the table-driven or parametric approach to design will enable changes to be made merely by altering stored data rather than requiring program modifications which may need more recompiling and testing. Examples are changes to routing, to the sequence of processes on certain message types, to formats and reports, messages and displays, to operator keyboard sequences, etc.

In spite of all the consideration given to the operational requirement before design commenced, it is unfortunately common to find that, by the time the system is ready for commissioning, things have changed. While we have emphasized that it is the engineer's responsibility to think ahead and foresee technical problems, pinning down grey areas and hammering out details of design in advance, some major changes are hard to foresee. For instance, the user's company might be taken over by another with a different system, an air force may change its weaponry, or other fundamental changes in the user's *modus operandi* may occur. Such possibilities cannot be fully catered for, but the designer does have opportunities to ensure the structure of the system is less bound up with pecularities of the application, remaining general where possible.

More commonly, however, it is not until the user actually has the system in operation that he realizes what he really wanted, and finds many things he insisted on are quite unnecessary while other facilities cause embarrassment by not quite matching the real requirement. To help by suggesting ways to avoid or reduce such situations is the prime purpose of this book.

When, however, these problems do arise, how are they best resolved? The answer is surely in exactly the same way as we have advocated for the initial design, namely to establish explicitly the requirement, agree the functional specification to meet it together with cost and time scales, and then design, implement, and prove the function. Whether the change is carried out before or after the proving of the original design is a matter for decision in individual cases, but it should be an explicit decision taken in the knowledge that late changes immediately implemented may delay getting any initial system into use. Is it worth that delay or could such cumulative delays prevent real trials which might show the need for more important changes? Unless there are seen to be fundamental errors or essential changes, one may decide to use the original design and only after its assessment in use to incorporate changes. Otherwise experience shows a tendency for systems never to reach operational use if they are continually modified. Changes therefore should be batched, using the system as it is meanwhile.

Further temptations arise when new or better equipment is announced. If this is during development, should one revise the design to incorporate the latest model? If it occurs after commissioning and one is extending the system, does one add on compatible equipment or change the whole installation to the newer type? In the first case, during development, the decision is surely that of the designers and implementers, not that of the user who has agreed costs and merely wants the requirement to be met. So the designer must decide if any rework and alterations or uncertainties in equipment delivery are warranted.

In the second case, choosing whether to extend equipment of existing or compatible type or to change to new and different types, the decision is surely that of the user, who will pay for it. Such a user may be well advised to obtain cost estimates for both approaches and to decide on that basis which if any course is the best to meet his requirement. Just because new equipment is announced does not mean, even if it is cheaper to buy, that it should take the place of existing equipment which is well proven with spares holding, maintenance contracts, and trained staff. The cost of administering the change and the upheaval to ongoing operations have to be considered. As for the original system, the user should assess the benefit and the total cost of changes.

Clearly there are some step functions. Where changes are required that are beyond the capability of existing equipment, through limits on size, throughput, or response being exceeded for example, a new approach may be necessary rather than upgrading or optimizing the current installation. In such cases one may be able to take advantage of the major change and incorporate further facilities which might individually have been too expensive to add to the old system. Indeed, when an installation is replaced, it is often found that there have been so many changes in technology, in the operational requirement, and in relative costs that a complete reassessment is necessary just as for the original installation. A well-considered replacement will therefore take time, and meanwhile the current system can continue to be used.

Eventually, the changeover from the old to the new system has to be carried out. This replacement can be an expensive and traumatic experience in the same way as the cut-over to the first real-time system. It is hard to switch over a whole system at once and still allow fall-back to the old system if there are troubles, particularly in an extensive process-control system or where a database is involved. Parallel running is likewise difficult. The problems and cost of phasing out an old system in favor of a new one can be substantial and are additional to the capital cost of the new system. One has to consider rather carefully whether the increased benefit is worth this upheaval and cost or whether the current proven system could continue with enhancement.

The cost and problems of removing a system are reduced if the designer of the original system does have in mind the eventual need to replace his system by another. If, for instance, interfaces between types of equipment coincide with boundaries of main functions, there is a greater chance of being able to replace part of the system. If memory-management techniques in the software are separated from the application software, storage devices may be enhanced or expanded or quite different in a new system without requiring application algorithms to be reprogrammed. Likewise, separation of input and output facilities from the main processing could allow faster transmission facilities to be substituted, or even the addition of a front-end. Where parts of the system can be upgraded, one can avoid the giant step functions of having to change to a whole new system.

The most obvious way of providing for enhancement is to ensure that the initial system is not pushed to its limit. One avoids either packing store that is already a maximum size for the machine or using all the available CPU time. If a configuration is chosen which leaves elbow room and time in hand for further tasks, many enhancements can be simply incorporated with only normal software cost. Where it is recognized that the requirement may change within the lifespan of the equipment, it is increasingly common for the specification to state that only perhaps 25% of CPU time and 50% of maximum store capacity at each level are to be utilized in the initial system. This does not necessarily mean that the equipment need be over-expensive; in relation to total system implementation cost, the price of the processor hardware is a small fraction. It is up to the user to specify at the stage of Chapter 2, in the operational requirement, how much spare capacity must be provided and acceptance tests should show that it is available.

Another kind of enhancement sometimes arises, where a small real-time system needs to be integrated into a wider system. Sometimes the original system is reduced to a front-end for the central system which does all the processing, or sometimes it merely passes certain information to the central computer and receives directives back. If a designer has foreseen such possibilities, the user may later be saved considerable trouble. Local processing can become a part of a distributed system for example.

When a decision about improvements has to be made there would seem to be some benefit in separating the user and the implementer, not in discussions on requirement, but on decision of benefit and justified cost which are the user's decision, and on design and methods of implementation which are not. It is not for the designer to urge the inclusion of further operational facilities, or to judge costs against benefit, nor is it for the user to decide how the requirement is to be met. A firm budget and specification can help to avoid those situations where either the user or the designer wants to slip in extra facilities or changes. One needs not only this discipline, but also an agreed method of working between user and supplier. This is similar but distinct from the procedure for making corrections. Once the modification procedure for making enhancements is established, the changes can be more efficiently carried out.

We have urged the intending user to think ahead hard, to reduce the need for late corrections and for specification changes. We have urged that the designers of the real-time system use a modular design to make corrections easier and that they anticipate the types of change and expansion which are likely to occur. The user can help, and also help save himself money later, by requesting provision of spare capacity and indicating in the operational requirement the types of change that could occur in his future operational policy.

7.4.5. Life after Delivery

To summarize, the stages in commissioning the installed system are as follows.

Rerun the "factory" acceptance tests if necessary to check that the real-time system's technical performance still meets the functional specification.

Try out the new operational procedures with the equipment, using only test data for this "shakedown" phase.

Carry out field trials as if for real with as much of the system and procedures as possible and with staff already trained.

Cut-over the new system into real operational service.

Once the system is in actual use the following should be carried out.

Monitor its performance and compare against the forecast.
Decide solutions to evident shortcomings and establish maintenance.
Evaluate the benefit of enhancements and phase them in.
Plan ahead for easy upgrading.

Whether or not a turnkey system is obtained, the user organization must remain responsible for these activities and will need to allocate specific management staff.

7.5. The Book in a Nutshell

This book is about both management and design. It emerges that the right way of doing either is much the same. First of all it is essential to define precisely what one is setting out to achieve, how much of it, and by when.

Only then can the best method of achieving it be determined. To do so one has to iterate a number of promising designs, evaluating the total real cost and full benefits of each. In this way one establishes not only the best design, but also whether this best design is beneficial enough to be undertaken. To do all this one has to be able to envisage in advance both how the design will work when implemented and its future environment. It is precisely this complete envisaging in advance which has in fact been defined as design. Design is hard, expensive, and time-consuming work, but you cannot afford not to do it, for muddling through somehow, crossing bridges as one comes to them, can cost a hundred times more. A wide knowledge of relevant experience is a prerequisite for successful design. This book attempted to provide a distillation of such relevant experience in the field of real-time systems, together with pointers to further sources of information.

Bibliography

Computer Architecture

Chu, Y. *High Level Language Computer Architecture*. Academic Press, New York, and London, 1975.

Hortenstein, R., and Zaks, R. (eds.) *Workshop on the Microarchitecture of Computer Systems*, North-Holland, Amsterdam, 1975.

Proc. 2nd Annual Symp. on Computer Architecture. IEEE Computer Society Publications Office, Long Beach, Calif. and ACM, New York, 1974.

Lipanski, G.J., and Szygenda, S.A. (eds.) *Proc. 1st Annual Symp. on Computer Architecture*. IEEE, New York and ACM, New York, 1973.

Organick, E.I., *Computer System Organization*. Academic Press, New York, and London, 1973.

Proc. 3rd Annual Symp. of Computer Architecture. IEEE, Long Beach, Calif., 1976.

Symp. on High Level Language Computer Architecture 1973. ACM, New York, 1973.

ACM-IEEE Symposium on High Level Language Computer Architecture. ACM, New York and IEEE Computer Society, Northbridge, Calif., 1973.

Computers in Telecommunications

Software Engineering for Telecommunication Switching Systems, IEE Conf. Publ. No. 135. IEE Publications, Hitchin, UK, 1976.

Bear, D., *Principles of Telecommunications Traffic Engineering.* Peter Peregrinus, Stevenage, UK, 1976.

Hills, M.T., and Kano, S. *Programming Electronic Switching Systems.* Peter Peregrinus, Stevenage, UK, 1976.

Handbook of Data Communications. N.C.C., Manchester, UK, 1975.

Flood, J.E. (ed.) *Telecommunications Networks.* Peter Peregrinus, Stevenage, UK, 1975.

Data Communications

Proc. 1976 Symposium on Computer Networks: Trends and Applications. IEEE, Long Beach, Calif., 1976.

Proc. Fourth International Zurich Seminar on Digital Communications. IEEE, Long Beach, Calif., 1976.

4th Data Communications Symp. 1975. IEEE, Long Beach, Calif., 1975. *Text and References for Commuter Networks: A Tutorial.* IEEE, Long Beach, Calif., 1975.

Green, P.E. *Computer Communications.* IEEE Press, New York, 1975

Proc. 1975 Symposium on Computer Networks: Trends and Applications. IEEE, New York, 1975.

European Computing Conf. on Communications Networks: On-Line 75. On-Line, Uxbridge, UK, 1975.

Proc. 1974 Symposium on Computer Networks: Trends and Applications. IEEE, New York, 1974.

2nd International Conference on Computer Communication 1974. IEEE, Long Beach, Calif., 1974.

3rd Data Communication Symp. 1973. IEEE, New York, 1973.

Davies, D.W., and Barber, D.L.A. *Communication Networks for Computers.* John Wiley, New York, London, 1973.

Winkler, S. (ed.) *Proc. 1st Int. Conf. on Computer Communications: Impacts and Applications*. IEEE, New York and ACM, New York, 1972.

Martin, J. *Systems Analysis for Data Transmission*. Prentice-Hall, Englewood Cliffs, NJ, 1972.

Martin, J. *Introduction to Teleprocessing*. Prentice-Hall, Englewood Cliffs, NJ, 1972.

Martin, J. *Teleprocessing Network Organization*. Prentice-Hall, Englewood Cliffs, NJ, 1970.

Effective Computer Usage

Management Auditing of Computer Operations, Tutorial. IEEE, Long Beach, Calif., 1976.

Graham, J. *Making Computers Pay*. Allen and Unwin, London, 1976.

Burnham, P.M., and Morris, E.P. *Effective Computer Management*. John Wiley, New York and Chichester, UK, 1976.

11th IEEE Computer Society Conf. — How to Make Computers Easier to Use. IEEE, New York, 1975.

The Evaluation of the Performance of Computer Systems. OECD, Paris, 1975.

Adams, E.B. *Management of Information Technology*. Petrocelli Books, New York, 1975.

Thompson, T.R. *Management and Computer Control*. Gee, London, 1973.

Grindley, K., and Humble, J. *The Effective Computer*. McGraw-Hill, New York and London, 1973.

Conf. on Organisation and Management of Computer-based Control and Automation Projects. IEE, London, 1973.

Microprocessors

Barna, A., and Porat, D.I. *Introduction to Microcomputers and Microprocessors*. John Wiley, New York and Chichester, UK, 1976.

Healey, M. *Microcomputers and Microprocessors*. Hodder, London, 1976.

Soucek, B. *Microprocessors and Microcomputers*. John Wiley, New York and Chichester, UK, 1976.

Applied Workshop on Microprocessors, Tutorial. IEEE, Long Beach, Calif., 1976.

Unique Aspects of Microcomputer Applications, Tutorial. IEEE, Long Beach, Calif., 1976.

Microprogramming

7th Workshop on Microprogramming 1974. ACM, New York, 1974.

Husson, S.S. *Microprogramming: Principles and Practices*. Prentice-Hall, Englewood Cliffs, NJ, 1970.

MICRO 8, Eighth Annual Workshop on Microprogramming. IEEE, Long Beach, Calif., 1976.

Microprogramming, Tutorial. IEEE, Long Beach, Calif., 1976.

Miscellaneous

Fifth Texas Conference on Computing Systems, IEEE, Long Beach, Calif., 1976.

Trends and Applications 1976: Micro and Mini Systems. IEEE, Long Beach, Calif., 1976.

Arms, W.Y., Baker, J.E., and Pengelly, R.M. *A Practical Approach to Computing*. John Wiley, New York and Chichester, UK, 1976.

Bennet, A.W. *Introduction to Computer Simulation*. Holt, Rinehart, and Winston, New York, 1976.

Minisystem '76: A Technical Conference Sponsored by Honeywell Information System. Honeywell Information Systems, Publications Distribution Center, Brighton, Mass. 1976.

Belzer, J., Holzman, A.G., and Kent, A. (eds.) *Encyclopaedia of Computer Science and Technology*. Marcel Dekker, Maidenhead, UK, 1975 onwards.

Proc. 1974 National Computer Conference. AFIPS Press, Montvale, NJ, 1975. (Major topics — microprocessors, computer networks, software, database management, storage technology, interactive graphics, future prospects in data processing.)

An Understanding of Coral. Computer Analysis and Programmers (Reading), Reading, UK, 1975.

Maguire, B.W. *Handbook of Computer Maintenance and Troubleshooting.* Reston, Reston, Va., 1974.

Martin, J. *Security, Accuracy and Privacy in Computer Systems.* Prentice-Hall. Englewood Cliffs, NJ, 1974.

9th IEEE Computer Society Conf. – Micros and Minis: Application and Design. IEEE, New York, 1974.

Beizer, B. *The Architecture and Engineering of Digital Computer Complexes,* vols. 1 and 2. Plenum Press, New York and London, 1971.

Parallel Processing

1975 Sagamore Computer Conference on Parallel Processing. IEEE, Long Beach, Calif., 1975.

SIGPLAN Notices, vol. 10, no. 3, March 1975. *Proc. Conf. on Programming Languages and Compilers for Parallel and Vector Machines.* ACM, New York, 1975.

Sagamore Computer Conf. on Parallel Processing 1973. IEEE, New York, 1973.

Real Time – General

2nd Conf. on Trends in On-Line Computer Control System. IEEE, New York, 1975.

Pritchard, J.A.T. *Introduction to On-Line Systems.* N.C.C., Manchester, UK, 1973.

On-Line 72 Conf. Proc. On-Line, Uxbridge, UK, 1972.

Real-Time. Infotech, Maidenhead, UK, 1971.

Software Design

Second International Conference on Software Engineering. IEEE, Long Beach, Calif., 1976.

Graham, J. *Systems Analysis in Business.* Allen and Unwin, London, 1972.

System Design

Blackman, M. *The Design for Real-Time Applications.* John Wiley, New York and Chichester, UK, 1975.

CAP's Approach to the Design and Implementation of On-Line Systems using Manufacturer's Software. Computer Analysts and Programmers, London, 1974.

Using CICS for Performance and Integrity. Computer Analysts and Programmers, London, 1974.

Water, S.J. *Introduction to Computer Systems Design.* N.C.C., Manchester, UK, 1974.

Martin, J. *Design of Man-Computer Dialogues.* Prentice-Hall, Englewood Cliffs, NJ, 1973.

Yourdon, E. *Design of On-Line Computer Systems.* Prentice-Hall, Englewood Cliffs, NJ, 1972.

Rogers, D. *Creative Systems Design.* Anbar Publications, London, 1970.

System Integrity

1976 International Conference on Reliable Software. IEEE, Long Beach, Calif., 1976.

Protection of Information in Computer Systems, Tutorial. IEEE, Long Beach, Calif., 1975.

1976 International Symposium on Fault-Tolerant Computing. IEEE, Long Beach, Calif., 1976.

Int. Conf. on Reliable Software 1975. IEEE, New York, 1975.

Simpson, R.M. *A Study in the Design of High Integrity Systems.* University of Newcastle-upon-Tyne, UK, 1974.

IEEE Symp. on Computer Software Reliability 1973. IEEE, New York, 1973.

Systems Software

Minicomputer Realtime Executives, Tutorial. IEEE, Long Beach, Calif., 1974.

Tsichritzis, D.C., and Bernstein, P.A. *Operating Systems.* Academic Press, New York and London, 1974.

Huberman, A.N. *Principles of Operating Systems.* Science Research Associates, Henley-on-Thomas, UK, 1976.

Graham, Robert M. *Principles of Systems Programming.* Wiley, New York and Chichester, UK, 1975.

Hoare, C.A.R., and Perrott, R.H. *Operating Systems Techniques.* Academic Press, New York and London, 1973.

Sayers, A.P. (ed.) *Operating Systems Survey.* Auerbach, Philadelphia, Pa. 1971.
Cohen, L.J. *Operating System Analysis.* Spartan Books, East Lansing, Mi., 1970.

Gauthier, R.L., and Ponto, S.D. *Designing Systems Programs.* Prentice-Hall, Englewood Cliffs, NJ, 1970.

Time Sharing

Wilkes, M.V. *Time Sharing Computer Systems.* (3rd edn.) Macdonald and Jane's, London, 1975.

Auerbach on Time-Sharing. Auerbach, Philadelphia, Pa., 1973.

Watson, R.W. *Time-Sharing System Design Concepts.* McGraw-Hill, New York and London, 1970.

Index